DAVID BRINKLEY

*11 Presidents, 4 Wars, 22 Political
Conventions, 1 Moon Landing,
3 Assassinations, 2,000 Weeks of
News and Other Stuff on Television
and 18 Years of Growing Up in
North Carolina*

Published by Random House Large Print
in association with Alfred A. Knopf, Inc.
New York

LIBRARY OF CONGRESS CATALOGING-IN-PUBLICATION DATA
Brinkley, David.
    David Brinkley : 11 presidents, 4 wars, 22 political
conventions, 1 moon landing, 3 assassinations, 2000
weeks of news and other stuff on television and 18 years
of growing up in North Carolina / by David Brinkley.
                    p.   cm.
            ISBN 0-679-76506-9
    1. Brinkley, David.   2. Television journalists—
United States—Biography.   3. Large Type Books.
                    I. Title.
        PN4874.B6695B75   1995
            070'.92—dc20
        [B]   95-22852   CIP

Manufactured in the United States of America
10 9 8 7 6 5

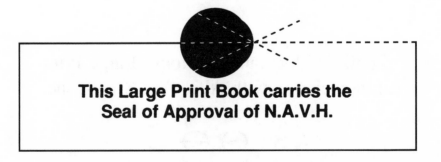

**This Large Print Book carries the
Seal of Approval of N.A.V.H.**

I

SUMMER 1930. The Cape Fear River docks at the foot of Walnut Street in Wilmington, North Carolina. Clear. Warm. Sunny. Mark Twain would have found no romantic adventure here. No humor. Unlike his Mississippi River, the Cape Fear hardly went anywhere. From the Atlantic Ocean ships struggled to Wilmington through miles of dangerous shoals and vicious currents where for centuries ships ran aground and sank, hence the river's name. Beyond Wilmington there was only shallow water and no room for Twain's steamboats and their paddle wheels, gamblers and fancy women.

As a young boy I wandered down to the docks occasionally to watch the ships come in from all over the world and sometimes to observe local adult males amusing themselves and perhaps expelling some personal demons by shooting the big, ugly wharf rats running around the docks. Their weapon of choice was the .22 rifle loaded with the cartridges called shorts, because they were cheaper than the longer and more powerful cartridges and had less destructive power, but enough for a rat if it was hit right. If instead of a quick kill it died slowly, all right. "The bastard," they said aloud after each kill.

This tells less about the extermination of dangerous predators than it tells about the open, tolerant, easygoing attitudes in that time and that place, my hometown. A man walking down to the docks carrying a rifle attracted no attention at all. If anyone thought anything it would not be believed he was on any kind of criminal errand because there simply were not any criminal errands to be on. That was where I was born and grew up and where I learned to be trusting and accepting. Like other Americans, I have had to change my mind and learn doubt and suspicion. And I have absolutely hated having to change.

A more pleasing sight on the Walnut Street docks was to watch the Sprunt family's compress in action. Cotton arrived by truck and train from farms in upstate North Carolina already formed into bales and wrapped in burlap. They came down to Wilmington to be shipped overseas. But first the bales had to be squeezed down to about a third of their original size so as to fit the maximum number in the hold of a freighter. This required a compress, a giant, hissing steam-driven machine, and a team of muscular, sweating black men, singing rhythmically and splendidly as the machine hissed and steamed, hissed and steamed, as the men moved cotton bales in and out of the compress, all this seen through a thin, white cloud of steam. The bales came out one-third of the original size but, oddly, weighing the same. It could have been the ''Old Man River'' scene in *Showboat*.

Another day, my friend Ned and I saw a large freighter pull in from Britain and tie up at lower Walnut Street. A hatch was opened, a deck crane reached down into the hold and lifted out an automobile, an English MG convertible, swung it outward and set it down on the dock. Whereupon the ship's youngish captain and his wife walked down the gangplank, got into their MG and drove away in the direction of Wilmington and Wrightsville Beach. I thought I had seen a man who really knew how to live—traveling in comfort and luxury on a big merchant ship to any port in the world, carrying cargo to pay for it, having your car lifted ashore and then driving anywhere you wanted to go. I almost wished I could have shown him our local sights: the house at Third and Market where Cornwallis lived while he waited to lose the last battle of our Revolution to George Washington, allowing him to usher into history a place to be called the United States of America; the city's glorious azalea gardens; the Greek Revival mansions lining Market Street until—in a lapse of taste and judgment—the city permitted many of them to be demolished; the grave of a woman who died on a sailing ship en route to America and was, at her request in her will, buried in a barrel of wine; the site of the first battle of the Revolution, at Moore's Creek, where it was established that the English colonists in the New World did not want to remain English.

The Brinkley family folklore passed down to me

was that in the English colonial settlement of Wilmington, at about the time George Washington was born, a squirrel buried an acorn on what eventually became Princess Street. It took root. Two hundred years later we lived at 801 Princess in a vaguely Victorian house under the branches of an oak tree older than our country, lying in bed at night listening to its acorns bouncing and rattling on the red tin roof.

In the early years several Brinkley families lived up and down the coast of Virginia and North Carolina, one of them in my time piloting the automobile ferry *John Knox* back and forth across the Cape Fear River. Some others lived a mile or two outside of Wilmington in a village called Brinkleys, which they named for themselves before the Civil War. It was a small place, but early in the twentieth century when Wilmington was wired for electric lights the village insisted it should have them, too. At least it wanted electricity in the high school gymnasium for basketball games at night in a place having few other amusements. But the electric utility company said it would be years before it could run its lines out to Brinkleys. The place was too small to justify the cost. The village responded by borrowing money and buying its own electric generator made by Delco and installing it in the high school. When it was ready the entire town turned out to witness the arrival of what surely would be a new and exciting world of electric light, replacing the oil lamp with its unfortunate habit of turning over, breaking its glass reservoir of kerosene, starting an oil-fed fire and, since there was no running water, burning down the house. All across the rural South there stood brick chimneys, lonely sentinels left standing when the modest wooden houses that once relied on them for warmth burned to cinders.

The Delco's switch was thrown, the gymnasium exploded into brilliant light, the crowd cheered and applauded and milled around the basketball court happily discussing the new electrified future including, best of all, basketball at night. It was all so splendid that after an informal survey of the crowd it was decided there in the gymnasium to change the name of the town from Brinkleys to Delco. So it remains today.

Southern families since the country's beginnings have frequently, habitually, named their children for English kings and queens. My own parents were William and Mary. My two sisters were Mary and Margaret. My two brothers William and, a southern favorite, Jesse. My name, David McClure Brinkley, was taken from my mother's favorite Presbyterian minister, Dr. Alexander McClure. The Englishness in the mid-South dates back to the earliest pre-Revolution days. The first battle of the American Revolution was near Wilmington at Moore's Creek, and it was fought between loyalists who wanted this country to remain a British colony and those who wanted independence from England. The first political tea party, the dumping of English tea in the river to protest George III's taxes, was not in Boston. It was in Wilmington's Cape Fear River, but the history textbooks were written in Boston.

In her early years when my mother, whom we called Mama, invited friends to 801 Princess for Sunday dinner, served in midafternoon, usually there was a Presbyterian minister or two being served a chicken or two. In addition to the usual bustling around in the kitchen and dining room, there was one more detail to be attended to. My oldest sister, Margaret, then about five, refused to sit at the table with adult guests or with any adults at all. She hated the smell of their tobacco smoke and found their conversations boring. She asked for, and was given, nursery-size furniture, a small table and chair to be placed under the dining table. There she sat and ate at her own little table. The adults sat at the dining table, and Margaret sat under it, out of sight. As the adults ate and talked, suddenly and seemingly from nowhere came a child's voice asking her mother to lean down and hand her something from the table or asking what she should wear to school tomorrow. Family friends were accustomed to this Gothic oddity, but to newcomers it was so bewildering and somehow upsetting that they found it difficult to converse. A few made excuses and left early.

SOME MILES OUT, where the bays, sounds, the Atlantic Ocean and the stands of longleaf pine and live oaks lined the North Carolina coastline, a splendid Italianate mansion stood facing Wrightsville Sound. It was the residence of Pembroke Jones, Wilmington's wealthiest squire in the 1920s. He managed to make money from the swamps around the Cape Fear River and their huge production of snakes, mosquitoes and rice. He paid his plantation help to kill the snakes—ten cents for a rattler, twenty cents for the more deadly water moccasin. For the mosquitoes he bought citronella by the quart and built birdhouses to attract crowds of purple martins noisily and happily swallowing mosquitoes. As for the rice, Jones milled it and sold it abroad during World War I and at the same time ran a shipbuilding yard on the bank of the Cape Fear River. Soon he was selling his rice and delivering it to Europe in his own ships. Some countries not only bought the rice but also bought the ships it came in. If there was a certain commercial symmetry here, in these tax-free days there was also a certain commercial profit, a great deal of it.

Accordingly, Jones pursued a social life far grander than customary in our small southern town.

There the usual nightly ritual was to lounge on living room furniture done up in cut velvet, drink homemade wine or bootleg whiskey or pitchers of something in funny colors and called punch, while conversing of business, the weather and how the fish were biting off Wrightsville Beach. This was far too tame and too boresome for Pembroke Jones. By now he was entertaining his New York friends—Astors, Whitneys, Vanderbilts and Wilmington's Wrights, for whom Wrightsville Sound was named.

The live oak tree, one of nature's wonders, thrives in the sandy soil and salt air of North Carolina's Atlantic coast, lives for centuries and over time accumulates a silky mantle of Spanish moss, turning a woodland into a beautiful Impressionist landscape in black and pale shades of gray and green.

This was the setting where Pembroke Jones served dinner to his guests—up in a tree among the branches of a live oak. The ramps he had ordered built rose gently, with handrails, making an easy walk up to a platform built around the trunk and over the oak's sturdy branches. It was not your great American picnic of chicken sandwiches and hard-boiled eggs and ants. No. It was china, crystal, silver, damask, long-stemmed pink roses with baby's breath and lilies of the valley, strings of pink lights strung through the branches. A local historian, Lewis Philip Hall, described the scene: ''. . . the guests at dinner up in a live oak tree festooned with Spanish moss. To the east, far out over the marshes and creeks, the distant Atlantic shimmered under a full moon. In a nearby grove of pines, the choirs from local black churches lifted their splendid voices in ancient spirituals while thousands of fireflies sparkled in the shadows.''

From the Jones compound a shell road led out along the shores of the sound. Shell roads were made with oyster shells. When they were spread over dirt roads and then crushed by automobile tires and wet by the rains, the lime in the shells formed a hard, smooth surface in some ways better than the asphalt now being put down by the county. They were bright white and visible at night, and along this coast oyster shells were so freely available that a shell road cost almost nothing. The early settlers found huge mounds of shells left by the pre-Columbian Indians.

Down the coast a mile or two a shell road led through the woods to another locally famous institution, Uncle Henry's Oyster Roast. Since early in the century Uncle Henry had served oysters in what could barely be called a restaurant and served them only in his own way. This was his recipe:

> Start with an inch-thick steel sheet like those the repair crews put down to cover holes in the streets. Set it up outdoors about two feet off the ground. Build a fire under it. When the steel is hot, dump a bushel of oysters on it. Throw several layers of burlap over the oysters. Pour a bucket of seawater over the burlap. Let the steam fly,

carrying the smoke and fragrance up into the pine trees. When the oysters are cooked, they pop open. Lift them off the steel plate with a flat-bladed spade and dump them into a bushel basket.

By now the customers are waiting inside a simple wooden building, little more than a shed, seated at plywood tables under bare lightbulbs. Each diner is assembling his own little bowl of choices from the condiments on the table—melted butter, vinegar, lemon juice, Tabasco sauce. Two or three young boys come in, smelling of smoke and carrying baskets of oysters. They stand behind the customers' chairs opening the oysters one by one and dropping them into the bowls of condiments faster than they can eat them. All they can eat for a set price.

Occasionally, Mama was willing to go to Uncle Henry's, even though she, the fiercest Prohibitionist since Carry Nation, thought it was sinful, criminal self-indulgence that people arriving there carried bottles of whiskey in brown paper sacks. Prohibition's cold hand lay across the land, but so did the blue smoke from the bootleggers' distilleries. While Margaret ate under our dining room table, Pembroke Jones's guests ate up in a live oak tree, and in a shed at Uncle Henry's they ate the oysters almost as fast as they were plopped into their bowls.

On a spring morning in the late twenties, the Wilmington *Morning Star* printed the stunning news that New Hanover County sheriff David Jones had boarded a boat in the Cape Fear River and found it loaded with good, clean, well-made Canadian whiskey, packed in sawdust and wrapped in burlap and bearing a label saying the contents were automobile parts. It appeared that a truck had been expected to come down to the docks, secretly pick up the whiskey and haul it upstate where businessmen prospering in tobacco, textiles and furniture were willing to pay top dollar for prime whiskey. But somebody, perhaps a competitor, tipped off Sheriff Jones. He seized the whiskey, seized the boat and arrested its captain. After the briefest of legal niceties, recorder's court judge George Harris ordered the whiskey destroyed as the law required. Sheriff's deputies were observed carrying the burlap bales up the steps to the courtroom as the courthouse idlers stared in awe, whispering among themselves. The judge ordered the deputies to set the bales outside on a sloping tin roof behind the courtroom and to smash the bottles with hammers and let the whiskey run down into the storm drains. A crowd gathered. The judge ordered them to stay off the roof. Too much weight, he said. But John Marshall, editor of the afternoon paper, who had been a reporter when the liquor was seized, did climb out on the roof, detected no smell of whiskey, dipped a finger into the puddle running out of the bales and tasted it. It was water.

Afterward, he dropped by Judge Harris's office downstairs and reported this. Said the judge:

"Damn it! I told the boys to leave one full bottle in every case to make a little odor of alcohol. The whiskey's back there in my closet. Take a bottle."

WILMINGTON'S OUTBREAK of criminality included a sordid episode of thievery at 801 Princess Street when I was six years old and in the first grade and Mama caught me stealing a quarter. I noticed that Margaret had left her handbag standing open on a living room table with an assortment of coins in plain view. There was nobody else in the room. No witnesses. No trail of evidence. It seemed a clear chance, the perfect crime never to be solved and the miserable sinner never brought to justice. I calculated these odds as best a six-year-old could, took a quarter, walked across the street to Montgomery's store, bought five Baby Ruths, hid on the back porch and ate all five. Here I was, stuffed with chocolate, peanuts and sugar, happy and safe, I thought. But then it all began to unravel. Margaret missed the quarter, worth dollars in today's money, and at the dinner table, looking straight at me, wondered aloud where it went. Mama noticed I ate almost no dinner and asked if I felt all right. I didn't. I felt the world was closing in on me. The Baby Ruth wrappers had been found where I carelessly discarded them. A call to Montgomery's brought the final, crushing evidence.

"Yes, Mrs. Brinkley, David did come in today.

Bought five Baby Ruths. Didn't charge them. Paid cash. Is anything wrong?''

Yes, everything in the world was wrong. I was about to become the Al Capone of Princess Street, and I knew it. I was called in, confronted with the evidence and invited to plead guilty. I squirmed and said nothing, the term ''nolo contendere'' being unknown to me. Guilty as charged. Whereupon Mama took to her bed and cried for three days, saying over and over, ''I hope God will forgive me for raising a thief.''

My father, the kindest man I ever knew, feared my mother as much as I did. He pulled me aside out of her hearing and said, ''It's all right, son. I'll give Margaret's money back. Just don't *ever* do that again.''

The Princess Street crime wave had been broken, but it remained a low point in my life, an agony of guilt and fear that still drifts through my dreams.

NONE OF US could anticipate when Mama could or would let down enough, give enough of herself to show some small sign of kindness or generosity, since she seemed to love babies, dogs and her flower garden but nothing or no one else. I remember only one exception. I could not understand it then and cannot now. One day in May she was rocking on the front porch at 801 embroidering something while I sat out there reading. There was, as usual, little or no conversation. Approaching our corner was a two-wheel cart being pulled along by an ancient, sore-footed mule and being driven by an elderly black man who was shouting, or singing, over and over the word, ''Strawberr*eeeeeeeees*.'' Then, as now, eastern North Carolina grew the finest strawberries in the world, arriving in May in a burst of sweetness and redness unequaled. Those he was offering for sale from his cart were fifteen cents a quart, two quarts for a quarter. The driver apologized, ''A little high this year because of the rain.''

As he turned his cart left from Eighth Street onto Princess his mule was frightened by the clanging of a passing trolley car. He reared up on his hind legs and tilted the car on its side, spilling strawberries halfway across the street. Instantly, Mama was out of her chair. ''Come on, David. We're going to help him.''

We ran into the street. Dr. Dreher next door saw what was happening and came out to help. So did the Blakes from across Eighth. Others came. It began to look like a block party. Together we lifted the cart back on its wheels. Mama shouted to me to drag the garden hose out from our front yard and turn on the water. She stood in the middle of Princess Street, her ankle-length housedress soaking wet, using our hose to wash the strawberries as they were picked up and put back into their little wooden baskets. A trolley car arrived on its way downtown. The motorman stopped it, got out and helped lift the strawberry baskets back into the cart. A scene from *Our Town*. In about half an hour the strawberry man was back in business and on his way toward Ninth Street and back to his chant ''strawberr*eeeeeeeee*s.''

It was one of Mama's rare moments of warmth and humanity. What prompted it? We never knew, but before it was over she had rallied most of the neighborhood to come and help, including two black families who lived on the next block. In southern towns in these old days, meaning into the twenties and thirties, neighborhoods were racially integrated as they had been since the Civil War. Slave owners in the cities often built small houses nearby for their slaves, and when they were freed they stayed on where they were with no fuss and no one paying any attention. And two families of former slaves had stayed on a block or two from Eighth and Princess, and their descendants still lived there in their same small houses, and no one gave it a thought when they came out to help with the strawberries. Like the other neighbors, they were needed and they came.

TWO YEARS LATER, when I was eight, I awoke one morning to be told my father had died of a heart attack during the night. Or, as Margaret put it to me, ''Papa's gone to heaven.''

I hurried downstairs to find Mama. She was already in the pantry dumping the wine my father had carefully and lovingly made over the years. As she poured his wine down the sink she wore a thin, cold smile of satisfaction, of victory. A woman who had hated alcohol all her life and had fought bitterly with my father because he liked it too much had won her fight with him. Finally, finally.

Mama was forty-two years old when I was born in 1920. At that time, among her women friends in the small-town South, it was thought to be hardly decent for a married woman to be pregnant at the age of forty-two. Slightly scandalous, in fact, and seen as the product of lascivious behavior unseemly for a woman her age. Word reached Mama that her women friends, all members of her St. Andrew's Presbyterian Church, were saying out of her hearing that by her age married women were expected to be finished with having babies. Given that she was born in 1879, just fourteen years after the Civil War and the murder of Abraham Lincoln, her friends' disapproval probably was a medical remnant surviving from the early nineteenth century, when the average life span was shorter, when babies were delivered by midwives or by the family doctor who arrived in a one-horse carriage carrying a small black bag and calling for hot water and towels, when childbirth was hazardous and infections frequent and sometimes fatal. And in the early practice of medicine it was known that mothers older than forty or so often had problem babies. For that or some other reasons unknown to me, my mother's women friends—gray-haired, thin-lipped, cold-eyed and waspish—all thought she had committed a sin. While saying nothing to her directly, they made sure she heard about what was being said at St. Andrew's gatherings, leaving her to suffer the painful knowledge that there was ugly gossip behind her back. Cruelty in the service of the Lord. When Mama, a Presbyterian, married my father, an Episcopalian, these were the same women who privately denounced it as a "mixed marriage." My sisters told me later she cried uncontrollably when I was born because I was a terrible embarrassment to her. I had made her the victim of gossip. I was not wanted. I now believe that for every day of my life at home with her, every time she looked at me, when she could not avoid looking at me, I reminded her of the agony and suffering that came with me when I was born. I regret her suffering, but I must say I am thankful that abortion was not available at that time in that place. If it had been, I would not be here.

Dr. Alexander McClure, the pastor of St. Andrew's, was tireless in trying to help her through her unhappiness when they had all come home from my father's funeral. He came to our house day after day and sat with her, talking so softly that in the next room we could not hear what he was saying, and at the age of eight I was unable to make any judgments about her, but in thinking back on this in later years, I did see that when he talked to her, holding her hand, she looked calmer and more serene than I had ever seen before. Was she in love with him all those years? Maybe. I don't know. But I do know that since my father's death was the first in our immediate family and since he died quite young, at fifty-two, no one had ever thought to buy a cemetery lot. Mama had to do it. She chose a space for him and all of our family among the moss-draped live oaks and dogwoods in Wilmington's ancient Oakdale Cemetery. And in what seems to me now to have been the one grand and operatic romantic gesture of her life, she chose one only a few feet from a burial space reserved for Dr. McClure.

AN EAGERNESS to write, or try to, said to be an ailment endemic among southerners, infected me in high school. Why? I don't know. I believe it was William Faulkner who was asked why the American South produced so many writers, good and bad, and who replied: "Because we lost the war." Meaning, I've always thought, that in the post–Civil War South, a devastated land cast into deep poverty, there was nothing else to do. Businesses and jobs had been destroyed, and writing required nothing more than a cheap pencil applied to cheap paper.

Whatever the history, another day burned forever in my mind was when I wrote a little story about something or other and walked upstairs and showed it to Mama. After a brief glance, she threw the paper in my face and said, "Why are you wasting your time on this foolishness?" It was another scar slow to heal.

It all changed a few years later. The one-hundred-watt local radio station, WRBT, announced on the air it would have an essay contest on the topic "What WRBT Means to Wilmington," the winning entry to be awarded five dollars. With a cynicism I had never known I possessed, I gave this some thought and concluded that what WRBT meant to Wilmington was that it was a small nonnetwork radio station where an advertiser could buy a one-minute commercial for two or three dollars and where the remaining airtime was filled with the playing of 78-rpm records by Paul Whiteman and cheap OKeh and Vocalion records of small dance orchestras that sounded to me as if they consisted of two C-melody saxophones and a tuba. I wrote out an entry in pencil, asked Margaret to take it to her office, where she had a secretary type it and make it look nice, and sent it in. It said that what WRBT meant to Wilmington was free entertainment along with an interesting, valuable and money-saving flow of information from the station's advertisers, "information no one in Wilmington should miss." Dick Dunlea, the station's manager, thought that was just wonderful, exactly what he had in mind. He announced on the air I had won the essay contest and the five-dollar prize. Instant fame and riches! Winning a more or less literary competition open to all! My name announced on the radio! Announced right after Paul Whiteman's record of "Dardanella"! Plus about four dollars more cash than I had ever had in my life.

A broadcaster today might envy Dunlea and WRBT. Wilmington was not much of a city, or market, as it would be called today, with a population of about thirty-five thousand, but the station had an audience share of 100 percent, since it was the only one in town. And it was the only one on the dial. There was none other close enough to Wilmington to be tuned in by anyone but the tinkerers with backyard antenna towers fifty feet high, the hobbyists who built radio gear in the garage and who liked to report that last night they managed to tune in Chile, or somebody talking in a funny language that sure sounded like Chile. So, to listen to the radio was to listen to WRBT.

Now my friends at Hemenway grade school regarded me as a famous writer whose literary skills had made him into a well-known figure worth a good deal of money for my age, about twelve. Even Mama warmed up very slightly and used her most extravagantly effusive language in response to my great achievement. She said, "Oh, it's all right." For her, that was an emotional outburst.

Life in the 1930s in a southern town of thirty-five thousand with one one-hundred-watt AM radio station with no network affiliation and no news wire? How could it broadcast the news? It couldn't. That difficult and expensive service it left entirely to the local newspaper. Live coverage of important news events? Election nights? Franklin Roosevelt's fireside chats? The beginnings of Hitler's conquest of Europe? The World Series? So far as WRBT was concerned, none of this ever happened.

Wilmington stood about in the middle of the southern states so deeply addicted to baseball that year after year they produced far more than their share of major league stars, but even so it was a city with no sports teams of its own other than that from the local high school. And so it felt truly deprived, denied and underprivileged, and particularly so during the World Series. The radio network broadcasting the games could not be heard in our town, and WRBT, with no network affiliation, could offer nothing. With an unaccustomed willingness to spend money, the *Star-News* rose to this challenge. It hired a Western Union wire to bring the World Series by telegraph, in Morse code, play-by-play to the paper's office. What came in were the barest bones, the briefest and most cryptic possible descriptions of each pitch and each play. Strike one came in over the wire as "S1." When a batter hit a grounder to the shortstop and was thrown out at first, the Western Union operator sent this information: "63O"—meaning the ball was hit on the ground to the shortstop, position six, and then thrown to the first baseman, position three, and the

batter was out. Had the runner managed to beat out
the throw to first, the wire would have read ''1B''
—a one-base hit. A generation of small-time radio
announcers broadcast baseball games by starting
with these tiny, dry bits of information and embel-
lishing them with chatter about events in the game
that sounded good on the radio whether or not they
actually happened, often describing a game far more
exciting than the one being played. It recalled for
me a remark by the grand old sportswriter Grant-
land Rice. He sat in a press box watching a game
and at the same time listening to NBC's announcer,
Bill Stern, sitting at a microphone nearby and describing it on the radio and adding juicy details as
he saw fit. His description, but not the game, was
frenzied with excitement. Rice wrote: ''There were
two entirely different games played here today—
one on the field and another on NBC radio.'' One
of the early and much-admired practitioners of this
obscure art form was a radio announcer who later
went on to a somewhat higher calling, Ronald
Reagan.

Now the World Series approached, and the *Star-
News* with its Western Union wire was ready. The
paper could have and probably should have turned
its baseball wire over to WRBT and had one of its
announcers broadcast the game to the entire city.
But no. This new and exciting technology was being
brought to Wilmington by Rinaldo B. Page and his
newspaper, and he was absolutely not willing to

share the glory with Dick Dunlea. So, how to use the play-by-play?

This was the answer they settled on: They built a wooden platform out over the front sidewalk at the level of the paper's second-floor windows. They bought or rented from God knew where a contraption consisting of a very large upright green board printed with a white graphic of a baseball diamond maybe six feet high. In front of it, a white tennis ball suspended on a taut wire. On a platform behind the diamond was an arrangement of cables and pulleys that allowed the operator, out of sight, to move the tennis ball around the diamond as the Western Union wire dictated. For each pitch, the tennis ball on the wire was moved from the pitcher's mound to home plate. If it was a ball or a called strike, the tennis ball went back to the pitcher. If a hit, the operator moved it around the field to wherever the incoming wire said. The paper had no sports staff to speak of, having few local sports events to speak of; Lamont Smith, the paper's editor, said he would do all the announcing himself, shouting from a second-floor window through a megaphone. The paper invited the entire town to turn out for this new and exciting marvel and to watch the game from the post office lawn across the street. Even the postmaster, Wilbur Dosher, came out and strolled through the crowd, complaining as he went that this was all so exciting he was watching the *Star-News* re-creation of the game and taking time out in the

midst of a fight with the U.S. Post Office Department in Washington. It was trying to take away
some of the monetary credit for his rising volume
of mail and transfer it to a bigger city, Charlotte,
upstate. He said, "They want to grease a fat sow's
ass with Brookfield butter."

But with the World Series about to begin, nobody
cared about that. People brought folding chairs and
set them up on the grass across Chestnut Street, pic-
nics, blankets on the grass, pints of whiskey in
brown paper sacks; hawkers moved through the
crowd selling peanuts while Lamont Smith bel-
lowed the play-by-play out of his upstairs window.
For nine innings a copyboy ran back and forth
across Front Street to Skipper's poolroom to bring
Smith cans of Krueger's ale. That was how I and
the townspeople of Wilmington, North Carolina,
"saw" our first World Series game.

IN THE BEGINNING of radio, about 1912, federal
licenses for local stations generally could be had
almost for the asking, since the idea of commercial
advertising on radio had not yet been imagined and
only recently President Herbert Hoover had spoken
angrily against it, saying it should never be allowed.
Accordingly, many of the earliest broadcast licenses
were awarded to the tinkerers out in the garages of
America, playing around with wires and coils and

breadboards and crystal sets with cat's whiskers. A Washington, D.C., license was given to an optometrist named M. A. Leese. He is long since deceased, but his initials live on in a modern radio station, an ABC affiliate, WMAL. The first licensee in Richmond, Virginia, was a bicycle repairman.

These were not your creative programmers. They were not actors, musicians, journalists. They were hobbyists and experimenters in electronic gadgetry. All they knew was to play 78-rpm records with their ticks, pops and scratches. And the fairly typical small-town radio station, WRBT in Wilmington, was equipped with two microphones and a turntable. That was it. That was all it needed for its announcers to read commercials and to cue up the records of the dance bands. The announcers usually worked for nothing, for the honor of it, for the local celebrity it brought them, and for the hope eventually to reach the big time and do the midnight dance band remotes from New York. These were an interesting artifact of American popular culture in the thirties. The ritual called for an announcer with his left hand cupped behind his ear, the better to hear his own velvet tones, talking over the audience's shrieks, giggles and alcoholic laughter and saying something like "Ladies and gentlemen, from the Burgundy Ballroom high atop the Sherry Netherland Hotel, a bare quarter mile from Times Square in New York City, NBC brings you the scintillating rhythms of Jan Garber, Idol of the Airlanes.''

The sound quality was uniformly terrible because the microphone setup was slapdash, hurried, unrehearsed. The music as heard on the radio was badly out of balance because the instruments nearest the one microphone, usually the saxophones, were the loudest, and the others farther back could barely be heard.

One of WRBT's unpaid announcers, Howard Ozment, thought that just being on the air, seeming somehow to be in the company of such famous figures as Benny Goodman, Tommy Dorsey and Artie Shaw, made him an important figure around town and also made it easier to get girls. But in a small-town radio station with no network and no news wire, with few facilities and little money, there were no other benefits. WRBT was able to survive with nothing more than unpaid announcers reading three-dollar commercials and spinning records while dreaming maybe, somehow, someday, of standing in the spotlight in some version of the Burgundy Ballroom.

Near the end of the thirties, WRBT decided it could no longer ignore the news. Hitler had invaded Poland. Al Dickson of the *Star-News* agonized for hours about his headline for the next morning's paper and settled on THE GERMAN ARMY MARCHES. There was talk of another world war and a military draft only about twenty years after the last one. The station had to do something. An affiliation with NBC or CBS was out of the question. The big networks did not want and would not accept one-hundred-watt stations. Dick Dunlea turned to the *Star-News* and asked to make some kind of deal. The paper had the services of the Associated Press bringing news from the war fronts and from around the world. He said to Rinaldo Page, the paper's publisher, ''My boys can go on the air and read commercials for Kingoff's jewelers selling wristwatches and so on, but they can't deal with the news. Can't pronounce the foreign names. They don't know where Poland is. Wouldn't know what to say about it if they did. Can you folks help us out? Can you do something with news on the air?''

Page offered Dunlea five minutes of news off the AP wire in mid-afternoon every day, written and read on the air by me, for no pay, of course. I did it, the first words I ever spoke on the air, and it was perfectly awful. I did not know how to write words to be spoken, and once they were written I did not know how to read them. I got by with a profound incompetence because the local audience knew no more about it than I did. In a one-station town with no network people had never heard a news broadcaster who was any good and so had no way of knowing how bad I was. It was the first of many times luck has been with me when talent was not.

I am thankful that in these first years tape recording had not yet been invented.

THE LOCAL NOTORIETY from the WRBT essay contest even led to the offer of a paid Saturday job in the A&P store. This in the middle thirties when Franklin Roosevelt was still battling the depression, and a job, any job, doing any work at all at any pay, in any place, was ardently to be sought. The unemployment rate across the country then was approaching 30 percent, and a job, if found, was coveted, raising as it did the possibility, or hope, of buying a new car and new clothes, the unvarying stuff of teenage dreams. Mr. Swindell, the A&P manager, later told me he offered me the job because in the WRBT essay contest I ''wrote so well about Wilmington business I thought you might do well in retail groceries.'' And when I was older, he said (I was then twelve) I might even be eligible to join the Wilmington Rotary Club—the shining vista of American success and prosperity laid before me, along with enticing dreams of a new car, my choice of a Ford, Chevrolet or Plymouth.

One entering the Wilmington A&P at Sixth and Grace walked into a dense cloud of assorted odors and fragrances, a retailer's sachet, in these years when nothing was wrapped in cellophane and there was no air-conditioning to pump out the air and the smells of bananas, Eight O'Clock coffee, apples and dust to the outdoors. But the A&P believed it had created a slick, modern progressive merchandising system with its policies of cash only and no deliveries. This eliminated charge accounts and their collection problems and ended the angry customers' complaints about groceries delivered by pickup truck over bumpy streets on hot days and arriving in a mess of cracked eggs, soured milk and melted butter. Instead, A&P customers rolled their groceries home, often in their children's red-enameled Radio Flyer coaster wagons.

Mr. Swindell explained to me that the A&P sold butter in two forms—''print'' butter in quarter-pound sticks wrapped in paper printed with the dairy's name, and a cheaper butter that came in bulk in wooden tubs set on the floor open to dust and insects. When bulk butter was sold, it was scooped into pressed cardboard trays and weighed on a scale with a sliding balance out of the customers' sight. Mr. Swindell explained to me that when I weighed butter for black customers, ''you should set the balance about here,'' he said, placing the balance weight at thirteen ounces. If the weight was out of sight of the customers, it was also out of sight of the store manager. I always set it for a pound at nineteen ounces.

Inside the Wilmington A&P in the early thirties, the nineteenth century was alive and well but soon to die. A man named Michael Cullin was building a new chain of supermarkets in the Midwest called

King Kullen, featuring for the first time in retailing the oxymoronic term ''self-service.'' This radical idea had not yet reached Wilmington. Here, store clerks wearing white aprons stood behind the counter, each with a pencil behind his right ear. When a customer came in with a grocery list, A&P policy was to ask for the list to be handed to a clerk to save time in assembling the order. But most shoppers refused and insisted on asking for one item at a time—one can of early June peas, then one pound of Gold Medal flour—forcing the clerk to run around the store, back and forth, collecting the groceries one item on each trip. Speed and efficiency? Not yet invented. When it was all done at last, the clerk used his pencil on a brown paper bag to total the order, collected the money, made change and bagged the groceries—each with a high probability of errors in his arithmetic or, for those so inclined, petty chiseling. It was a wonder the A&P survived. It never paid me enough to buy much of anything—$1.25 a day.

PRINCESS STREET'S yellow-painted trolley cars ran out to the end of town, through the suburbs for nine miles, bouncing and swaying over creaking wooden trestles to Wrightsville Beach, accessible only by trolley or by a half-mile footbridge over the sound and always crowded with bait-casting fishermen trying to hook a few half-pound eight-inch spot and perch. Those not fishing were crabbing. This required a scrap of meat for bait, tied on a string with a weight and lowered into the sound for a few minutes and then slowly raised to the surface. Most times, two or three crabs would be found clinging to the bait, and the crabbers used long-handled nets to dip them out of the water. When the time, tide and temperature were right a bushel of crabs could be caught in an hour or two. This in the thirties and forties when the East Coast beaches, with the arrival of the automobile, were coming to be crowded, polluted and their waters overfished. Wrightsville escaped most of this because from its beginnings in the nineteenth century it was isolated, off in a corner of the North Carolina coast, no big city nearby and not easily accessible. Local residents then were able to keep the beach mostly to themselves, and on weekends there might be fifteen people on its clean white sand. Wilmington residents of even modest prosperity could have a house in town and a shingled cottage built up on stilts on the beach, a fifteen-minute drive from downtown. My own family, not rich, lived at 801 Princess in the winter and in a small house on the beach in summer. We moved to the beach in May and back to the city in late September. For a schoolboy with a summer job at the beach making a little money working as a soda jerk—milk shakes ten cents, fountain Cokes five cents—with girls all around in swimsuits that then seemed skimpy, the beach, the surf, Lumina with big bands playing every night, it was heaven. It even made Mama tolerable. I knew of no place on earth where such a great life could be had so easily and cheaply.

A WORLD turned for me in Mrs. Burrows Smith's English class at New Hanover High School. When I wrote a few pages of something and showed it to her she actually read it, commented on it, told me what she thought, and when it was good she said so and when it was not good she told me what was wrong and how to improve it. After some months, she said to me, "David, I think you ought to be a journalist."

It was the first time that idea ever occurred to me. I had not known it, but the high school had a program called Cooperative Education or some such name. It allowed a student to leave school two hours early in the afternoon and to work in some local business as a sort of intern, the only pay being the opportunity to learn a little something. They sent me to a job at the *Star-News*, morning and afternoon papers, circulation about ten thousand. I worked there in the early afternoons, without the smallest idea of what I was geting into, but I quickly came to love it.

A pleasant, gray-haired woman on Wilmington's North Fifth Street owned a century plant, a type of cactus said to bloom only once in a hundred years.

She called the paper and said the century plant sat on her front porch and it would bloom on the following Tuesday night. Al Dickson, the managing editor and a great man, high-strung, often smoking two Camel cigarettes at once, always worried about something, probably from a lifetime of working on bad newspapers, handed me at the age of seventeen the first news assignment of my life. Go over to the north end of town, he said, and do a story about the century plant—interview the owner and her neighbors and all that. "Could be a nice little local story."

In doing a little advance research, I found the office dictionary said "century plant, a Mexican agave, cultivated as an ornamental, *erroneously believed to flower only once every century*" [emphasis added].

"Erroneously believed?" My first big story dead even before I got to it? I called Will Rehder, Wilmington's longtime florist, and asked him, "Do you know anything about the century plant? Supposed to bloom every hundred years?"

"What do I know about it? Not a damned thing."

I asked myself, should I tell Al Dickson about all this? Stomp on a story because of what the dictionary says? And what Will Rehder says? Wouldn't that be a hell of a way to start a journalism career? Yes, it would. So ignore all that and go to North Fifth Street and report whatever happens. *Whatever* happens. If the plant blooms, mildly interesting. If it does not and the neighborhood is disappointed, maybe even more interesting. And what does Will Rehder know anyway? He sells roses and gladiolus and Easter baskets full of shredded green wax paper with plastic rabbits nesting in it. He's never sold a century plant in his life. And, again, anything may happen. You're a reporter? Go and report.

I arrived to find a wonderful scene—a block of North Fifth Street crowded with people. Popsicle vendors working the crowd, the fire department's emergency floodlights, their diesel engines roaring, lighting up the block and the gingerbready front porch where the Mexican agave sat in a large pot looking like not much. At the bottom of the plant there was a little scraggly circle of spiky, sharp, pointed leaves and then a bare stalk going straight up for about four feet with a few tiny green sprigs growing out of it at the top. It looked like a broom handle growing a little hair.

I asked the woman, "When your century plant blooms, where will the bloom be? On top of that stalk?"

"How would I know? I'm not a hundred years old."

"How do you know tonight's the night, the end of a hundred years?"

"My grandfather bought this plant in Mexico. Before he died, he was told this plant was about sixty years old and that was forty years ago."

About sixty years old forty years ago? Some-where around a hundred, or so it was said by an unknown Mexican long since dead? The plant could be almost any age. And of its true age the woman had no idea and neither did anyone else. Not only that, the dictionary said "erroneously believed."

Here was all this mess and confusion on the first assignment of my life. I could not see how to get out of it. I was afraid it would get me fired. As it turned out, I didn't have to produce anything. Al Dickson called and said there was mechanical trouble in the composing room, he had to put the paper to bed early and he couldn't wait for my plant to bloom. "Knock it off and go home."

I stayed around anyway. This might be an even more amusing story than if the plant had bloomed on time, whatever the time was to be. What would the battalion chief say to his firemen who had worked overtime to set up the floodlights? Would he tell them city hall had screwed up again? Actually, when asked, he said, "Buncha damn fools in city hall, all of them. What will I tell my men? Tell them to come back in another hundred years?"

How about the people who kept their children up late to see a miracle of nature that never happened? They were all furious, the children screaming. The woman who owned the plant and started all this? What would she say? She said, "I'll never trust a Mexican again."

It was Sociology 101 out there—a small-town

street full of people, including the kind who write angry letters to the editor signed "Concerned Citizen" or "Outraged Transit Rider." I found an older man wearing khaki pants, high-top tan shoes, gray mustache, a shirt with a Prince Albert pipe tobacco can in its pocket and a green felt hat. I quoted him: "Look at this damn mess. Popsicle sticks and Eskimo Pie wrappers all over. Coca-Cola bottles. Broken glass. Because of that damn fool woman the taxpayers have to pay to clean this up? What's all this going to cost us? Don't we pay enough already? And that damned century plant never even bloomed?"

So, the next morning all this nonsense made an amusing little story for the paper, and to everyone's astonishment it was picked up and carried across the country by the Associated Press, even getting three column inches in the Los Angeles *Times*. Al Dickson could not believe it. Lamont Smith, the editor, called me in and said when I got out of school I could have a job at the paper if I wanted it.

THE *Star-News* was a nice enough small-town newspaper, about 10,000 copies a day in a town of 35,000—about average. The *News* in the afternoon did a little better than the *Morning Star*, since these were the years before anyone even dreamed television would kill off nearly every afternoon paper in the United States. This was a family-owned paper as most were then, the owner, Rinaldo Page, a short, red-faced man who always seemed to me to be hurrying to get something done, whatever it was, before it was too late. His number-two executive was J. Walter Webb. When he was arrested for driving drunk it was pointed out to him that the paper's policy unfailingly was to print the names of those arrested for driving under the influence, an iron rule in the 1930s in North Carolina where Prohibitionist sentiment never really disappeared and where it was assumed these drunken sinners must be punished by exposure in the press even if they were never tried in court. In a small town where everyone knew everyone, this was a sin close to mortal. So what was J. Walter Webb to do now? If he used his position to keep his name out of the paper it would become scandalous gossip embarrassing to him as well as to the *Star-News*, and if he put his name in the paper he probably would have to cringe and resign before the lightning bolts of righteousness flashing down from the Protestant-Prohibitionist pulpits on Sunday morning. J. Walter Webb weaseled his way out of this by having the paper report the arrest of John W. Webb. That was his correct name, but nobody in town knew it. Probably some out-of-town visitor drinking at the beach, the gossip went.

The *Star-News* reporting staff numbered three, and the photographic staff numbered one. Of the three reporters, two were paid. I was not. Later, however, my pay zoomed upward in a giddy spiral, reaching eleven dollars a week. But in the meantime, I was working for the experience.

One of the paid reporters was Bob Matthews, who had been taught, or mistaught, somewhere that the central fact of journalism was "names make news." Some names, sometimes, yes. But Matthews's idea of a news story was a piece of copy saying little or nothing but accompanied by a long list of names, something like this: "The Membership Committee of the Sorosis Club held its monthly meeting in its clubhouse on Third Street last night and voted to make no changes in its policies, and those present included: . . ." and here Matthews listed every name he could find, sometimes filling an entire column.

When I asked why they printed all this junk, the answer always was "Mr. Page likes it." The journalism lesson here was entirely clear: if you own the paper you can print any damned thing you like.

The one-man photographic staff consisted of Roderick Sparrow, a nervous, high-strung and diminutive man whose most notable facial feature was a set of teeth so perfect, so large, so straight, so prominent and so eye-catching it appeared they would be about the right size for a set of dentures for a Clydesdale. Sparrow's camera was called a Graflex, a body about the size of a shoe box with a black chimney rising about a foot up from the top. Look down into it and you could see a ground glass with a picture upside down and backward, so cumbersome and so complicated that anything that could not be held motionless for several minutes was difficult to photograph. When Eleanor Roosevelt came to visit a federal agricultural experiment station at Willard, North Carolina, about forty miles from Wilmington, the paper sent Sparrow to photograph the event. He returned with a stack of negatives, every one of them made after the subject had moved out of the frame. Sparrow's other Great Performance was when he invited the whole staff to a party at his house in the suburbs. Everyone would get a picture to take home, and every table lamp in his living room had a photoflood bulb screwed into it, providing enough light for casual and informal photography, he said. Maybe so. Photoflood bulbs make a bright light, yes, but they also produce tremendous heat. And so in about fifteen minutes his living room began to heat up and the guests to sweat through their clothes. In another few minutes Sparrow's lamp shades started to smoke and then to burst into flame. Regrettably, as usual, he got no pictures.

The other paid reporter was Sam Ragan, by far our best. He is still active and the owner of a weekly paper in Southern Pines, North Carolina, and a splendid man in all respects. He smokes a pipe, wears his hair a little longish, writes poetry and prose, both beautifully, and is at this writing the poet laureate of North Carolina. In his person and his manner he calls up every southern dream of romance and beauty among the live oaks and pines and the quietly sad longing for a southern past that none of us now alive ever knew, if anyone other than Margaret Mitchell ever did. I believe Sam is the only member of the *Star-News* staff who was there when I began to work fifty-odd years ago and who is still around to know of my great respect and affection for him.

LIKE EVERY southern city able to spend the money, Wilmington's city hall was high Greek Revival—columned portico, Corinthian capitals, monumental granite steps. On the ground floor was the police department, on the second the mayor's office and the attendant bureaucracies and on the third floor were the public library and Miss Emma Woodward, the librarian and maybe the brightest woman in town. She looked like Joyce Carol Oates with her large, round, black, heavy-framed glasses that seemed almost to extend from upper lip to forehead of her classic southern/English face that needed only an oval frame to resemble a cameo— not quite beautiful but altogether wonderful. She talked the way a bird chirps—fast, high-pitched words running together in bursts followed by a little silence. Quick burst, silence, quick burst. Some southerners drawl. Others talk so rapidly their words are almost disembodied and high pitched because they come entirely from the front of the mouth without chest tones, and they pour out like a spilled bag of marbles.

During the many days, years, when the atmosphere at home was strained I retreated to the public library five blocks from home and roamed through the stacks trying to read everything in sight. Watching this, Miss Woodward called my English teacher and said I needed more than the high school could give, and she offered to take me over herself with courses in English and history and more, supervised by her. She became my personal tutor—taking my papers home at night, reading and grading them and discussing them with me the next day. Why did she do all this?

"David, because it's a relief from spending my days running what amounts to the town's lending library checking out and checking in cheap novels by Margaret Widmer and Ethel M. Dell. This is more fun. This is what I went to school for."

For more than three years, we read and talked through the afternoons, and after I left school, she gave me a sort of diploma. She handed me the tome Oswald Spengler's *Decline of the West* and said, "This is a free copy the publisher sent. You take it. Nobody else in the county will ever read it."

IF YOU DROVE southward through Wilmington you passed Doc Hall's drugstore and saw this huge sign painted ten feet high on his store's outside wall

IF YOU'VE GOT THE ITCH
AND A DOLLAR
I'VE GOT THE CURE

and you entered a blue-collar, low-income, rough-and-tumble, crime-ridden neighborhood called Dry Pond, so named because until it was drained it was swampy in summer and dry in the winter. Doc Hall, the pharmacist, was its unofficial, unelected mayor. Not only did he offer to help itchy customers at a bargain price, he also specialized in fitting trusses to old geezers unwilling or unable to have their hernias repaired surgically. In a neighborhood where at times money could be made lifting heavy cargoes on and off freighters docked in the river, hernias were common, expensive surgery was not, and Doc Hall had a room in the back devoted entirely to trussing up hernias. And he offered other services: during Prohibition his soda fountain provided regular customers two ounces of whiskey concealed in a milk shake. An ordinary milk shake was ten cents. This special offering, sold under the counter and sold only on such special occasions as paydays, birthdays, Christmas, cost thirty-five cents. Other services included this: regular customers whose incomes were erratic, which was most of them, were allowed a few dollars of credit at interest rates of 10 percent a week, more or less, depending on Doc's personal assessment of the credit risk. Interest rates for less than a week of credit—''Just until payday, Doc''—were negotiable.

A typical payday for Dry Ponders in the middle thirties came when a freighter sailed up the Cape Fear River to discharge a cargo of bananas in Wilmington. Six or eight Dry Ponders were hired to unload the ship by shouldering the bananas, one bunch at a time, and carrying them about a hundred yards to a warehouse. The pay? A penny a bunch, maybe enough to square accounts at Doc Hall's. His store clearly was Dry Pond's one essential institution, dealing with the pain and struggle of small-town working-class Americans in the last, lingering days of the Great Depression.

IN SEPTEMBER 1940, when World War II raged in Europe while the United States was still at peace, but barely, I enrolled at the University of North Carolina at Chapel Hill, but changed my mind at the last minute. I thought it wise to go into the Army as a volunteer first—the draft was soon to begin—and to get my military service behind me before starting college and then having to interrupt it before I could start a more serious career in journalism. I signed up at a recruiting station in Wilmington, they put me into the nearest National Guard unit, already absorbed into the regular U.S. Army, Company I of the 120th Infantry. I was astonished to find that from its National Guard days the company was composed almost entirely of men from Dry Pond. And its first lieutenant was Mike Hall, Doc Hall's son. Soon we were shipped out to Fort Jackson, South Carolina, where the Army was trying to assemble all its southern forces in one place. We were, we told ourselves, a regiment of rifle-carrying mud-slogging infantry foot soldiers always out front in battle and always the first to die. Probably true, but as new young soldiers, having never witnessed blood or spilled any but having seen a few war movies, we were entranced with our own bravery, untested as it was, and liked to discuss our opinion that because we were always out front in battle, we were the bravest. No doubt.

To the other enlisted men, I was a curiosity. Not a Dry Ponder. A resident of Wilmington and Wrightsville Beach. Able to use a typewriter without looking at the keys. Had even written a little stuff for the local paper. I was one of *them*—the them they imagined to be rich, owning instead of renting, living a life of no heavy lifting, driving their own cars, and how come they always had their clothes pressed and their shoes shined? I did not meet all their imaginary standards, but they thought I did, and in time we got along. And I became their trusted friend when I was appointed supply sergeant. I learned the 1940s peacetime Army was so strapped for money its regulations required all missing military property to be paid for in cash. And I learned that every Dry Ponder was charged with so much Army property he had lost or stolen he could never hope to pay his way out of debt. I worked over the records I inherited, found them to be an impossible mess, and in the process of straightening them out I found various ways to get the men all clean and out of debt to the Army. It was the kind of dubious, chiseling, more or less honest game they all understood, and they all thanked me, since in their ethic those who were somewhat privileged were expected to help those who were not, even if the rules had to be bent a little. And so the word went down the row of canvas pyramidal tents lining the company street where we all lived for a year that the new supply sergeant was not a Dry Ponder but was all right nevertheless.

From there on, Company I was what the peacetime Army always was—dull and boring. But after about a year, the Army medics told me I had a kidney ailment, which I did not have and never have had, but they insisted, and I was handed an honorable discharge, medical. I left the Army and took the Greyhound bus back to Wilmington and back to work for the *Star*.

ON A SATURDAY night in 1940 a dozen or so middle-aged and older men, well dressed, looking prosperous and making sure their prosperity was visible, came into Hall's store in a group. They needed no credit and wanted no whiskey-flavored milk shakes. They were former Dry Ponders who had long since moved out of the neighborhood to live in the more socially presentable parts of town, a few even to Forest Hills, the town's pretty, leafy suburb. Rather than dropping out of Tileston grade school as so many Dry Ponders had, they had gone on to finish some kind of schooling and gone into business downtown, dealing in insurance, investments, real estate, law. And they had stopped by Hall's for a minute to pay their respects to Doc and to recall with slightly forced laughter their youthful memories and then to walk down the street to the fiftieth reunion of the Brigade Boys Club.

The club consisted of a basketball court and a few modest facilities contributed by the town's do-gooders in the hope of keeping the young Dry Ponders amused and off the streets when they were not hanging out at Hall's or idling noisily on street corners and starting fights and contemplating acts of petty thievery. Now, on its anniversary, the club invited all its old members back to celebrate with a dinner of cold sliced ham, potato salad and odds and ends served on paper plates, followed by a couple of speeches.

The *Star*, doing its civic duty, felt this was an event worth a little coverage and sent its youngest, greenest reporter, me. The speeches ran to sentimental memories of youth in Dry Pond and at Hall's and good times at the Brigade Club. A former club president, trying not to cry, recited with emotional difficulty a line of poetry by Florence Percy that had somehow survived since its publication in *The Saturday Evening Post* in 1860:

> *Backward, turn backward, O time in its flight*
> *And make me a boy again just for tonight!*

When it was noticed that I was not a Dry Ponder and not a member of the club and when I was seen making a few brief notes, a certain nervousness spread through the crowd, and I saw they were all staring at me. Finally, one came over and asked, "Are you a reporter?"

"Yes."

"From the *Star*?"

"Yes."

"Are you going to put this meeting in the paper?"

"Yes."

When that word spread, a pathetic little procession of club members called me aside, asking that if I printed the names of those present, would I please leave their names out.

"Why?"

Some lied and said they had told their wives they would be somewhere else and were afraid of being caught. But the real reason, and a few finally admitted it, was that it would hurt their business and social relationships in Wilmington's upper crust if it became known their origins were in Dry Pond.

I asked Al Dickson how to handle this and he said, "Hell, it's not enough of a story to worry about. Hardly worth printing. Use the names of the officers who made speeches and that's enough."

The end of this little tale is that Company I landed in Normandy after D Day, June 6, 1944, and was fighting its way into France. Whereupon, on July 25, 1944, a fleet of American bombers from the Eighth Air Force flew over from England carrying tons of bombs intended for the Germans. When the American pilots could not find their assigned targets through the cloud cover and the thick dust raised by previous bombings, they had to drop their bombs anyway. They fell and exploded directly on the 120th Infantry's Thirtieth Infantry Division—one of the great, bloody mistakes of the war with a very heavy loss of life in an unutterable disaster. Out of 250 men, 245 died. The same attack also killed General Lesley J. McNair, the chief of Army Ground Forces. Not one of my friends in the 120th did I ever see again. That was Dry Pond's contribution to the war. No one gave more.

MARGARET grew up, came out from under the dining table, married her second cousin, William West, who worked in some obscure capacity in a motion picture studio in Hollywood, moved there with him, died there and was brought back to Wilmington for her funeral. Mama somehow held herself personally to blame for a betrayal of decency in outliving her own daughter. And so we all watched and decided it was guilt that led her to mount a massively excessive funeral, including a wake the night before for a very large crowd in her living room. Present were many people none of us had ever seen before.

The noise level rose. When I retreated to the front porch one of William West's friends, some kind of movie director, walked over to me and said, "Mr. Brinkley, I've never been in the South before and I find it surprising."

"Why?"

"Because I've seen all these Tennessee Williams plays and movies about the South and its drunkenness and cruelty and what I see here now is a gathering of pleasant, attractive people."

"They are that, yes, but more than that. In the corner of the room in the black dress, Margaret's and my mother. For thirty years she tortured her husband, my father, and finally forced him out of their bedroom and forced him to sleep in another bedroom alone. Then there's an usher from my mother's Presbyterian Church. She caught him stealing out of the collection plate. And next in line there is the town nymphomaniac."

"What did you say her name was?"

I told him. The next time I noticed, the two of them had disappeared and neither of them showed up the next morning for Margaret's funeral.

II

ON A SATURDAY NIGHT at Lumina, the grand old dance pavilion at Wrightsville Beach, Kenny Sargent was driving the women crazy. He was up on the bandstand singing one of his standards, "Under a Blanket of Blue," calling up warm, smooth and moist fantasies of making love out on the beach sand . . . *"Wrapped in the arms of sweet romance."*

Behind him, Clarence Hutchenrider played clarinet figures of soft, fluid perfection, and Billy Rausch blew the longest, purest tones out of his trombone.

> *A summer night's magic, enthralling me so*
> *The night would be tragic*
> *If you weren't here, to share it, my dear . . .*

They, along with the Glen Gray Casa Loma Orchestra, were arrayed across the bandstand in white-tied splendor, already well known to the Lumina crowd from their movies, radio's *Camel Caravan* and their Decca records. They had come to Wrightsville to play a one-night stand, traveling by bus as all the big bands did then, twelve or fourteen players in the bus seats, sleeping, reading, drinking, all their instruments stuffed into the baggage compartment below.

Lumina stood on, or actually in, the Atlantic Ocean, since it was on raised pilings, and at high tide the breakers rolled in, roaring and sizzling over the white beach sand and on up under the dance floor. The soft-edged pastel beauty of the ocean-front, the sounds of the surf, the music, Sargent, suave and handsome and, it seemed, singing to each woman alone about making love on the beach. It simply was wonderful. For two or three women swept up in erotic fantasy, it was too much. They groaned and fainted and had to be carried out to the cool salt air in a memorable display of thighs, satin garters and silk stockings. One young woman pushed up to the bandstand and reached up to tug on Kenny Sargent's sleeve and, in my hearing, in-vited him after the dance to come to her house down the beach where, she said, he could "relax, put your feet up, look out at the ocean under the full moon and I'll give you a drink."

He asked her, "Where are the people you came here with?"

"Forget them. I've sent them all away. It'll be just you and me under a blanket of blue."

In this and other ways, Lumina was the center of summer social life for Wilmington and the small towns all around. For me, at fifteen, it was even more than that—the first summer jobs of my life. First, as a soda jerk at the fountain just off the dance floor and overlooking the ocean where a six-ounce glass of ice, a one-ounce squirt of Coca-Cola syrup, plus carbonated water drawn with a flourish from a faucet shaped like a chrome-plated swan's neck, produced a "fountain Coke," the aqua vitae of the prewar South. At intervals other dancers took time out to stroll over to my soda fountain to ask for a bottle of Canada Dry club soda, or sparkling water, to mix with their illegal whiskey concealed in brown paper sacks. Mr. Reynolds, the proprietor, carefully explained to me that the carbonated water from his soda fountain was identical to the brand-name product that came in bottles and sold for twenty cents. Therefore, he said, we should collect the empty bottles and refill them from the fountain and sell them again for twenty cents at a profit margin of 100 percent.

Was this cheating?

"No," he said. "Carbonated water is carbonated water. Ours is better than theirs. Theirs is put in bottles and hauled down here to the beach on a truck. Ours is made fresh right here. And so ours is better." With these contortions the moral dilemma was resolved in Mr. Reynolds's favor, and I refilled Canada Dry bottles from my fountain.

Later, I was promoted to the tune of twenty-one dollars a month and given several jobs. One was to take tickets at the gate from dancers, who were charged forty cents admission. On the rare nights when the men were asked to wear black ties I was told to turn away anyone not properly dressed, particularly those wearing tuxedos and white shoes, which was often, or even worse wearing the gray suede crepe-sole shoes then fashionable among the young and highly endorsed by our fashion bible, *Esquire* magazine, though not for evening. The magazine's prescribed dress for males of high school and college age aspiring to a degree of dudishness in these years was a gray suit in a small, muted glen plaid, a blue shirt with the white collar then considered somewhat exotic, gray suede shoes with squishy crepe soles and a gray porkpie hat with a blue feather in the band. So, in these times, what was life about? It was about acquiring these clothes and then parading them around for the girls to admire. At the time, that seemed enough. Aside from taking tickets at Lumina's gate, another of my summer jobs was occasionally to switch on a mirror-covered ball suspended over the dance floor so that it rotated while I aimed a spotlight at it, changing colored filters and causing the tiny mirrors to throw little spangles of colored light all over the dance floor. Before the discotheque was invented this was a new and exciting idea that made the dancers stop, marvel at this spectacle of what were not yet called production values.

On Lumina's roof, five stories above the beach and the ocean, was a huge sign with six letters about eight feet high spelling out in 126 electric lightbulbs LUMINA. I knew it was 126 because I counted them when I was given the daily job of climbing to the roof carrying a bushel basket of sixty-watt light-bulbs and replacing the ten or twelve that burned out every day, being rather proud that my extremely specialized handiwork could be seen for miles. My older brothers laughed at the sight of me climbing around on the roof with a basket of lightbulbs. Laughable, no doubt, but it did buy me a glen-plaid suit and a blue shirt with a white collar. Not even *Esquire* could ever persuade me to wear a porkpie hat.

Wrightsville Beach at night was all sweet, all beautiful, but its days were dwindling down to a precious few. The war was raging in Europe now. Musicians were being drafted to play in military bands, and soon these would be remembered as the last nights of peacetime frivolity.

Now working for the *Star*, I came home from a Saturday night dance at Lumina with Kitty McKoy, I found the United Press had called to offer me a job in its Atlanta bureau with the promise of an eventual assignment to New York. News spread around the *Star*, and people congratulated me for a position I was not sure I wanted. More money, yes, but not much, the UP being notoriously stingy. And moving to Atlanta? Leaving Wilmington where I knew everybody and moving to a city where I knew nobody? And while I realized the UP had better jobs than any I would ever find in Wilmington, I also assumed they would go to its more senior people and not to a twenty-one-year-old just hired. But Al Dickson's advice was quick and brief: "Take it. Take the job. Move to Atlanta. Just an overgrown country town. But you won't stay there long. They'll move you around. With the war you'll have a lot to do. Stay here and in a few years you'll have my job and you'll grow old making seventy-five a week. You can do better. Take the job."

I did, but before I left Lamont Smith was fired. Management gave no reason, but we assumed he had spent too much time in Skipper's poolroom drinking Krueger's ale and watching the pool players. All of us on the staff liked him, drunk or sober, and I did not forget and have not forgotten now that he gave me my first real job in journalism.

About ten of us walked in a group over to Smith's house to commiserate and to say we were sorry and to offer him a few modest gifts— a case of Krueger's and a few cartons of cigarettes. He stood on his front porch and thanked us, saying he had no idea where he would go to work, but would miss all of us and our good times together, and, finally, "You can give me a few beers if you want to, but I can't let you buy my cigarettes."

What did that mean? It meant that in the small-town South in 1942, beer was regarded as a luxury and therefore suitable for gift giving, but for tobacco addicts cigarettes were a necessity for human survival and therefore inappropriate as a gift. Had

Smith put it into words, he could have said, "You can give me roses, but not bread."

I PILED BOOKS and clothes, all I had, in the back of a 1939 Ford two-door bought used through the Morris Plan Bank for $250, and drove to Atlanta to enter into my new life. The UP's bureau in 1942 was in the grimy old Western Union building beside the railroad tracks. Bureau manager Ted Lewis assigned me to write for the radio wire, a news service the UP sold only to radio stations, television at that time being a distant curiosity mainly seen in the pages of *Popular Mechanics*.

The United Press staffers, accustomed as they were to living on pride rather than money, assumed that all the announcers who read our radio news on the air were ignoramuses knowing nothing of the world or of journalism or much of anything else, including the English language. And in their disdain they were not altogether wrong. How could they know anything, we said to each other in tones of self-satisfied confidence, when one minute they would read news of blood and death and disaster on the war fronts and then slide smoothly into introducing a record by Carmen Cavallero and his schmaltzy piano, followed by reading commercials for laxatives, soap flakes and Carter's Little Liver Pills? And so the UP's instructions for writing for the radio wire were less than demanding and in fact were quite simple: "The more clichés the better. Make it easy and breezy. That's what radio announcers like. Easy and breezy."

That silly phrase made no sense to me. With the country at war, the draft calls increasing, the first young bodies arriving for burial at Arlington cemetery, sugar rationing beginning soon and more rationing promised, the American people being asked to sacrifice as they never had before, Edward R. Murrow's baritone voice coming in on CBS radio from London with his moving descriptions of the Germans' bombing attacks (". . . below and behind me there is a dripping sound. A fragment of a German bomb has punctured a can of peaches on a grocer's shelf"). What was easy and breezy about all that? Nothing. Miss Emma Woodward's strictures on English usage kept coming back to me.

But the UP continued to try. The lead story coming down the wire from Washington one night was that sugar rationing would soon begin. Surely that was big news. But when it came out through the UP's easy and breezy filter, it read: "OPA administrator Leon Henderson announced today he would yank the nation's sweet tooth for the duration."

My bureau manager said I ought to poke around the state capitol for a day or two, meeting the reporters from the Atlanta *Journal* and *Constitution*, both United Press clients, and attending Governor Eugene Talmadge's press conferences when and if he decided to have them. I went to his office, expecting to ask a secretary or some kind of assistant when there might be a press conference. I found his door standing open and his office crowded with what looked like a crowd of subsistence farmers loafing around, sitting on the windowsills and the radiators now cold, most of them wearing bib over-alls (here pronounced ''over-hauls''), high-top shoes and no socks, smoking, chewing tobacco and spitting in the general direction of the brass spittoons and usually missing, splattering the governor's marble floor. One sitting on a radiator was smoking a White Owl cigar then retailing for five cents, while the governor sat at his desk, seemingly oblivious to the Hogarthian scene before him, shuffling papers and muttering on the telephone. His only sign of political rank was that when he chewed tobacco he used his own, personal spittoon, not shared with the others, a privilege of rank. He was a graduate of the University of Georgia and had earned a law degree in 1907, but seemed intent on seeing that nobody knew it. Instead, he calculated that in a Georgia still mostly rural with mostly dirt roads, political success lay in playing the role of the rural primitive. I introduced myself to him and told him I was new in Atlanta working for the United Press.

He said, ''Are you foreign-born?''

''No, sir. I was born in North Carolina.''

''That's foreign-born. Outside of Georgia.''

He had adopted red suspenders—called galluses

—as his political trademark, wore them all the time and constantly attacked what he called "the fertilizer trust," and accused Armour and Swift of having evil designs on extracting too much money from the honest Georgia farmer trying to raise a few pigs. Beyond that, he boasted that he had been elected and reelected governor without ever carrying "any town that had a streetcar line."

I asked him why.

"Any town big enough to have streetcars will be too big for honest, hardworking farmers. Too big and too rich for my voters." Big cities, he said, were full of "foreign-born professors."

Around the state he affected the look and the dress of a farmer struggling to pay his feed bills, but the one time I saw him outside of Georgia he was straight, flat-out Brooks Brothers—natural-shoulder suit, horn-rim glasses, button-down shirt, striped silk repp tie—and looked like a man who had married a rich widow named Mattie Thurmond, which he had. Soon after their wedding she inherited 1,500 acres of prime farmland. Now independently prosperous, he had his way with the state government by firing everyone who disagreed with him and saved on the cost of the state penal system by opening the jails for hundreds of convicts. After I had spent half an hour trying to talk to him above the noise of all the visitors lounging around his office smoking and spitting, a man walked in carrying a briefcase and wearing what looked to be a Robert

Hall blue suit, walked over and told the governor he was from the Federal Bureau of Investigation and needed to talk to him in private. In private? Where? Behind Talmadge's desk was the governor's private bathroom, the only hideaway available. The two of them went in and closed the door. For a few minutes I heard them laughing, and when they came out both refused to say what they were talking about. I left.

With the draft, the UP had trouble keeping its bureaus manned, and every week or so it lost another manager. In my lifetime of modest talent and immodest good luck, at this point I was lucky again. The UP moved me to its Nashville, Tennessee, bureau and appointed me manager. Surely a resounding title at the age of twenty-two, but less than it appeared. I would manage a one-man bureau, the one man being myself. And giving me the title simply was a way to evade the new wage-and-hour law and avoid paying me overtime. Laughable as it was, this made me, in the eyes of the law and Washington bureaucrats, an executive, and the result was that I could be made to work any number of hours, and so for a fifty- to seventy-hour week I was paid $42.50. The UP's other money-saving dodge was to rent a small office somewhere on the premises of a client, in this case radio station WLAC, a fifty-thousand-watt CBS affiliate, and then to squeeze the rent down by assuring the manager that having a UP correspondent working on or near his studios would often be useful. Meaning that he could be called on at any time to help with WLAC's own local news coverage, without pay, of course.

There being very little news in Nashville, I had free time for two years to pursue Virginia Mansell, a splendid young woman working at WLAC doing fashion commercials on the radio for Loveman's department store. She was a new graduate of Emerson College in Boston, a speech and drama major, and my first serious woman friend. She quickly set to work on my speech pattern, ridding me of the southerner's habit of emphasizing the wrong syllables, as in ''se-DAN'' for a four-door car instead of ''SEE-dan,'' and other southernisms that sounded good enough in Wilmington, North Carolina, but not good enough for talking on the radio, as I was now doing in a small way on WLAC, keeping the UP's cheapskate promise. And I still talk as she taught me to talk. And I was lucky again in having a woman friend willing to teach me some version of standard, unaccented English, Emerson style.

We spent every evening together, I liked her enormously, and now from the perspective of years I know I loved her before I truly knew, at the age of twenty-two, what that actually meant, and around the station in a few months there was talk of marriage and I found the idea intriguing but daunting. Marriage on $42.50 a week? While I contemplated this, the UP settled the question for me by moving me from Nashville to Charlotte, North Carolina, to replace somebody lost to the draft. And in wartime, to get from Charlotte back to Nashville to see Virginia was nearly impossible. The new gasoline ration was too small to allow me to drive. Airplane and railroad tickets required a priority. A year later I moved even farther away, to Washington and NBC News. Perhaps only Elizabeth Barrett could maintain a romance by mail, writing to Robert Browning, ''How do I love thee? Let me count the ways.'' So Virginia gradually slipped out of my life, and I never saw her again, but I have never forgotten her for a day, and her teaching has been helpful to me ever since. It was one of several failures in my life when I was slow to understand what to do until it was too late to do it.

(Virginia married, had children, lived in Torrington, Connecticut, and died there some years ago. I do not know any of her children or descendants, but if any of them would write me a note at ABC News in Washington, D.C. 20036 I would be grateful and in return would send a few notes and snapshots.)

LIFE as the United Press bureau manager in Charlotte in 1943: One morning at 3:00 a.m. the phone rang beside my bed. It was the UP news desk in New York saying a Mexican newspaper client wanted ''about a hundred words on the Mexican Hat Dancers' performance in Charlotte tonight.'' I asked for a little more information, but the deskman knew nothing more.

The Mexican Hat Dancers? Vaguely I remembered hearing of them somewhere, sometime. But I knew next to nothing about them. I was aware that the UP had many newspaper clients in Latin America and was always attentive to them. But if the Mexicans had danced in Charlotte tonight, where? In a theater? A school auditorium? At one of the colleges? Which one? Who in town would know anything about it? Even if I knew someone to call for information, was I willing to awaken him at 3:00 a.m. in pursuit of news as puny as this? No. I went through the local papers looking for any mention of Mexican Hat Dancers. Nothing. While I struggled with this the New York desk called again and said it was late, and the client was impatient, and how was I doing? I said I would have a story for the client in five minutes. I did have it in five minutes because, feeling some guilt but seeing no alternative, I made up a sort of story and sent the New York desk this little scrap based on no information whatever:

> CHARLOTTE, UP—The famous Mexican Hat Dancers performed here tonight in a local auditorium before a large and appreciative audience. The dancers in their colorful costumes performed many of their traditional numbers with numerous interruptions for applause.

And so on for a paragraph or two. Short on facts, yes, but I never heard anything further from New York or from the Hat Dancers or anyone else, since I knew then as I know now that no one ever complains about a flattering news story, even if it is inaccurate.

In Charlotte, as usual in smaller cities, the UP finagled an office inside the studios of WBT, a client. I found that if there was very little news in Nashville, there was even less in Charlotte, and soon I was eager to get out and was thinking seriously about going back to Wilmington. In those early years of World War II, there was very little demand for the routine news from small southern cities—politics, local calamities, floods, fires and Rotary Club Ladies' Nights. I persuaded Jack Knell, WBT's news director, to talk CBS News in Washington into offering me a job in its Washington bureau. They did have a job for me, he said. Wonderful. I took the first train to Washington and reported, as instructed, to Bill White at the CBS bureau in the Earle Building at Thirteenth and E. Not wonderful. White refused to see me, sent word out he had never heard of me and had no job to offer. What happened? I never knew. I asked the receptionist to take a message back to White for me: "Go to hell." I walked four blocks over to NBC News at Fourteenth and New York, was hired in ten minutes and worked there for thirty-eight years.

Washington in the fall of 1943 suffered from

shortages of everything—housing, food, clothing, cigarettes, cars new and used, shoes, telephones, gasoline, taxis and whiskey. Diabolically, demand was highest for whatever was in shortest supply. Housing was the worst. Washington had houses and apartments to accommodate its normal peacetime population of about seven hundred thousand. Now that number was nearly doubled with all the new people government had brought in to run the war and to do the paperwork. There was never any shortage of that. Every night of the week, a thirteen-car train left the Washington railroad yards loaded with wastepaper. Once I asked an official of the RF&P railroad where all this paper was going. Sorry, he said, wartime security did not allow him to say. The paperworkers (Washington never manufactured anything; once it did have a potato chip factory, but it moved across the line into Maryland, where the labor laws were less demanding), the paper shufflers and typists were flooding into town on every train and every bus every day, every hour. The military services built plywood shacks for their new staff members. They were regarded as temporary offices and housing, to be demolished after the war, were called tempos, and some of them sat there temporarily for forty years. They were flimsy and ugly, but the military people working in them at least had a roof over their heads. Civilians, having to shift for themselves, were mostly young women moving in from small towns all across America looking for the only commodity not in shortage, jobs. There were thousands of jobs paying $1,440 a year, in more recent dollars, about $15,000. But no housing.

Every major news agency in Washington, including NBC, felt it needed a regular correspondent to cover the White House and Franklin Roosevelt's press conferences. He held two a week, one in the afternoon for the convenience of the morning newspapers and one in the morning for the afternoon papers. These in the years when the country still had afternoon newspapers. The working people of America would arrive home in the late afternoon to find the day's newspaper lying on the front steps, and there was no competition from television. In most cities the healthiest and most profitable were the afternoon papers. When I came to Washington, the *Evening Star* was the richest, fattest newspaper in the United States until it sickened and died. When television began offering news in the early evenings and often at all hours of the day and night, its news was faster and more recent than news hauled around the city in trucks and then thrown on the front steps, or into the shrubbery, by young boys on bicycles. Soon nearly all afternoon papers began to falter and fold, and today there are only a handful left.

Carleton Smith, NBC's Washington manager, considered Roosevelt's conference schedule, consulted with his superiors in New York and resolved that the network had to cover the White House. But first, it being his nature, Smith resolved that his correspondent must be tall, white, Protestant and neatly dressed. He appointed me. I met all of his visible requirements, but he never asked if I was fully informed, had intimate knowledge of all the national and world affairs the White House dealt with every day. Had he asked, the answer would have been no, I was not. Fresh from United Press bureaus in small cities in Georgia, Tennessee and North Carolina I didn't know much. But I knew how to ask questions, to listen, to read, to learn. And the most useful source for me was the *Evening Star*, and for an interesting reason: the paper was so fat with advertising, had so much space to fill between the ads, that it had to struggle to find enough news material to fill it up. Therefore, it printed everything every day. Anyone who read it carefully for a few months would complete the equivalent of a graduate course in world affairs. I did. When I went to the White House representing NBC, I was hesitant to ask a question out of fear I didn't know enough and my ignorance would be revealed. For the first several months I never asked a question. I was intimidated by the presence of such famous figures as James B. "Scotty" Reston of *The New York Times*, Merriman Smith of the United Press and others. There were still a few White House correspondents who affected the look of the statesmen they supposedly were covering—wearing homburg hats, striped pants, pince-nez glasses with dangling black silk ribbons. I always thought they looked like statesmen on their way to an international conference, where they would sell out another innocent and unsuspecting country.

At my first press conference, for my first look at President Roosevelt live and close up, we gathered in a semicircle around his desk, smoking cigarettes and dropping ashes on the presidential rug, knowing he would not complain because he was smoking a Camel himself. I was shocked at his appearance, having seen him only in black-and-white newsreel pictures where he looked reasonably healthy, good-natured, outgoing and relaxed, and now seeing him thin, drawn, with virtually no color in his face. It was gray.

I was entirely unprepared to be NBC's White House correspondent. I knew the usual nuts and bolts about political life in Washington, but the subtleties and nuances were foreign to me. Among the famous and experienced reporters, senators and cabinet members were routinely referred to by their first names, and often I had to pretend I knew what they were talking about when usually I did not. But I learned.

WITH WASHINGTON'S critical need of housing, President Roosevelt fancied himself an architect. He sat at his desk in the White House Oval Office working with a ruler, pencil and legal-size sheets of paper designing temporary housing. His architectural designs were ridiculous, and while nobody ever wanted to say anything to him, nothing he designed was ever built.

In my own case, the best I could hope for was maybe a rented room in a house in some decent part of town. Even that was nearly impossible. After a time one of NBC's announcers, a bachelor, offered to rent me his spare bedroom in his apartment at 2500 Q Street in Georgetown. That was fine, I thought, until he insisted on climbing into the bed with me. I asked him to get out. His response was that if he had to get out of my bed I had to get out of his apartment. I got out, while continuing with some awkwardness to write news scripts for him to read on the air. Inconveniences like this were frequent in those years. We consoled ourselves and romanticized it all by telling ourselves, ''Well, what do you expect? This is war.''

Government by now had taken over several Washington apartment buildings and turned them into offices, even using their bathrooms as work space. This was done by laying a sheet of plywood over the bathtub and placing a typewriter on it and, where the layout allowed, putting a cushion on the toilet seat to serve as a chair for the typist. Ridiculous, yes, but these women were young, eager, believing they were helping to win the war, as no doubt they were, feeling that as young women they were for the first time in their lives being taken seriously as individuals and allowed some responsibility. And $1,440 a year was more than most of them had ever made in their lives. Years later some of them remembered me from Washington radio in the war years and wrote to me, recalling their work and saying they now were married, had children, PTAs, suburbs and power lawn mowers. But they remembered with great fondness their wartime jobs in Washington. More than one has written ''when I think about those days, I cry.''

In the 1980s Alfred A. Knopf published a book of mine called *Washington Goes to War*. It had a detailed description of the lives, pains and occasional pleasures of the women who came to Washington to work through the war years and then went home. A great many of them sent me their copies of my book and told me how pleasurably they remembered their years in Washington and asked to have them autographed. I signed each one and wrote the inscription TO ONE OF THE GREAT WOMEN WHO CAME TO WASHINGTON AND HELPED OUR COUNTRY WIN THE WAR.

A mother in Illinois wrote to me and said her daughter recalled her time as a worker in wartime Washington as the great experience of her life and treasured the inscribed book I had sent her.

''And when she was found to have untreatable cancer of the pancreas, she asked to have your book buried with her. We respected her wish and as I write this, I have tears in my eyes.''

As I read it, so did I.

THE NBC NEWSROOM in 1943 supplied Washington news (White House, Congress and so on) to the network and general news to WRC, the Washington local station owned and operated by the network. That was where I was first put to work. I soon learned that to say so much as one word on the grand and glorious NBC network was to ascend to what NBC people thought was heaven, with RCA microphones replacing the harps.

But CBS was doing quite well now. It had Edward R. Murrow, whose broadcasts from London and the war fronts were the best, and NBC could not match them. Still, NBC believed itself to be the classiest network in the world, the company whose chairman, David Sarnoff, had originated the idea of broadcasting news and music to small boxes, or radios in private homes, and now talked of eventually doing the same with television.

Until the war forced an end to it, NBC believed it only fitting that after 6:00 p.m. all announcers speaking on its radio network were required to wear tuxedos. Formal dress, yes, even though the audience could not see them, but it was felt that the announcers would take their work more seriously and their words would carry greater weight and authority. That went away with the war, but NBC still required that without exception every sound heard on its network be live—no recorded anything, speech, commercials, music, even sound effects on radio plays and comedy programs. On Jack Benny's comedy program when he started up his ancient Maxwell automobile, the sounds of a coughing, wheezing, sputtering and backfiring car were all created entirely by an actor who made these hilarious sounds with his mouth. Frank Russell, NBC's Washington vice president and lobbyist, explained it to us: "If we allowed recorded material on our network, sooner or later all our programming would come in by mail from New York and Hollywood and we'd need nothing here but a record player."

I never had or wanted any part in these discussions of high corporate policy on such issues as live noise versus recorded noise. Instead, I was put to work writing news programs to be read by announcers, and for the first time I began to listen carefully to what they said on the air and how they said it. The stated requirements were not onerous. An announcer had to say the words in a pleasing baritone and pronounce them correctly, being careful to remember to get the commercials in. But there was no attempt to train them to speak with appropriate emphasis. Say the words, yes. Pronounce them correctly, yes. But nothing about emphasis to make the meaning clear. One example I have never forgotten:

Late in 1944, after the Allied landing in Normandy, the supreme commander, General Dwight Eisenhower, said he now believed he could smash the German Army *west of the Rhine River.* Big news. Eisenhower now thought he would not need to fight his way across the river, saving a good many lives and shortening the war by weeks or months. Big news, yes. But when I wrote it for the announcers, it came out on the air: "General Eisenhower said today he would *smash the German Army* [voice trailing off] west of the Rhine River." It was read wrongly and the meaning changed and the whole point missed by reading a sentence with the wrong emphasis, and the emphasis was wrong because the announcer was reading the words, not the meaning, because he did not know the meaning. I still hear these same kinds of errors on radio news today.

I began trying to correct this by underlining the words that needed emphasis to make the meaning clear. The right emphasis is crucial because I believe the ear is the poorest of all ways to absorb information. To miss the meaning of a report on the radio is to miss it forever. My underlining did not help much. One who has read scripts on the air for years has learned to coordinate eye, tongue, teeth and vocal cords in a way that seems right to him and finds it desperately difficult to change, and won't.

Later, when I was giving news on the air myself, I put this into practice and perhaps overdid it, trying a little too hard to place the emphasis where I thought it should be and, without intending it, developing a jerky, labored way of speaking that soon attracted the attention of the comedians and mimics who lumped me in with others they found easy to imitate: James Cagney and Cary Grant. I guess I was flattered. But it was annoying to learn that an announcer in Los Angeles, imitating me, was doing commercials selling cemetery lots. I had NBC's lawyers write to him and claim he was violating some law or other—it was not clear what law— since it is impossible to copyright a speech pattern. The lawyer found he could do nothing.

At this time, in 1944, a small ad in *Variety* offered $1,500 to anyone who could do a Brinkley imitation for a one-minute commercial. The story then circulated was that I applied for the $1,500 commercial job and was turned down because I didn't sound enough like Brinkley. Amusing, yes, but false.

Since I was through with my work in the newsroom at 12:15 p.m., I had the afternoons free to poke around Washington—the White House, the Capitol, the agencies—looking for news to put on the radio. A reporter scouting for news will, shamelessly, look anywhere at all, including the yellow pages of the telephone book, where sometime in the forties, I noticed a listing for the Anti-Cigarette Alliance. What could that be? Why would anyone be anticigarette? Weren't Clark Gable and Carole

Lombard and all the great stars smoking all over the screen? Didn't President Roosevelt smoke Camels by the carton? Didn't he use his cigarette holder tilted upward to emphasize his upthrust chin as a symbol of strength, hope and optimism? Didn't the magazine ads show the essence of calm and sophisticated satisfaction to be a lovely woman prettily balancing a cigarette in manicured fingers while the smoke floated away in languid curls? It was such a beautiful picture. Who could oppose that?

The Anti-Cigarette Alliance was in a shabby old building downtown, its outer office piled with old newspapers turning yellow. An ancient Underwood typewriter sat on a small desk, rusting and unused, its ribbon drying out. Presumably, any typing would be done by the fiftyish woman sitting there with chemically induced red hair and several gold teeth. Inside her black patent high heels she wore white ankle socks encircled with embroidery of red tulips. The inner office was inner only because it was behind a shoulder-high frosted glass partition. The redhead pointed a thumb toward the partition and said, ''Go on in.''

Inside was a bouncy little man, a halo of white hair over a pink, smiling face. He did not talk so much as he twittered like a sparrow.

''You want to know what the Anti-Cigarette Alliance is about, don't you?''

''Yes. It does seem odd. What's wrong with cigarettes?''

"What's wrong with cigarettes? Plenty. They'll kill you. Smoke them a few years and you'll have lung cancer, emphysema or heart trouble. I know you don't believe me. The tobacco companies with their clever ad agencies have made cigarette smoking look romantic and glamorous. And safe. It's not."

"How do you know all this? Why don't others know it?"

"They will. My friends in surgery tell me lung cancer was almost nonexistent until recently. Now they're seeing it more often in the lungs of smokers. The tobacco companies spend millions to promote cigarettes. We have very little money. We can't advertise. I pay myself twenty-seven fifty a week. Good thing my wife has a job in the government."

I wrote a little story about the Anti-Cigarette Alliance and its founder, and I regret to say I treated him and his ideas as a joke, when he was right, and right earlier than anyone else I knew. How did he know all of this long before the rest of us, long before it became the familiar and accepted wisdom? I never knew. He died soon after this. I will always be ashamed of ridiculing him; if his advice had been followed many people, including my two older brothers, might now be alive and enjoying life.

The NBC newsroom in Washington was modest. There were AP and UP printers, seven desks, all of them marked with cigarette burns, scratches, stains from spilled coffee, soda pop and bourbon whiskey.

At the desk next to mine was a staffer named Leif
Eid. He was Norwegian, always annoyed because
nobody knew how to pronounce his name. It
rhymed with "leaf reed." He was a fairly myste-
rious figure in the wartime Washington news community. Nearly all of us were small-towners who
had started work on our hometown newspapers and
one way or another found our way to Washington.
And most of us were helped along in this because
so many men were being drafted and we were hired
to replace them. Leif Eid was an exception we never
understood. He was an immigrant who had worked
as a lumberjack felling huge Douglas firs in the Pacific Northwest. How and why in wartime he made
it from Norway to the forests of the American West
he never would say, nor would he ever say how he
moved from the world of fir trees, axes and chain
saws to the NBC newsroom in Washington. We all
guessed he was there because when the war started,
the network had very few newspeople of its own.
In peacetime it had relied on a few big names like
H. V. Kaltenborn, Lowell Thomas, Morgan Beatty
and a few others who did fifteen minutes of news
and comment each day, and the rest of the time
NBC's individual stations were left to do their own
news with their own people. In peacetime this was
thought to be good enough. But the war forced the
networks to do more. The Washington station hired
Leif Eid because he already worked for NBC in
New York in its press—publicity—department,

where he had a high reputation as a writer, and moved him to Washington. If he could write press releases promoting entertainment programs, he could write news, couldn't he? Well, yes.

His manual labor in the forests had left him so heavily muscled he had his shirts and suits custom-made to fit him about like a sausage skin and to emphasize his formidable body. When he had nothing else to do, he went out and ordered shirts. Otherwise, he smoked, he drank, he dressed and he wrote. Above all, he wrote. He did ten minutes of news and commentary every evening at 6:05, just after an announcer billed as the Esso Reporter read five minutes of news ripped off the UP radio wire. Then for ten minutes Leif Eid did a program he had written himself, and in my judgment it was the best-written news material being broadcast anywhere. When I asked him about it, he said he tried in every line he wrote to achieve the crystalline clarity of E. B. White's essays in the *New Yorker*. We discussed this on quiet afternoons, and as he put it, "You write it and then you go back through it and comb the dandruff out of it, taking out every word that does not add something useful."

But the regrettable fact was that Eid could write it beautifully, but on the air he read it terribly. If Demosthenes learned to orate by filling his mouth with pebbles, Eid sounded as if he were talking with a mouth full of marshmallows. And he never went far in broadcasting because he could not overcome his stumbling, halting, confusing speech.

At another desk on the night shift was Raine Bennett, the islandologist. The what? The islandologist, the specialist in the history and culture of islands around the world. He explained that island people, wherever found, being more or less confined by the surrounding water, had become acculturated differently from those living on the mainland. I hesitated to ask him if this applied to the residents of Manhattan. And his great accomplishment, he thought, was that he had read and made notes on every *Encyclopaedia Britannica* entry dealing with islands and then combined this accumulated knowledge into an article on islandology, a term he invented, and sold the article to *Britannica*. If all this was true, the encyclopedia had bought back its own material, repackaged by Raine Bennett. His manner was that of a failed Shakespearean actor—flowing white hair, broad gestures, long, slender fingers constantly stroking the air as he talked, and in his speech he stretched out the vowels like saltwater taffy, and when he spoke to the rest of us in the newsroom, it was in a tone of genteel disdain. After all, he regarded himself as a scholar and the rest of us as the common clay of the working class. All sorts of strange creatures, left free by having escaped the draft somehow, washed ashore in wartime Washington. Bennett was one of the strangest.

Then there was the manager of NBC's local station, Carleton Dabney Smith, who hired me. He was so fastidious that when he sent a personal check to be cashed in the NBC accounting office, he would accept only new, unused bills. When one of his secretaries cashed his check and brought him the money, she said, "I'm sorry, Mr. Smith, but the girls in accounting said they didn't have any new bills."

Smith stared off into space, slowly touched his fingertips together, hesitated for a moment and responded softly to this intolerable outrage: "No new bills? Then perhaps accounting should find some new girls."

Bob Doyle was the mail boy. He was Catholic, normally a crippling handicap in Carleton Smith's eyes, but in this case overlooked because Doyle's family was socially prominent in Washington. He sorted and delivered the mail, rolling a wire cart up and down the hallways, and at times he filled in on the telephone switchboard. In both capacities, he was a mine of inside information for the rest of us. Before he delivered the memos sent daily between New York and Washington in a canvas sack filled with unsealed interoffice envelopes, he opened and read all the interesting memos between New York and Washington executives. And at the switchboard, when Carleton Smith was on the phone with NBC in New York, he listened in and shared the information with all of us.

When Doyle moved onward and upward in NBC, in later years becoming the director of *The Huntley-Brinkley Report*, he was replaced as mail boy by a jolly, plump young man named Willard Scott. In time Willard graduated from the mail cart and began doing funny stuff on the Washington radio station and made himself into a character called Bozo the Clown. NBC bought him a pink Jeep convertible painted in circus colors and with a pink-and-white canvas awning with red fringe. In his clown uniform of orange fright wig, rubber-ball nose, greasepaint and a polka-dot satin suit he drove around town to hospitals and orphanages to entertain the children. One afternoon, returning to midtown from a hospital in the suburbs, he ran out of gas, pulled off the road and stood outside in his clown regalia trying to hitch a ride. Car after car, seeing this crazy sight, not only did not stop to pick him up, but shuddered and sped up to get away quickly from this odd and perhaps dangerous creature. After a half hour of this, an elderly black gentleman stopped, picked him up, dropped him off at NBC and—astonishingly, in a high degree of sophistication—never asked a question.

ONE DAY in the midforties, a large, odd-looking object arrived at the Washington studio. It appeared to us to have just landed from Mars or out there somewhere, and it was about the size of an automobile set on casters. On its side was a decal of the NBC trademark, the three chimes famous for years for sounding at the end of every program, *ding, dang, dong*. The three notes were and still are G, E, C—for General Electric Company, one of the founders of RCA and NBC. This new object was so big it could barely be rolled through the door. It was our first television camera.

The word "television" initially appeared in *Scientific American* in 1907, meaning, of course, "distant vision." NBC's David Sarnoff insisted all his life that the word was pronounced wrongly by all those who called it "TELE-vision," emphasizing the first part of the word, when the logic of it was not "tele," a Greek combining term meaning "distance," as in "telescope," "telephoto," "telephone." We'd had "tele" for a long time in radio. What was new was tele-*vision*, for distant seeing, and so he thought the word's emphasis should be on "vision." In every speech, he went on about the pronunciation he wanted and never got. But he got everything else. When World War II ended several big companies were eager to start television broadcasting, RCA the first among them. But there remained the question of technical standards—how many horizontal scanning lines the television picture should have and other technical questions. These had to be accepted unanimously. Otherwise, home receivers would be able to tune in some channels but not others. Obviously, there had to be a single standard for the entire United States and, as it turned out, most of the world. RCA had a system ready. So did Philco. So did Zenith. But none of the three would work with the others. It was the duty of the Federal Communications Commission to settle the dispute among these industrial giants. But the commission's chairman, James Lawrence Fly, was an ardent, devoted New Dealer and something of a fool from the unthinking left. He was basically antibusiness and quite pompous about it, hating the thought that the big electronic companies might make money out of television, while offering no ideas on how it could be otherwise financed. His obstinacy and arbitrary delays held up the arrival of television in America for a year or more. And the FCC never did set the technical standards. The television industry itself formed a group called the National Television Standards Committee (NTSC) and agreed on how many horizontal lines would form the television picture and other issues. The FCC at last accepted its findings, and the NTSC standard drives American television today.

That put the networks on the air, but what put them in business in a big way was the experience of a small manufacturer of lipstick called Hazel Bishop. In the year before her television commercials were broadcast her profit was $49,257. Three years after her first advertising appeared on television, her lipsticks made a one-year profit of $10,100,682. The advertising agencies looked at these figures in awe and stupefaction and what had been seen as an interesting and perhaps promising novelty was now regarded as the most effective advertising medium in history, and the commercial money began to flood in.

In Washington we tried to do television out of the NBC radio studios, all we had at the moment, but found it was impossible because the ceilings were too low. Television required bright lights hung from the ceiling. The heat from a five-thousand-watt klieg light hung from an eight-foot ceiling, about two feet above the TV performers' heads, would have blistered their scalps. And the early TV cameras were so insensitive they required extremely bright lights that produced heat so unbearable it overloaded the air-conditioning, and a new building designed for television had to be built. And this was how the broadcasting of news on television began, the first truly new way of disseminating news since Gutenberg's inventions allowed the printing of newspapers in the fifteenth century.

Perhaps it is difficult to see now, but those of us standing around in television's beginnings could not help wondering what the human mind could do with a new device, a new technology, that allowed picture and sound—movies, of a sort—to be sent simultaneously across the entire United States and eventually around the world. What was this? Was it radio with pictures? The shape of the television screen from the beginning was roughly the shape of the movie screen. Whatever its size—inches, feet or whatever—the screen had to have a ratio of four wide by three high. The earliest designers of television equipment chose this shape because they anticipated broadcasting a lot of movies as well as film from our own newsreel cameras. NBC's film cameras were monsters designed for Hollywood, not for moving around to places where news was being made. They were so heavy it took two muscular men to lift one, and it was assumed we would have film cameras like them sometime in the future, all of them making pictures of the same size and shape. A bit of luck here, since the engineers told me that in the entire world there were only two manufactured items that were precisely the same size in every country around the globe. One was the valve on automobile tires. The other was thirty-five-millimeter film.

This convenient fact led NBC to hire cameramen from the existing newsreel companies to make news film for us. Technically, this worked perfectly. For journalism it did not work at all. The newsreels were accustomed to spending three or four days moving news film from the camera to the movie theater screen—transporting the film to a laboratory for developing, editing, laying in the ridiculous background music they insisted on using, printing multiple copies for the theaters and then distributing

them to movie houses in fifty states. It was a slow,
tedious process. Take the music, for example. Each
newsreel company had a library of music on thirty-
five-millimeter film with sound tracks only, no picture, two or three minutes long and filed and labeled
by content, or tone, with such labels as MARTIAL,
FUNEREAL, SPORTS, KIDS. Each musical piece was
on two pieces of film—one for use at the opening
and another for the closing. If a newsreel story was
ninety seconds long, at somewhere close to forty-
five seconds the music editor had to switch from the
opening music to the closing music, trying to make
the change unnoticeable, and so to have some kind
of coda or closing flourish to hit exactly at the end
of the story. The newsreel's negative film of the
picture, the film with the music track, along with
the stentorian voice-of-doom narration by somebody like Westbrook Van Voorhees, had to be combined on a single reel of film to be copied and
shipped out. This work was then regarded as something close to high art and held in even higher
regard because by newsreel standards it had to
be done quickly. Sometimes in maybe three or four
days.

The newsreels were never any good for television
because they were too slow. In the earliest days
those of us doing news on the air felt we were competing with the newsreels and took some pride in
pointing out we had news on the air days before it

got into the movie theaters, and NBC's earliest television news programs—quite crude—were introduced with the boastful line ''Today's news today!'' That was a bit deceptive. While we could indeed get film on the air quickly once we had it in hand, getting it in from around the country and around the world was as slow for us as for anyone else. For foreign stories, the ''Today's news today'' slogan should in honesty have been ''Yesterday's news or the day before yesterday's news today.'' Only God knows how many miles of our foreign news film never got on the air at all because it never made the switch from one airline to another in the London airport.

The newsreels never worked for television for another reason, their editorial content. Because they were so slow and cumbersome and their equipment was so heavy and difficult to move, they could only cover staged, scheduled events that allowed them to arrive a half day in advance and spend hours setting up their gear—such events as ship launchings, sports events, beauty contests, horse races and politicians making speeches on political issues the movie studios wanted to support, such as one of their favorite causes, lowering federal taxes on movie theater tickets.

Since the newsreels were owned by the movie studios, they were blatantly loaded with promotional pieces about their new productions, like this:

Open high and wide looking down on a street scene in Hollywood in front of a movie theater, floodlit for the opening of a new film. Pan the camera over to the theater's marquee where we find the name of the new movie emblazoned in brilliant light. Cut to the street. Music up. A white Rolls-Royce glides into the frame. A studio functionary in white tie and tails bounds up to the car, opens the door, bows and hands two dozen white roses to the star, Dolores del Somebody or Other, as she steps out of the car wearing a white sable coat in warm weather. Up comes the narrator, who seems barely able to contain his fake excitement, describing the scene as Dolores sweeps inside, smiling prettily and carrying her roses while the camera again pans up to the marquee and holds on the new movie's title long enough for the dumbest member of the audience to read it four or five times. Music up and out. No program with even a passing interest in news would ever have put that on the air, since it was a flat-out commercial. But the movie studios' newsreels carried it on until the day they died.

But when all the theaters dropped the newsreels, the studios kept their immensely valuable film files. Now, today, you want to make a television documentary on the rise of Adolf Hitler? Or any other figure from before World War II? Since Hitler died in his bunker before television cameras came along, there is only one place to buy film of Hitler. The price to a network for one-time use of newsreel film? One thousand dollars a minute. So they are out of the theaters, but not out of money. Ours.

TELEVISION NEWS was alive but not well. In the radio years the networks had a roster of well-known newsmen—Kaltenborn, Robert McCormick, Elmer Davis, Thomas and others—all of them admired figures accustomed to attracting large radio audiences. But not one of these famous figures was now doing the news regularly on television. Why? Because they knew how to read a news script on radio, but they did not know how to deal with television. They were afraid of it and reluctant to try anything new. Kaltenborn once said to me, "I hate television." He and others were slow to understand that no television audience would sit still for fifteen minutes to watch him doing what he had done for years on the radio—a middle-aged man sitting at a desk and reading from a script he held in his hand. As yet there was no reliable prompting device. The first was a primitive machine set on top of the TV camera that slowly unrolled a long sheet of yellow paper with a TV script typewritten on it in big letters. But it had the annoying habit of jamming in the middle of a sentence, and, even worse, if the broadcaster stopped for even a moment for a change of subject, or to swallow or to clear his throat, the prompter continued unrolling the paper without a halt, so when the poor soul was ready to talk again the prompter had moved on and left him behind and unable to catch up. Here was the newest RCA television camera, the highest expression of the technology of the day, having to work with a prompting device not much beyond the technical level of the slingshot. It was several years before anybody made a prompter that worked. But even if it had worked, it was still too much to expect the audience to sit through fifteen minutes of a man reading off a prompter, what later came to be called a talking head.

So the older, richer, more famous newsmen from radio days were not to be seen, and not one of them, not one of the famous newsmen from radio, was able to make the transition to television news programs. Murrow continued his radio news show and did some great television documentaries, including his famous one attacking and beginning the destruction of Senator Joseph R. McCarthy, but never television news. So what happened?

In the NBC newsroom in New York a man previously unknown and called John Cameron Swayze was working in New York local radio. The NBC legend was that Swayze was not invited but ordered to move over to television on pain of being fired if he refused. He moved. Then it was found he had one talent previously not recognized as valuable— the ability to memorize news copy and recite it back to the camera in letter-perfect order and without needing a prompter. Beyond that he had a plain, open face, a pleasant midwestern speech pattern he brought with him from Kansas City, an inoffensive down-home manner and style. He began to attract an audience, competing as he was with Douglas Edwards on CBS and, later, John Charles Daly on ABC. The necktie industry persuaded him to accept five free ties every week on condition that he never wear the same tie on the air twice. Pretty soon his fifteen-minute program picked up an advertiser, R. J. Reynolds tobacco, and was named the *Camel News Caravan.* They were among the first advertisers on a network news program, and they came in with a few demands. One was that never, ever, would the news film on the Swayze program show a NO SMOKING sign. It would be nice, they said, to always have a lighted cigarette smoking in the ashtray on Swayze's elbow. With one exception, nobody could be shown smoking a cigar. The exception was Winston Churchill, then a heroic figure of such magnitude that nobody, not even an advertising man, would dare restrict him in any way.

In these postwar years, American military forces were still stationed around the world in a hundred places, and the Reynolds Company insisted on having Swayze announce on Friday nights that some thousands of free cartons of Camels had been "sent to our boys around the world." During his vacations I filled in for Swayze and had to hold up a Camel cigarette carton and do the little spiel about free cigarettes for our boys overseas. On occasion I infuriated the ad agency people by mistakenly holding the Camel carton upside down. The Anti-Cigarette Alliance still had work to do.

Time passed and a public increasingly at home with technological wonders began to anticipate color television. Dr. Peter Goldmark, the CBS scientist who invented the long-playing record, applied himself to this new challenge and in time came up with a color television system of sorts. It consisted mainly of a motor-driven rotating wheel with a series of mirrors and pieces of colored glass. It did, indeed, produce a pretty color picture. But its disadvantages were overwhelming. It was totally incompatible with existing black-and-white TV sets, meaning the CBS system instantly would make every existing set obsolete. Since the color picture would have to be viewed through one half of the rotating wheel, the wheel would always have to be more than twice the size of the picture. To build the twenty-one-inch TV set in common use today would require a rotating wheel about five feet in diameter. Where would you put that in the living room? Not only that, since the CBS apparatus required an electric motor driving a rotating wheel there certainly would be some noise. If the wheel was not lubricated often enough it would squeak, and in the sitcoms and *New Yorker* cartoons we would have had wives saying to husbands, ''Honey, you forgot to oil the television.''

Ridiculous as it was, it did in fact produce a

good-quality picture, if small. And the Federal Communications Commission appeared to be ready to approve it as the official television system for the United States.

David Sarnoff was aghast, but this setback mainly was his own fault. He had become so accustomed to winning he could not contemplate losing anything, ever. Weeks earlier, against all his engineers' advice, he insisted on demonstrating for the FCC and the press and others the RCA color system then under development. He explained that it was not finished, not ready, and assumed that the press and others would make the necessary allowances for RCA's unpreparedness and wait patiently for it to be ready. He went ahead with his demonstration. He was wrong on all counts. It was a blunder so serious it almost ended his hopes and dreams and possibly even his career. His demonstration showed a half-finished RCA system so crude it should have been kept out of sight until it was finished. The pictures were fuzzy and dim, the audience saw purple bananas and women with green lipstick. The press was viciously critical. *Variety* ran the headline RCA LAYS A COLORED EGG. No one was willing to make any of the allowances Sarnoff expected. After this disaster the FCC was not certain Sarnoff could ever produce, so it voted to approve the CBS system.

Sarnoff was stunned, refusing to believe the FCC had accepted for the American people a color television system he regarded as primitive, even ludicrous. He announced that RCA would not manufacture receiving sets to run on the CBS system. Zenith, Philco and other manufacturers agreed. For about another year color TV was at a standstill, nothing happening. In time, Sarnoff came up with a color system that worked, produced good pictures and in theory would allow screens of almost any size, and existing sets could receive the color pictures in black and white. The FCC approved the system we use today. By 1953 the size of television pictures are now limited only by the requirement that they be carried into a house through a door.

News in color would appear first on John Cameron Swayze's news program. The announcement was made with great seriousness. The press was invited. The BBC sent newspeople from London to observe. For this grand occasion, NBC moved Swayze into studio 8H, its biggest then and now. So big that Arturo Toscanini used 8H to conduct and rehearse the 120-piece NBC Symphony Orchestra, Sarnoff's pet. Swayze's desk was moved in from the smaller studio he used every day. Plus chairs for the reporters, dozens of them. Ad agency people. NBC executives. Visitors. The first news broadcast in color in the history of the world was about to begin. The air was electric. Swayze walked in, immaculately dressed and coiffed with that day's new necktie and his fresh white carnation. He looked around and said to the director, Ralph Howard Peterson, "It's warm in here. Is there a refrigerator for my carnation?"

IN MARCH 1946, before Swayze needed to worry about cooling his flowers, President Truman's private train sat on a siding in Washington's Union Station, for security reasons carefully parked out of sight behind a line of empty cars. His private Pullman, the *Ferdinand Magellan*, passed on to him after Roosevelt's death, was hooked to the rear end. About noon, through the damp, acrid smell of its plume of steam, it slowly began pulling out of the station and out toward the midwestern United States, where its passengers would soon make a little history. Traveling in the private car were the president; his guest Winston Churchill; his press secretary Charlie Ross; naval aide Clark Clifford, resplendent in his blue uniform encrusted in gold stripes and medallions; Admiral William D. Leahy, former chief of staff to Roosevelt; General Harry Vaughan, Truman's lifelong friend and now his military aide; Colonel Wallace Graham, his personal physician; and a few of us reporters, English and American.

Several weeks after the end of the war in Europe, Churchill had been voted out of office, saying, "My countrymen have given me the order of the boot," and as a private citizen in the months since the war he had come to think that the world, and particularly the United States, was not well aware of what was happening in Europe and did not understand that the Soviet Union's Joseph Stalin was aggressively and brutally spreading his power westward, routinely murdering those who stood in his way, while randomly violating the agreements he made at his Yalta meeting with Roosevelt. And Churchill was disturbed to see the U.S. Army being sent home from Europe, threatening to leave Britain as the only military power standing between Stalin and the Atlantic Ocean. The British, after two massively bloody wars in one generation, were severely weakened. Churchill regarded the United States as the only power left in the world able to stand firmly against Stalin. But he also realized that Americans were so happy to have the war behind them they had turned their attention inward, as was always their natural and historic preference, enjoying the booming prosperity of peacetime. And he thought that Americans and others needed to hear again the rolling thunder and heat lightning of Churchillian oratory, calling their attention and the world's attention to Stalin's nasty, murderous spreading of his Communist power across the face of Europe. He announced he would visit the United States in the spring, mainly because he wanted his message to be addressed primarily to the Americans.

Dr. Franc McCluer, president of Westminster, a small college in the small town of Fulton, Missouri, saw his chance. He called on an alumnus, friend and classmate, Harry Vaughan, to urge Truman to invite Churchill to speak at Westminster. Truman did invite him and offered to go with him to Fulton and introduce him. Churchill thought this was perfect, speaking to the world with the president of the United States standing beside him. The deal was made— Westminster College in the late winter and traveling there with the president and some of his staff aboard the *Ferdinand Magellan.*

I and the others in the press were put into cars up forward—a Pullman with roomettes, an ingenious and highly uncomfortable space-saving invention of the Pullman Company. At night, the seat folded down into a narrow bed, and what was now the foot of the bed rested on the toilet which, if needed during the night, required folding the bed back up and then down again. Still farther ahead were cars for the Secret Service bodyguards and a double-length railroad car once used by the Ringling Brothers and Barnum and Bailey Circus, now owned by the White House. On this trip it carried the presidential limousines, two of them.

It was a jolly scene in the private car back there at the rear end of the train. Clark Clifford was the bartender. He said later he was surprised to see that, despite all he had heard, Churchill drank very little, nursing one glass of Scotch for hours. Had Clifford known, he would have understood Churchill on an ordinary evening did in fact drink prodigious quantities of whiskey or cognac or both. But the Great

Orator was aware he would be tested the next morning when he addressed the audience in Fulton and an audience around the world by radio. There was no television, at Churchill's request. He said TV's lights were too bright when he was trying to read his speech.

Press secretary Charlie Ross came up occasionally to give us reporters some details on what was going on in the *Ferdinand Magellan*. What he did not tell us was that the president and Churchill had started a poker game with themselves and some of their staffs. Ross never told us much about this, and we did not know much about it until years later when Clark Clifford wrote his memoirs, *Counsel to the President*. Churchill, he wrote, turned to Truman and said, "Mr. President, I understand from the press that you like to play poker."

"That's correct, Winston. I've played a lot of poker in my life."

Churchill said he had learned the game while in South Africa as a correspondent covering the Boer War. He left the car for a moment and returned wearing the blue jumpsuit he had made famous during the war, a suit similar to what Americans called a coverall, a garment zippered up the front and quick and easy to get into and out of and often seen on garage mechanics with advertising embroidered on the back. While he was out, Truman said to the others that Churchill had been playing the game for forty years, surely was a wizard at it, and the reputation of American poker was at stake, and so he expected every man present to do his duty.

But they were surprised to learn that Churchill played poorly, did not know the game well enough to compete with the tough, hardened Missourian poker players traveling with Truman, men who had grown up together and played poker all their lives. Soon it was clear that Churchill was a lamb among wolves.

When he went out again briefly, Truman said to the others, "Now we see he doesn't know the game well enough, so I want you all to play customer poker. Don't embarrass him. He's our guest. Let him win. Just carry him for the evening."

They did. Ross folded poker hands he knew would have been winners. Churchill won several hands he should have lost. And so the president of the United States and the wartime prime minister of Great Britain rolled across the midwestern United States at the poker table with the staff following the president's orders to fold their good hands and let Churchill win the money.

Up in the press car, we heard nothing of this until Ross told us Churchill had dropped out of the game and retired to work on his speech. The covey of Washington veterans in a car up forward were astonished at this. Most of us had barely ever heard of a politician writing his own speeches. Politicians did not write speeches, they read them. They hired people to write them. Speechwriting was a well-paid and more or less honored profession in Washington with established ground rules. If a speech delivered by the president went well, earning applause and good notices, the politician took all the bows. If it went badly, the speechwriter took the blame. Too many failures and he was out.

One reporter, Harold B. Hinton of *The New York Times*, said, "Writes his own speeches? Maybe that's why they're so good."

Hinton and all of us knew that was not why they were so good. They were so good because Churchill's use of the English language seemed to have come pure and pristine and from the King James Version of the Holy Bible, its sentences written in a.d. 1611 and still standing like stone arches so perfectly built and delicately balanced that removing one stone, or one word, would cause them to collapse. All of us alive at the time had been moved and heartened by his wartime speeches. We told ourselves his oratory had kept the British in the war long after they had been defeated but did not know it, by recalling their past ages of grandeur and heroism.

The morning after the poker game the Truman-Churchill Express pulled into St. Louis and stood in the station for a few minutes. Charlie Ross let me and the others get off the train to stand and watch Truman appear on the observation platform on the back end to wave to the huge crowds waiting for him and, they hoped, Churchill. Truman they had known before. Churchill they had seen only in the newsreels. And the American people held him in the highest respect and affection in these years soon after the war, and they began to clamor for him to appear. But he did not. He never said why, but we assumed he saw this as Truman's scene and he did not want to interfere or appear to overshadow the president.

None of us knew or could have known that this —Truman out on the train's back platform and responding to the crowd—would become his way of running for president two years later. "Whistle-stopping" it came to be called, and this was where it began.

The next morning in 1946, in Westminster's gymnasium, mostly used for basketball, here came the president, Churchill and their retinues in academic robes running from purple to scarlet to Truman's black. The audience filled the gymnasium and spilled out to the lawn and down the streets in all directions to hear the speech, amplified through loudspeakers. We reporters were seated at the front, on the speakers' left, about six feet away. Members of the press are expected to remain aloof from the news they are covering, since they are there to represent their readers and viewers, not to be a part of the audience and not expected to join in the applause if there is any. Nevertheless, while I had often seen Churchill in pictures and films, I had never observed him in person. And while I had heard a few and read many of his wartime speeches I had never sat at his feet and watched him speak. And I thought at the time I was seeing more than a statesman. I was seeing an actor who did not make a speech or deliver a speech. He *acted* a speech. He threw his whole body into it but somehow managed to do so without excessive gestures or histrionics. The words alone were enough, his speaking style the highly distilled product of a thousand years of upper-class English language and rhetoric. The audience sat still, quiet, entranced, eager to applaud but afraid to. The clapping of hands would have somehow seemed almost vulgar. Further, he was not talking to those of us in the hall. He was talking to the world.

But first, he spoke to the faculty of the college, just after he was given an honorary degree: "I am glad to come to Westminster College this afternoon, and am complimented that you should give me a degree. The name Westminster is somehow familiar to me. I seem to have heard of it before. Indeed it was at Westminster that I received a very large part of my education in politics, dialectic, rhetoric and one or two other things . . . it is also an honor, perhaps almost unique, for a private visitor to be introduced to an academic audience by the president of the United States. . . ."

He said there was a "shadow fallen across the scenes so lately lighted by the Allied victory. . . . I am sure you would wish me to state the facts as I see them to you, to place before you certain facts about the present position in Europe.'' And here his statement that would resonate down through the years: ''From Stettin in the Baltic to Trieste in the Adriatic, an iron curtain has descended across the continent. Behind that line lie all the capitals of the ancient states of Central and Eastern Europe. Warsaw, Berlin, Prague, Vienna, Budapest, Belgrade, Bucharest and Sofia. All these famous cities and the populations around them lie in what I must call the Soviet sphere, and all are subject in one form or another, not only to Soviet influence but to a very high and, in many cases, increasing measure of control from Moscow.''

His conclusion was that the United States and Great Britain should stand in friendly association to stop ''the expansive proselytizing tendencies of the Soviet Union.''

At the last minute, he deleted from his speech a reference to United States power and ascendancy and deleted a verse by Lord Byron, which he wrote out from memory as follows:

He who ascends to mountain tops shall find the loftiest
*   peaks most wrapped in clouds and snow.*
He who surpasses or subdues mankind must look down on
*   the hate of those below.*
Though far above the sun of glory shine
And far beneath the earth and ocean spread
Round him are icy rocks

*And fiercely blow contending tempests on his naked head
and thus reward the toils which to those summits led.*

He said later he cut this from his speech because
he decided it was unduly pessimistic and he wanted
nothing pessimistic or negative in his remarks to his
American hosts. And, he said, ''Not every word of
this Byron verse fits the scene because the prevail-
ing sentiment of the world toward the United States
is not hate but hope.''

The reaction to Churchill's speech, at least
among some of the editorial pages, was not hope
but hostility. The Chicago *Sun* said Churchill's object was world domination, through force of arms,
by the United States and the British Empire. ''To
be sure, he speaks again of his regard for Russia
and Stalin, but such words are hollow in an address
of threat and menace.'' The *Times* of London,
whose misunderstanding of history went back to
Neville Chamberlain's offering of ''peace in our
time,'' came in with a comment so silly that, if
shortened, it might have been pulled out of a Chi-
nese fortune cookie. Its editorial blamed Churchill
for appearing to ''contrast 'western democracy' and
'Communism.' '' It said while democracy in the
West and ''Communism are in many respects opposed, they have much to learn from each other,
Communism in the working of political institutions
and in the establishment of individual rights, western democracy in the development of economic and

social planning.'' This was one of the world's grand old newspapers, somehow able to see what nobody else in the world was ever able to see—communism displaying even the smallest interest in ''individual rights.'' In the United States, the *Nation*, unrelievedly left wing, said Churchill had added ''poison to the already deteriorating relations between Russia and the western powers.'' The conservative *Wall Street Journal* said Truman had been ''remarkably inept'' in associating himself with the Churchill speech.

None of us, including me, sitting in the Westminster gym and listening to Churchill's speech had any notion the reaction would be so hostile. The ugly words about the Fulton speech continued throughout Churchill's visit to the United States and beyond. They never stopped entirely until Russia began sending its tanks in to dominate one European country after another, killing anyone trying to resist and proving that in Fulton, Missouri, Churchill had been right.

III

As the 1948 presidential nominating conventions approached, the Republicans to meet first, it was never clearly established that anyone actually *liked* Thomas E. Dewey, the cold-eyed governor of New York, but he had become a figure in the Republican party through his reputation as a gangbuster. He had sent a number of famous hoodlums to jail while padding his crime-buster résumé by arresting and prosecuting a lot of whores and petty criminals who jumped the turnstiles and rode the New York subways without paying. In 1948, crime was not nearly the public concern it was to become later. And the exploits of New York's big-time gangsters were reported in almost affectionate detail by the city's tabloids, while Dewey followed and took care to be seen following the straight, stern, upright path of righteousness. His other political asset was a notably mellifluous speaking voice. He had even thought of becoming a professional singer, but concluded that a career built on a fragile pair of vocal cords was too risky. Then it was pointed out to him that if he went into opera, he would be a baritone, and most of the good arias went to the tenors. And they told him he was not tall enough, that if he sang a duet with one of opera's statuesque sopranos, he would have to sing directly into her bosom, not an attractive picture. So he chose politics. He hated but pretended to ignore Alice Roosevelt Longworth's comment that in his perfect suits and meticulous haberdashery, hair professionally coiffed, homburg hat and small mustache, shoes shined twice a day, he "looked like the little man on a wedding cake."

Even so, as the Republicans gathered in Philadelphia to choose their nominee for president, Dewey—who had run respectably against Roosevelt in 1944—was far out in front. The other famous contenders included Senator Robert A. Taft of Ohio, Governor Earl Warren of California and Harold Stassen, formerly the boy-wonder governor of Minnesota.

The establishment Republicans wanted Taft. He was safely and reliably conservative. He was from the Ohio heartland. He was the son of a Republican president. He was all blue suits, white shirts, bare scalp, rimless glasses, vest and gold watch chain. And it was said he looked like "a composite picture of 16 million Republicans." Before World War II he had been isolationist, opposed to sending American troops into any foreign wars for any reason whatever. And what really made the conservative heart beat faster was that he vociferously advocated small government and low taxes. That was why his party loved him. Not because he could match Dewey's campaigning skills. He couldn't, and his handlers felt they must somehow overcome the effete

image of Taft in his gentlemen's club lounging in
a leather chair reading the financial news and waiting for the butler to bring his vintage sherry. They
thought he needed to be seen more as a man's man
given to such masculine pursuits as tramping
through the woods carrying a shotgun and looking
for game. So, one of his campaign photographs sent
out to the press and to me in television showed him
standing in a woodsy setting wearing a dark three-
piece suit, felt hat, shiny black shoes, and holding
out at arm's length with clear distaste a wild turkey
shot by somebody else. And if Dewey's speaking
voice sounded like a cello quartet, Taft's was rusty
hinges on a henhouse door. But no matter. The Republicans were enraged at having been forced to
watch Franklin Roosevelt elected president four
times, in the White House from 1933 until he died
in 1945, being replaced by his vice president, Harry
Truman, who was still another Democrat and now
running again himself. It was too much for the hard-
line Republicans to stomach, and they seemed ready
for Taft.

Otherwise at the convention, there was Stassen,
the classic overachiever, beginning as a boy taking
on a newspaper route and tripling the subscriber list
in two months. In college he was Mr. Everything
—first in this and chairman of that. In the grand but
erroneous American tradition it was assumed that
one who succeeded in private life certainly would
be successful in public office. And so Stassen went

on to election to local offices, to governor and now here in Philadelphia in 1948 a candidate for president. He probably should have stayed in Minnesota. He was seen as a regional politico, not well known outside his own Midwest. Then he blundered badly and agreed to a network radio debate with Dewey on the topic "Should Communism Be Outlawed?" Stassen took the affirmative. Communism was so evil, he said, it should be abolished by law. Dewey asked, how? With Orwellian thought police? Opening mail? Tapping telephones? House searches at midnight? Blacklists? Stassen floundered and could not deal. Dewey was not lovable, perhaps, but he was quick, cutting and adept at slitting the jugular with a cold knife and watching as his opponent's blood formed a puddle on the floor. Stassen lost the debate and lost the nomination. On the first ballot, he was a weak third with 157 out of 1,094 votes. Earl Warren peaked too soon with little to offer beyond the fact that as California's attorney general he aggressively demanded that Japanese civilians, born in the United States of Japanese ancestry, be locked up. He got 59 votes. But shortly when Dewey offered him the nomination for vice president, he took it. He said he accepted because he had been assured that the president would allow him a substantial, meaningful role in the new administration. We all thought if Warren was dumb enough to believe that, he was too dumb to hold office. Every presidential nominee says his vice president will be given a serious, important role in the new administration, but this serious and important role almost never materializes. A strong, totally self-centered politician like Tom Dewey sharing his hard-won power with a vice president? Don't count on it.

On the third ballot Dewey won, and Stassen and Taft were out, but not down. Taft was back to try again four years later. For another forty years Stassen kept trying for the Republican nomination. He was a candidate in one out of every five elections since the election of George Washington. He ran and ran and tried so hard for so long and failed so often he became an embarrassment, a pathetic figure wearing an ill-fitting toupee and still hoping and grasping for what was no longer there, if it ever had been.

IN 1948 television made its first appearance at a political convention. The two parties did not know what to make of the new medium, and we did not know what to make of a convention, since none of our crew at NBC had ever covered one. It appeared mainly to be a crowd of middle-aged white men aimlessly milling around in a huge hall, talking, smoking cigars and shaking hands, and occasionally pushing through the crowds to get out to cadge free drinks from a bar operated by the Association of American Railroads, and after a stop at the men's room to return to the convention floor only to find that the speaker who had been so boring he drove them out of the hall in the first place was still on the rostrum and still talking. The television picture in 1948 was available only in a small area of the East Coast, and even there it could be seen only in the tiny number of households owning television sets. Nevertheless, NBC sent cameras to Philadelphia, only a few since at that time it only had a few. John Cameron Swayze, whose knowledge of politics was limited, went with them to explain the proceedings to what little audience there was. He and the cameras arrived to find a less than effusive welcome. The Republicans would allow only one camera in the convention hall and said NBC must install it in a cubicle high up among the rafters. There would be nothing up there but Swayze and a few pigeons. So many steps had to be climbed to get up to the camera booth that many Republicans, when invited up to be interviewed, squinted up into the half-dark spaces just under the roof and declined to make the long climb. Since the party leaders were not young athletes most of them were never seen or heard from.

In view of this, in view of the convention camera's being physically inaccessible, and the television picture's being seen only in a small area of the East Coast and nowhere else, and Dewey's being nominated once more and going on to lose the fifth election in a row to still another Democrat, both the Republicans and television might as well have stayed home.

THE NEXT MONTH, the Democrats met in the same Philadelphia hall, with Swayze and television still up in the rafters, but the party had more serious problems than television reporters and pigeons. The southern states were furious that race and civil rights were coming to be an irresistible political force, more and more difficult to ignore as they had ignored them for years. The convention was near to revolt, the southerners feeling like strangers in their own land, and there was even talk of a third-party candidate who would be more amenable on questions of race.

Roosevelt had won four elections in a row and served in the White House longer than any president in history, but in 1948 for the first time in sixteen years the Democrats had to choose a nominee for president. Until then it had been Roosevelt and no argument. In 1944 he had been elected for the fourth time even though his doctor, Admiral Ross McIntyre, knew it was nearly impossible for him to live through another term. But he was secretive and deceptive about Roosevelt's rapidly declining health until the day he died in Warm Springs, Georgia, and his vice president, Harry Truman, replaced him. Arguably, Truman had not been Roosevelt's first choice for vice president. When he wrote out a list of his preferences, Truman was not at the top. Supreme Court justice William O. Douglas was. But Robert Hannegan of Missouri, Democratic national chairman and a friend from the old days, moved Truman's name to the top of the list without telling Roosevelt what he had done. Hannegan no doubt overstepped his authority, but Truman did, in fact, have a record of solid and impeccably honest performance in the Senate. However, neither he nor anyone else could offer anything like the overpowering presidency the country had lived with for twelve years.

Roosevelt being the social snob he was, he frequently berated reporters covering the White House at his press conferences over the years. He made no attempt to hide his opinion that we were all poorly educated in what he called redbrick colleges, and so we could not possibly know enough or understand enough to report to the American people accurately and fairly about the activities of their president, a C student at Harvard. He even ridiculed the far better educated Walter Lippmann. As a way around the press, Roosevelt resorted to what he called his fireside chats, delivered from a tiny studio in the White House having no fireside. He felt it was the only way he could reach the people directly, without reporters—and their publishers he always detested—twisting and distorting his views.

During the few months Truman served as vice president, Roosevelt ignored him almost totally. He never invited him for dinner, and for lunch once and once only. If he was not quite contemptuous of him, it was clear he saw Truman as a routine, uninteresting politician from the Midwest, the product of a crooked political machine run by the Pendergast gang but who even so had somehow built his own political career with honesty and integrity.

As the White House correspondent for NBC, I was able to observe both of them as presidents, and I came to think Truman was at least as adept a politician as Roosevelt was, and in some ways more so. Both of them, in their public utterances, played the role of the nice man next door who liked to chat over the back fence and could always tell you how to look after your tomato plants. Roosevelt did this in his fireside chats, using the vernacular of the workman in overalls, home from the plant and talking with his wife at the kitchen table covered in oilcloth. So did Truman, who in public liked to play the proletarian and refer to his wife, Bess, as ''the boss.'' In Roosevelt's case this folksiness was put on. Truman lacked the social polish of Harvard and the glittering New York salons, he had done farmwork and had no inherited wealth, and so in his case it was genuine. And it got him elected president in 1948.

Not long after Truman took office, he announced he would for the first time as president visit his hometown and his relatives in Independence, Missouri. Several of us White House reporters flew with him in a four-engine, propeller-driven World War II transport plane, the *Sacred Cow*, and the flight was a nightmare. A tremendous storm moved in and bounced the plane around the skies, hailstones rattling on the wings, people sick and vomiting in the aisles, the pilot repeatedly assuring the passengers, the president and the rest of us, that we were in no danger. Nobody believed him but, to the surprise of some, we arrived alive. Truman had arranged for all of us on this trip, and others later, to stay in the grand old Muehlebach Hotel in Kansas City. A time or two, the president came over and joined our nighttime poker games while the manager, Barney Allis, overwhelmed at having a president of the United States under his roof, welcomed all of us with fourteen-year-old Scotch and apples stuffed with Roquefort, all of it far better than any of us were accustomed to.

As I later learned, a few of Truman's old friends from the fading and dying Pendergast machine had arranged for each White House correspondent flying in with Truman to be given a car and driver, each driver to be a pretty young woman. Pendergast had in fact chosen Truman for the U.S. Senate and then used his considerable political power to elect him. The young woman driving me explained that she was, or had been, a cocktail waitress in the Chesterfield Club, an establishment owned and operated by Pendergast, where the pay was good and the tips were spectacular, "Because," she said, "it's a club where men come without their wives. And the wives don't come because when we work in his club Mr. Pendergast has us wearing high-heel shoes and nothing else. The girls enjoy it once we get used to it.''

I was certain Truman knew nothing about all this. Nor did he know that each woman driver had been instructed to accommodate each of us in the visiting press corps in any way we desired, sexually or otherwise, mine said. But she apologized profusely and asked me, ''Please don't let Mr. Pendergast know that just when all of you came off the president's airplane, I got my period.''

On one of these nights in Kansas City, Hearst's International News Services correspondent Bob Nixon, Merriman Smith of the United Press and I were in a game of draw poker with several other players, including Truman. The president played skillfully and carefully without a lot of chatter, or ''coffeehousing,'' as he called it. That is, seemingly aimless conversation in mournful tones of resignation and self-pity intended to deceive the other players about the strength of his hand and to entice them to stay in and put more money in the pot before he won it.

On one hand Nixon and I ran the pot up to about eight hundred dollars. Even though he had long since folded Truman objected when the pot rose into the hundreds. ''Too rich for a government employee,'' he said. And he was right. It was too rich for any of us, more than Nixon or I could afford. As it turned out, I won the pot with four eights, and Nixon lost with a full house. But nobody was hurt financially because Nixon never paid me.

BACK IN WASHINGTON, the real Truman could be seen when his daughter, Margaret, sang in public. She had wanted a career as a singer, and when this became known she was invited to give a concert at Constitution Hall.

The next day, Paul Hume, music critic for the Washington *Post*, wrote a highly critical review, saying her singing was pretty bad and far short of any professional standard. Truman, the devoted father, was infuriated and wrote a nasty note to Hume, threatening him with bodily harm for criticizing his daughter. Hume said nothing, but he did manage to make the letter public. All of us smart alecks broadcasting news and comments gave Truman a mild chastising for what we all said was an exercise in bad taste, threatening a newspaper critic for writing unfavorably about his daughter's singing. On NBC, I joined in this chorus of condemnation. But then I had the same experience. My son, Alan Brinkley, now a professor of history at Columbia University, sang for a time in the chorus at his school in Washington. They were invited to sing carols on Christmas Eve in the National Gallery of Art, a substantial honor. They sang. His mother and I went to listen.

We thought they were just fine. But Paul Hume did not. Seemingly, he applied the professional standards of the Metropolitan Opera to schoolkids singing Christmas carols. I was furious and ready to write Hume, call him a damned fool and threaten to finish whatever Truman started. I never wrote the letter. I'm still sorry I didn't.

BY 1952, time for another convention, with Swayze presiding over the nightly news program in New York, I had begun doing the Washington report on each night's *Camel News Caravan* and finding that we were still confused about what to do with television news. One ludicrous example from a broadcast in those early years:

> SWAYZE IN NEW YORK: Senator Wayne Morse of Oregon announced today he was leaving the Republican party and becoming a Democrat. Here's David Brinkley in Washington.
>
> BRINKLEY IN WASHINGTON (allowed five seconds to get into the film): Republican Senator Wayne Morse of Oregon announced today he was switching to the Democratic party. Here's Senator Morse:
>
> SENATOR WAYNE MORSE IN WASHINGTON (on film): Since the Republican party no longer represents my views . . . I am switching today to the Democratic party.
>
> BRINKLEY: Now back to John Cameron Swayze in New York.

That night, as on many other nights, I complained to Ralph Howard Peterson, the producer, that Swayze kept doing this, reading the script they handed to him and telling my news before I could tell it, switching to me to tell what he had already told, leaving both of us looking foolish.

The problem here was that we still thought we were in the picture business, still competing with the movie theater newsreels and still thinking, even though we all knew better, that news was whatever we could get on film and show, not tell. It seems absurd now because it was absurd then, but here we were, all of us young former newspaper reporters, trying to drive a new, highly complex machine that had arrived without an instruction book. Since we thought our job was to broadcast pictures, it might appear that my few words introducing Morse or any other short piece of film were superfluous because Swayze told all that needed to be told before he switched to me. So, why put me on at all? Why not have Swayze introduce the film and simply leave me out? Why? Because it took several seconds to get a film projector up to speed and, in effect, my job was to fill the screen with something, anything, until the filmed picture stopped blurring, rocking and jumping. During those seconds I could only tell again what Swayze had already told and then bring in Senator Morse, on film, to tell it again. Wonderful. But the projectors and cameras we used in television's early years had been designed for

Hollywood's motion picture industry, where these few seconds of delay were not a problem. In moviemaking, the actors would simply wait until the camera was up and running, and when the cameraman shouted "Speed," it meant the camera was ready and now William Powell and Myrna Loy could pour another martini or cowboy actor Hoot Gibson could kiss his horse. And that was why in about fifty seconds our modest little story about Wayne Morse got on the news three times.

By now, NBC had decided it probably could live without the news program I had been doing every night for several months. It was five minutes of airtime at 6:00 p.m. filled with scraps of film gathered during the day by a single cameraman, George Johnson, a nice young man totally inexperienced and untrained in journalism, working with a hand-held, spring-wound silent-film camera, a Bell and Howell Filmo, wandering alone around Washington during the day looking for something, anything, to put on the air that night. Whatever he brought in was broadcast while I sat in a tiny studio out of sight of the audience looking at a television screen and narrating film I had never seen before. Rehearsals? There weren't any. While the film ran and I talked behind it, an engineer somewhere else in the building played background music from a phonograph record. Background music? Yes, we still thought we were doing newsreels and they always had music, didn't they? Yes, of course. Predictably, this messy procedure brought to the screen some perfectly terrible programs.

This was the worst: One day, George Johnson brought in four small film stories. When they were spliced together, the first in line was a funeral of a departed dignitary in Arlington cemetery. The second and third stories I have forgotten. The fourth was about some kind of experiment with sheep at an Agriculture Department station in nearby Maryland. The film was delivered to the control room to be threaded into the projector. It was threaded in, but backward. Nobody noticed. At 6:00 p.m., the projector started, and somewhere down the hall an engineer started the music. What went out on the air was sonorous, funereal music suitable for a burial in Arlington while on the screen was a picture of a sheep upside down. I sat, stunned and confused, in the little studio looking at and listening to this mess and wondering what in God's name I could do or say. Nothing, as it turned out. Looking at an upside-down sheep I could do or say nothing but keep quiet and let it run out to the finish. But others said it for me. For years after, people on the streets and in elevators asked me, ''You ever get that sheep back on its feet?''

ALL ACROSS the South in 1953 the politicians—governors, mayors, county commissioners, police, others—were squirming in their swivel chairs, ner-

vously and even fearfully contemplating a case
awaiting a decision by the U.S. Supreme Court
bearing the title *Brown v. Board of Education*. It
promised, or threatened, as they saw it, the southern
states with a prospect they found entirely unimagin-
able—ending two hundred years of segregated
schools and forcing local school boards to place
black and white students in the same classrooms,
or "race mixing," as they called it. While they
awaited the court's decision, NBC sent me and a
camera crew cruising around the South looking for
comments and opinions from the pols on what they
would do if, as they feared, the court ruled that
schools must be integrated. One after another, they
offered the identical comment, "That goddamned
Earl Warren [the new chief justice] . . . ," followed
by a variety of opinions, all of them foreseeing violence and blood and death and doom in their most
horrible forms and even the end of American civilization as we had all known it.

Some friends at WSB, the NBC affiliate in Atlanta, suggested I go to Montgomery, Alabama, to
the Dexter Avenue Baptist Church and call on the
pastor—a largely unknown young clergyman with
the stately name of Martin Luther King. I found him
to be a handsome young man, a doctor of divinity
and Bible scholar, a descendant of Baptist ministers,
and with a warm, silken speaking voice. He was
curious about NBC's television camera, questioning
me about it, since he had almost never seen one

Knickers!!! The southern schoolboy's
uniform until he was thirteen and ready
for high school in Wilmington,
North Carolina.

Sergeant, 120th Infantry.
Every man in the picture
except me was killed
in Normandy after
D Day, 1944.

At my office at NBC in the
sixties. Ann brought John
in one afternoon for a visit.

Alan, our first son, and
Joel, our second, and an
easy shot into the
side pocket.

I've talked to millions, but Alexis, my only
daughter, is the best audience
I've ever had.

Our gang at a dude ranch in Wyoming:
John, daughter-in-law Shannon, Susan,
Joel, me, Alan.

I survived early radio at NBC, and it survived me. The grand old names in radio never made it in television.

Early TV and *David Brinkley's Journal:* making an episode in the Florida Everglades on a hermit who never came ashore.

Live television, no doubt. It came without
an instruction manual, and none of us
knew what to do with it.

In Greece, making TV's first documentary,
Our Man in the Mediterranean. John
Chancellor squints through the view-finder.
He directed. Very good.

This early, everything we did was a first—
good or bad. Here, *David Brinkley's
Journal*, TV's first magazine program.
Fairly good, not great.

We thought a rolltop desk looked good on
the set. It did. Antiques shops sold out
of them. I still use one.

The 1964 election night broadcast with Chet Huntley, reporting on Lyndon Johnson's landslide victory over Barry Goldwater.

With Huntley—our first Emmy. Success. Success. It's fun if you know it's temporary and don't inhale. Neither of us ever did.

Apollo 11: Our one and only news story
never seen before in human history;
exciting and a little scary. We were both
afraid it wouldn't work.

Home from Cape Canaveral and at
Wrightsville Beach with my poodles,
Ajax and Daisy.

While with Susan in Africa, a giraffe stuck
his head indoors, looking for food. We fed
him. Giraffes have black tongues.

Finally, a little time off. With Senator Abe Ribicoff and Secretary Henry Kissinger on the Yangtze River in China.

Susan and I walked (part way) up the Great Wall of China.

Nixon's task force tried to destroy Huntley and me, failed and sicced Spiro Agnew on us—a high time and great fun. We survived Nixon and Agnew. Then Gerald Ford. No genius but a nice man, easy for all of us in the press. But he lacked what it took for a second term. So did Jimmy Carter.

Regardless of party, most liked Ronald Reagan—funny, clever. While George Bush, a favorite of mine, awarded me the Medal of Freedom. Those present for the award: Evangeline, my daughter-in-law, and Alan; the President; me with a neck ribbon and medal; Mrs. Bush; Susan; Alexis; John; my daughter-in-law Sabra, wife of Joel, our Pulitzer Prize winner.

Our splendid cast on *This Week with David Brinkley:* George Will, Cokie Roberts, me, Sam Donaldson. They are the best.

Some black-tie function or other, improved by
the presence of Dorrance Smith, our executive
producer, with Susan and me.

Our studio background map was made of
wooden cutouts. Viewers complained
when Madagascar bumped out of place.
I had to straighten it.

before. I doubt it occurred to him and it certainly did not occur to me that in future years he would use television as no one ever had before, using it to rally an entire people to a cause that clearly would be difficult and dangerous. I asked his view of the case pending in the Supreme Court. Long overdue, he thought, and he was fairly confident the court would rule for integration. But he said he was fearful it was too much of a change too fast for white southerners to accept peacefully, and so there clearly would be violence. His plan, he said, was to play a role he called creative nonviolence. I did not understand that term at the time, since it had not yet passed into the American vocabulary.

As history shows, violence there was, and it fell to me to report it on the news every night. It was, as NBC's thinking went, my part of the country, and so it was a story for me to do. Before the arrival of many, many other networks, magazines and newspapers from around the world, I did it, and it was the most difficult work of my life. Telling the news as straight as I could was not enough. Nothing could satisfy some of the extreme and some not so extreme elements in the South. They, like others before and since, did not want the news straight. They wanted it slanted, but slanted their way, a human failing familiar to everyone in journalism. The mail was poisonous. There were death threats by mail and phone. In the southern press and in the street talk I came to be called Booker T. Brinkley.

Huntley, staying in New York and occasionally sub-stituting for Swayze, came to be called Hambone Huntley. The manager of an affiliated station in North Carolina, calling me a traitor to my home state and calling me, in the crudest terminology of the time and the place, a "nigger lover." He tried to get me off the air, but failed. Then he retaliated in the only way open to him. He hired a reporter, previously unknown, deeply unskilled and some-thing of a rural tinhorn. He put him on his local station each night immediately following my NBC news and gave him the assignment to "answer Brinkley's lies." Every night he came on just after our news program and carefully explained to the audience that I was a "turncoat southerner turned northern radical" incapable or unwilling to tell the truth about racial problems in the South, most of the troubles caused by "outside agitators" like me. He did his job so effectively he became an admired public figure. Whereupon he chose to turn his new popularity to his own advantage and run for the United States Senate. He ran. On the strength of his attacks on me, he was elected. His name: Senator Jesse Helms, Republican, North Carolina.

Until others arrived and took over—Frank McGee, John Chancellor—I was at a serious and possibly dangerous disadvantage here. When out-of-town reporters sent their stories to their papers in other cities, nobody here in these southern towns ever saw their papers, and nobody knew what they had written. In my case, I was there on the air in full view every night of the week trying to tell the news without being inflammatory. And very often when I left after a broadcast I slipped out a back door.

THE SUPREME COURT ruled in 1954 as expected, and soon the rough stuff began—marching, riots, shooting, burning. Even the Ku Klux Klan, long since dismissed as a gang of ignorant fools stomping around in the wet grass of cow pastures wearing white polyester sheets and burning crosses soaked in kerosene, now began to think they were respectable again. They weren't quite. But when they marched through the streets the police now left them alone.

The southern states had become a kind of war zone, and reporters poured in from all over the world, infuriating the South. The county sheriff in Troy, Alabama, asked me, ''How can I get all these goddamned reporters out of here? They're the cause of all this trouble. I'd kill 'em all if I could.''

He couldn't. But a sheriff in another town tried a new and clever trick. From the county jail, he pulled out the most attractive young black prostitute. She was told the sheriff had a job for her and if she did it well he would let her go free. Put her in a dress held together in front with one button and let her wear it with nothing under it. Took her to the door of a hotel room where a visiting reporter was staying. Then this little drama ensued: The woman knocks on the door. When the reporter answers she pushes her way into his room, drops her dress to the floor, and now, stark naked, she wraps her arms around him and forces a kiss on his mouth. Before he can free himself, the sheriff's deputies waiting in the hallway are shooting flash pictures. The sheriff thought he could use the pictures to blackmail the reporter, telling him they would not be sent to his newspaper if he would listen to reason and tone down his reports or, better still, quietly leave town. Clever, maybe. But it never worked because the newspapers knew the trick and would not print the pictures.

Another effort also failed. An Alabama newspaper printed a clearly false and clearly libelous report about some work I did on NBC. Normally, we ignore this kind of thing, but in this case I thought I should react. Otherwise it would go into newspaper files, never corrected, and resurface in some embarrassing way in the future. I wrote to the paper, pointed out the falsehoods and demanded a full retraction and apology within twenty-four hours or I would file suit for libel and ask for substantial cash damages. Carefully, I pointed out my suit would be filed in the jurisdiction where I had bought the paper, in a newsstand in the District of Columbia. The paper's lawyers saw quickly that my suit would be tried in a city predominantly black, and after a couple of the paper's racist editorials were read aloud in the courtroom, the paper would not have a chance. They saw what they had to do and devoted half the front page to a correction and apology.

BY 1952 when the Republicans and Democrats both held their conventions in Chicago, television was growing into a political force too big to ignore and too important to send up to the rafters with the pigeons. About 17 million homes had TV sets now, and the conventions were seen in sixty-four cities in thirty-eight states. This was before there were satellites, and we still used coaxial cables installed by the telephone company to carry our programs into most but not all of the United States. As yet only one cable ran all the way to California, and the three networks had to share it, with NBC, CBS and ABC all sending the same picture to the West Coast. While there was only one cable to carry the picture, there were plenty of wires in use since early radio days to carry sound and speech. The three networks had to share the one video cable, but each could send its own narration. Since no network was willing to carry the voices or names of reporters other than those of its own staff members, what was sent to California was the same picture with three separate narrations, each going only to the affiliated stations of one of the three networks. For competitive reasons, no network was willing to use news material generated by either of the other two, so the only picture we could send to the West Coast was the pool picture, set up by the networks jointly to cover the official proceedings inside the convention hall—the speeches on the rostrum, the opening prayers, resolutions of thanks to the local police and fire and sanitation departments and the roll calls. As for reports from outside the hall from the head-quarters hotels and for news items picked up from delegates on the floor and little feature stories and all that, each network did its own. But the pool was still interesting because its director, Bob Doyle of NBC, had an eye for engaging, amusing detail. During the dull spots when nothing was happening, and there were many of these, Doyle had his cameras roam around to find such close-ups as a portly state chairman asleep in his chair, a delegate splattering his necktie with mustard dripping off his hot dog, others reading the papers and ignoring the speeches. The mail told us the audience loved it. But the politicians did not, and in the next day's session each delegate found a printed notice on his chair warning that "you might be on television without knowing it. Please consider how you will look to viewers across the country and behave accordingly." The Republicans responded to this. Democrats responded barely, if at all. In this case, as in others, looking down on the hall through twenty-two conventions, I have seen, as if I were watching a psychologist's behavioral study, the differences between the two parties. Republicans arrived in the hall and started their sessions on time. The Democrats were always late. Republicans stayed in their seats. Democrats did not. They roamed the aisles visiting, shaking hands and chatting. The Republicans were neat and tidy, leaving not much litter. The Democrats left the hall looking like the top layer of a sanitary landfill.

At political gatherings when the whiskey is poured and the jokes begin, there are always laughs about the differences between the Democrats and Republicans, always with some small grain of truth. It is a favorite joke in a hundred variations. The best, I think, were assembled by Will Stanton and printed in the *Congressional Record*, entitled "How to Tell a Democrat from a Republican:"

> If a Republican catches a fish he has it mounted. If a Democrat catches a fish, he eats it.
>
> Republicans wear hats and clean their paintbrushes. Democrats do neither.
>
> Democrats give their worn-out clothes to the poor. Republicans wear theirs.
>
> Democrats put their newspaper's financial pages on the bottoms of their bird cages. Republicans read them.
>
> On Saturdays, Republicans go to their clubs. Democrats wash their cars and get haircuts.
>
> And [my favorite] Democrats name their children for political and sports and entertainment figures. Republicans name their children for the grandparent who has the most money.

Back on the convention floor, it was a Democrat, a southern governor, scheduled to speak to the convention, who came to Chicago two days in advance, and when his wife arrived later, she caught him in bed with another politician's wife. She threatened an immediate public announcement that she was filing for divorce, naming all the names. The party leaders were terrified of the publicity this would produce on the opening day of their convention with hungry reporters all over the place. They worked all night to persuade the governor's wife to hold back her announcement until the convention was over. She agreed to that. The party leaders tried feverishly to keep the whole affair quiet. They failed. And during the duller sessions the delegates now had something new to talk about. Talk they did. While a speaker on the rostrum explained how the Democrats had to save the country from ruination by the Republicans, I used NBC's binoculars for a close-up look at the delegates. Were any of them paying any attention to the speaker? So far as I could see, not one. A fairly ordinary sex scandal was far more interesting. As I roamed around the floor and talked and listened, I found a rough—very rough—consensus. The delegates were saying they thought this was one more example of what they believed to be true, that politicians more than others were prone to crawl into beds other than their own, and in all my time in Washington I had believed this, too. Why? The delegate-philosophers thought it was in the very nature of politicians to seek to dominate, to control, that politicians above all else sought power. Money, yes. But power above all. What else could it be when a candidate spent far more money campaigning for office than the office would pay him if he won?

> In order to obtain and hold power a man must love it. Thus the effort to get it is not likely to be coupled with goodness, but with the opposite qualities of pride, craft and cruelty.
> —Lyof N. Tolstoy, 1893

CHICAGO, 1952: Jacob Arvey, formerly the Cook County, Illinois, Democratic chairman, a machine politician if there ever was one. It was he who stepped aside and turned the political power over to Mayor Richard J. Daley. I had a talk with him, and he managed to shake some of my notions about political machines and the men who run them.

"You New York liberals think the machines, as you call them, are all corrupt. A political organization, as we call them, may be corrupt in certain situations at certain times. It depends. But at their best, they are most effective of all ways to run a big city. We don't survive by being corrupt. We survive by delivering service."

The service, he said, consisted of keeping track of the voters' wants, needs and problems and finding ways of helping them, or at least dealing with them somehow. He said this required an organization, an organization that the press always insisted on calling a machine.

"The press seems to have a taste for the word 'machine.' Maybe because the right word—'organization'—is too long to fit in a headline.

"Anyway, if Mrs. Brown, one of our voters, has a problem with the city hall, taxes, permits or something, we call down there and fix it. And she does not have to ride the bus to city hall and stand in line. If she has troubles in the winter, we help with her coal or oil deliveries. If her husband is out of work we tell the tax office to go easy on her and they do. We have a block captain on every block and he knows every man, woman and child on his block and they all know him and they all know where to go if they need help.

"We do all this every day and all we ask in return is Mrs. Brown's vote and we always get it. That's what you people call a machine. I call it an organization. An organization devoted to service.

"And again, I remind you, Tammany Hall, which you called a machine, did a little stealing here and there but never enough to empty the city treasury. Tammany Hall did not bankrupt New York City. The liberal reformers did."

SINCE THIS was the first convention I had ever attended or even seen, I didn't and couldn't do much. I did NBC's narration to the West Coast, talking over whatever picture popped up on the pool feed, never knowing what was coming next nor for how long. We did not yet know much about how to cover a huge, sprawling political event, but we did learn this: if you are to talk over a television picture, you must talk about what is in the picture. Anything else is confusing to the viewers, as if a newspaper printed a picture of a home-run hitter sliding into the plate and under the picture a caption telling something about the gross national product. Crazy as that would be, it was hard to avoid when I was talking behind the picture from inside a political convention hall, because in the slow, empty hours Bob Doyle kept the pool pictures jumping from the Kansas delegation eating roast-beef sandwiches to a musician in the band polishing his trumpet to the empty rostrum to the delegates from South Carolina complaining that their hotel's beds were too hard. I never knew what was coming next, who would be in the picture nor how long it would be on. If I tried to explain something even mildly complicated, the picture would switch to something else before I could get to the second sentence. The job was impossible to do well, and I couldn't. But, thankfully, I had to do it only one year. By the next convention there were more cables to California, and the impossible became the unnecessary.

By 1952 the networks had a somewhat reliable system of counting the audience and issuing ratings claiming to show how many people tuned in this or that program hour by hour all day and night. The press was critical, saying it meant the networks would concentrate on ratings at the expense of program quality. But no mass medium, printed or broadcast, can ignore its ratings or its circulation figures as a measure of success or failure. I recall articles in *The New York Times* by Herbert Mitgang accusing the networks of excessive and even sickly attention to ratings. On the opposite side of the same page was a *Times* house ad boasting about its growing circulation. Even so, talk of ratings was and usually is treated in the press not as a commercial necessity but as an unseemly aspect of commercial greed.

In any case the ratings, accurate or not, showed our audience for the 1952 conventions was a weak second, well behind CBS and Walter Cronkite. NBC had hired Bill Henry, a nice man from California and the Los Angeles *Times*, where he had worked as sports writer, reporter, Washington bureau manager and columnist. He worked alongside H. V. Kaltenborn, famous for having seen and done everything and then talking lucidly about it without a script. (He was also famous for claiming throughout election night in 1948 that Dewey would win over Truman as soon as the farm vote had been counted.) He simply talked. Even when he was wrong, as he often was, he sounded authoritative. As on December 7, 1941, reporting the Japanese attack on Pearl Harbor, he reassured his audience by saying that surely in a matter of hours or a few days at most the U.S. Navy would cross the Pacific and "devastate the islands of Japan" and end the war.

Soon after the conventions, the executives agreed they would do something about NBC's poor showing at the convention. But what? In those days NBC and ABC were deeply envious of CBS's Edward R. Murrow, by far the most admired figure in broadcast news. They sent scouts around the country to look at the newspeople on local stations, desperately seeking somebody who was, or appeared to be, another Murrow. They did this by checking into hotels, not telling the local stations they were even in town, and watching the local news on the hotel-room television. Was there a Murrow in town? This was how they found Chet Huntley, then on local television in Los Angeles. He was handsome. If the Marlboro man had been invented by this time, they could have photographed Huntley on horseback smoking a Marlboro. He had a serviceable baritone, looked good on the tube and was experienced in doing news on television. He was hired and moved to New York, where for a time he sat around and did occasional odd jobs, such as filling in on the *Camel News Caravan* when Swayze was on vacation. He and I both filled in there once in a while and found it to be about as uninteresting in New York's news headquarters as it had been at the

Washington end—simply writing and speaking little captions to introduce little pieces of film, about as exciting as writing the labels for the drawers of file cabinets.

WHILE NBC searched the country looking for a Murrow, I was still working in Washington doing little stories. I was asked to go out to the U.S. Bureau of Standards on Connecticut Avenue and see if there was a news story in a new machine just put on public display. It was called SEAC, for Standard Eastern Automatic Computer. I looked in awe but with absolutely no understanding at a machine maybe fifty feet long and two stories high and informally described as a "magic brain." It was, I was told, only the second computer built in the world. It was all black, covered with dials, knobs, meters, and for me it was totally incomprehensible. I called the New York news desk and told them the thing was black, hard to see, nothing moved, and since it was inside a Bureau of Standards building it was impossible to stand back from it far enough to get a picture of it into the television frame.

I asked New York, "You want it?"

"What does it do?"

"I don't know and there's nobody here willing to explain it."

"Well if we can't get a picture of it and we can't tell what it is, we may as well skip it."

We did.

Later I learned, along with the rest of the world, that the SEAC was an early, primitive, vacuum-tube model of a machine that would soon revolutionize human life. Still later I learned, along with everyone else, that since the invention of the transistor and the integrated circuit, the SEAC, even though fifty feet long, had less power than the personal computer now on my desk, fifteen inches wide. In time we knew better, but for a very long time we thought, or were required to think, that if we couldn't take a picture of it, it wasn't news. We did outgrow that, but we were still left with television's great strengths and great weaknesses. Would anyone like to try doing the stock market tables on a television news program?

WHEN the 1956 political conventions approached, NBC's news executives agreed on one point only —that losing the ratings to CBS and Cronkite was intolerable. John Cameron Swayze's *News Caravan* was leading the pack of early evening news programs, but they did not think he knew enough political history or knew enough of the political system's featured players and strutting prima donnas to carry the load of discussing and explaining them and the convention procedures for four days and four nights. Plus, Swayze's evening news program was carefully scripted, and he even had a little time to rehearse and memorize his stories, while at a political convention everything was ad-lib and nothing could be rehearsed. The pairing of Kaltenborn and Henry in 1952 had not worked. Both were experienced broadcasters, but they failed here for the reason now becoming familiar: both had grown up in radio and could not or would not adapt to the television medium, learn its needs and learn to use its strengths and steer around its weaknesses. A small example of this I remember from 1952: some forgotten senator finished an easily forgettable speech, folded his script, put it in his pocket and walked back down to his seat. Henry, the radio veteran, talked over the television picture as he walked, saying, "The senator finishes his speech . . . folds his script . . . and puts it in his pocket . . . and returns to his seat." That was narration for radio, not television. On radio there was and is a compulsion to talk because on radio, indeed, you *must* talk. If there is more than a few seconds of silence, known to broadcasters as dead air, listeners will put down their knitting, sensing that something is wrong. After Henry's and Kaltenborn's years on radio the habit was too hard for them to break. Very early, I discussed this with Reuven Frank, NBC's production genius who managed convention coverage and built it into the shape and style still followed today, and while we both opposed making a lot of rules, we did agree on one, one so simple, sophomoric and obvious it should never have been needed, but it was. The Frank-Brinkley rule was this: In talking over a television picture, never tell the viewers what they can easily see for themselves. If you cannot add anything useful to what is in the picture, keep quiet. It worked then and it works now.

For the 1956 conventions, NBC felt it needed somebody who already knew this, somebody who had made the effort to unlearn radio and had at least begun to learn television. Who was ready for this? Frank and Julian Goodman, a lifelong friend of mine and manager of NBC's Washington bureau, wanted Huntley and me. Everyone agreed on Huntley. He was new, he was experienced, he was good. Davidson Taylor, vice president in charge of news, wanted Huntley and Ray Scherer, our White House correspondent, not Brinkley. After all, I was from Washington. In his silly view, I was halfway down there in the South toward the corn-pone belt, living and working in a city full of verbose, tiresome politicians and, worst of all, *I was not in New York.* Taylor and the executives found it unthinkable that a big-time television name could be found in that boring gaggle of lawyers, lobbyists and accountants whose daily work was to find ways to squeeze more money out of the decent working people of America. Washington, they asked? Where was that? What they neglected to think about was that the largest single group of speakers and leaders at the convention would be from Washington, and I knew all of them. The issues to be discussed and fought over would be, or already were, Washington issues, to be settled in Washington if they were ever settled anywhere, and I, having lived and worked in Washington for years, had an advantage over those from New York. That never occurred to them. They were New Yorkers whose view of the world stopped at the Hudson River.

William R. McAndrew, one of the good guys among news executives, next in line below Taylor, wanted Huntley and somebody else he had not chosen yet. Why did everyone agree we needed two people while CBS did very well with Cronkite alone? Because we had nobody who had ever done a convention successfully, nobody they were confident could carry on for four days and four nights ad-libbing all that time while making some sense and keeping the facts straight and keeping the correct names and titles together while occasionally offering an insight or two. Finally, the question was passed on up all the way to David Sarnoff himself, and somewhere up in that management maze—I never knew where—the decision was made: Huntley and Brinkley.

Even after it had been decided, hardly anyone but Goodman, McAndrew and Frank was sure it was the right one. Sylvester L. "Pat" Weaver, vice president for television programs, was not confident. He knew nothing about news. All he knew was that he disliked Swayze. But he let the decision stand, lacking any other idea. Even so, there were such deep doubts about Huntley's and my ability to carry two massive political conventions on television successfully that NBC hung back for two months before it was willing to announce our names in public. And even after we were announced, Davidson Taylor thought Huntley and I would be too boring and would fill the air reciting dull facts nobody cared about. He tried to reduce the boredom by hiring a song-and-dance man named Barry Wood to teach us how to be lively and to tell how the next president was chosen, yes, but to tell it in an entertaining manner. Had he had his way, I think he might have liked us to sing the political news in close harmony while doing a tap dance. And in fact he did bring in two bright red blazers with the NBC chimes embroidered on the breast pockets and asked Huntley and me to try them on.

I asked him, "You get this out of Guy Lombardo's saxophone section? I won't wear it."

Huntley agreed, and the blazers went away. Since we would soon begin to set the tone and style for network news programs in the future, if we had worn those ridiculous uniforms they would have become the norm, and probably every young newsman coming along after us would have been expected to wear one. Ever since, I've wondered if that might have been our foremost public service. I do think

we saved a whole generation of local news broadcasters from having to come on the air looking like
animal trainers.

Barry Wood's nonsense aside, while we waited
for NBC to overcome its fears and announce publicly that we were chosen to report the convention,
there was a great deal of work to be done. While
Huntley was a respected friend and skillful news
broadcaster, he had only worked in the West, and I
knew he was not deeply, thoroughly informed about
American presidential politics. And always the
news broadcaster's nightmare is to have the camera
aimed at him, the red tally light on, meaning "on
the air," an audience of some millions waiting in
fifty states, and he does not have anything to say.
So I began assembling a notebook with brief entries
about every person, every candidate, every state
chairman, every issue that might come before the
convention delegates. Ad-libs? Yes. Extemporane-
ous remarks? Yes. But it is no secret in television
that the best ad-libs are always thought out and put
into notes ahead of time. Anyone with some facility
with the English language can ad-lib for a few
minutes, but not for four days and nights and not
after twelve or fifteen continuous hours on the air
and approaching the edge of exhaustion while taking care to avoid lawsuits and errors that once ut-
tered can never be called back. They need to be
written out, not to be read, but written out with
some degree of polish with captions to recall what

they are about. Two or three words will remind you of whatever the point is. One may wonder then exactly what *is* an ad-lib? Is it nothing more than words spoken and not read? If so, all of us ad-lib all day every day. But to have exactly the right brief and pungent remark ready at exactly the right moment, day after day, without having to rummage around in a pile of papers, takes planning in advance. And long before Huntley and I arrived in Chicago, I was working on my little notebook, writing ad-libs. On the air it worked. It worked so well that on the third day of the convention there was a newspaper column that changed my life forever. Jack Gould, television critic for *The New York Times*, then the most respected, most feared of all newspaper critics and the only one eagerly read by network executives, wrote an intensely flattering column. All these years later, I am immodest enough to reproduce it here:

> A quiet southerner with a dry wit and a heaven-sent appreciation of brevity, has stolen the television limelight this week at the Democratic National Convention. He is David Brinkley, who together with Chet Huntley has been providing the National Broadcasting Company's running commentary from Chicago.
>
> Mr. Brinkley quite possibly could be the forerunner of a new school of television commentator; he is not an earnest Voice of Authority imparting the final word to the unwashed of videoland. In-

stead of the pear-shaped tones he has just a trace of a soft North Carolina drawl. He contributes his observations with assurance but not insistence.

But during the many long hours in Chicago, where at times it has seemed there has been a national convention of commentators, Mr. Brinkley's extraordinary accomplishment has been not to talk too much. He has a knack for the succinct phrase that sums up the situation. Sometimes his incisiveness has been such as to catch cameramen and directors off-guard; he's finished his trenchant commentary but out of TV habit they wait for more. It is Mr. Brinkley's humor, however, that is attracting audiences. It is on the dry side and rooted in a sense of relaxed detachment from all the political and electronic turmoil around him. With a neatly turned sentence or two he frequently manages to put a given convention situation in an amusingly civilized and knowledgeable perspective.

Mr. Brinkley is the regular Washington correspondent on NBC's nightly "News Caravan" but this is his first important break . . . the sudden rise of Mr. Brinkley and the introduction of Mr. Huntley—the two work well together as a team, incidentally—is the first real change in the network news situation in a long while. This convention marks the first time the Columbia Broadcasting System, with such established stars as Edward R. Murrow and Eric Sevareid, has had real competition from NBC in the matter of news personalities.

The CBS pre-eminence always has been something of a sore point with NBC, but now even NBC might enjoy the irony of how it found the solution. Picking a chap from its own shop and then leaving him alone. But the larger significance of the happenings in NBC news may lie elsewhere. Who would have thought good old gray NBC could relax and laugh a little?

Within an hour after that *Times* column worked its way through NBC and was posted on the bulletin board, along with another, earlier column of generous remarks by John Crosby of the New York *Herald Tribune*, people began looking at me and talking to me differently, as if I had ascended to another level of being. In what amounted to a public installation ceremony by the hooded high priests and acolytes with sacred chants and incantations amid incense, smoke and flame, Gould had installed me in the television news pantheon, set like a stone bust in a niche standing alongside Murrow and Sevareid. All this for three small-town boys? Murrow from Oxford, North Carolina; Sevareid from Velva, North Dakota; and me from Wilmington, North Carolina—three towns whose combined populations were fewer than thirty-five thousand? I wondered what was to be made of that. I didn't know and still don't. I do know it was a stunning and unsettling experience to read that the *Times* thought more highly of me than I ever did of myself.

To understand how one newspaper column's extremely kind words could lift a moderately talented

staff member out of a pack of other moderately talented staff members and make him into a celebrity
of sorts requires an understanding of how television
networks are structured. At their top levels they are
not run by journalists. They are run by executives
skilled in finance, advertising and public relations;
by lawyers, accountants, compilers of the ratings;
by Washington lobbyists keeping a watch on the
Federal Communications Commission; by the ad
agencies deciding where to get the most from their
advertising dollars. They are run by bright, talented
and mostly decent people. And the broadcast management community usually sees a news program
as a nice thing to do, an effort they probably ought
to make and money they probably ought to spend,
but really not their reason for existence. Their reason for existence lies elsewhere, in entertainment
and advertising, not in journalism. And most admit
they don't know much about it. Since they held no
particular views of their own, if a Jack Gould said
it was good, that was all the affirmation they
needed. If he said it was good, it was good.

At times, for my own amusement, I have thought
back to the years when I was a young newspaper
reporter, and television as a public medium did not
even exist. Could it not have been decided then that
when it arrived, television's role would be entertainment only? Singers, actors, tap dancers and
stand-up comics? Would it not, after all, simply be
radio with pictures? And in radio's beginnings there

was no great devotion to news. Because in every sizable town there were still afternoon newspapers. Why put news on the radio when the news had already arrived and was lying out on the front steps?

A few broadcasters, contemplating the high cost of news coverage around the world, argued then, if feebly, that television actually could ignore the news and leave it to the newspapers. They were better at it anyway. They could print all the ball scores and the major league standings, the stock market tables, the movie schedules and the local scandals—stuff the networks could not handle.

Then this happened: NBC was so dominant in entertainment and in its overwhelming technical power to drive its radio programs into nearly every square foot of America that the young and growing CBS network was a weak second. But while Sarnoff and RCA were busily preparing for television, CBS was building the most formidable news department in broadcast history, offering listeners such resounding names as Edward R. Murrow, Eric Sevareid, William L. Shirer and Elmer Davis. When World War II stopped all television development and manufacturing, NBC and CBS were forced to go through the war years competing in radio only, and the American public, in its overwhelming demand for news of the war, turned to CBS for its superior strength in news. CBS then developed a highly successful news format all others eventually were to follow: the news roundup, switching from place to

place around the world for reports from its correspondents in one war front and then another. An
entire nation sat quietly at home and listened, often
using maps of Europe and the Pacific to help them
follow the news. After the years of war and radio's
often brilliant news from the fronts, nobody could
seriously consider television without news. Over
time, with the cold war, fears of nuclear war, the
murder of a president, the landing on the moon and
a thousand other events seen on television and in
time in full color, the afternoon papers died one by
one, and there was no more news on the front steps.
Now it was inside the house on the TV screen and
nowhere else. The evening news had moved to television. With a few exceptions—not many—radio
turned itself into an entertainment medium offering
rock music for adolescents while the Benny Good-
mans and Tommy Dorseys packed up their clarinets
and trombones and went away.

From the 1956 convention the NBC executives
and the staff—Julian Goodman, Reuven Frank,
John Chancellor, Ray Scherer, Herbert Kaplow and
Merrill Mueller, Huntley and I—all went home
winners. While the executives sat around upstairs
discussing their convention victory and dreaming of
a future of high ratings and sold-out commercials,
they decided Swayze had to go and that Chet and I
would take over the evening news program, no
longer to be called the *Camel News Caravan*. And

for a time to have no title at all. Reuven was to be moved over from the Swayze program and asked to design an entirely different news broadcast with Huntley in New York and me in Washington.

Entirely different? Yes, of course, but entirely different how? Particular news events may at times be entirely different, but usually they are only somewhat different. Whatever is in the news today most likely has been in the news before in one form or another, often with not much changed but the names of the guilty. No one at NBC could think of an entirely different way to report it. With our news program half in New York and half in Washington, the two of us throwing the picture back and forth between one city and the other might be mildly diverting, but not for long. While television, again, arrived without a rule book, journalism did too. There never was a generally accepted rule book, and still is not, because there can't be. The larger newspapers usually had style books, but mostly they were rules about typography, spelling, capitalization and nothing much about judging and assessing news, since this always was and still is, and must remain, the editor's personal judgment. There is no other way.

Now there was a lot of talk and passing of memos up and down the hallways discussing names for the new program. It never seemed to me to matter much what it was called, since nobody would tune us in to look at the title. Finally, they settled, more or less, on *The Huntley-Brinkley Report*. Adequate, perhaps, but no more than that.

On Monday, October 29, 1956, the new and much-anticipated program went on the air, and it was terrible. Frank said later, ''The first night sticks in my mind as the worst evening news program in the history of American network television. No kinescope recording was made and so [years later] I am at a loss for details, but I remember sitting at my desk when it ended, filled with abject despair.'' It was not that bad. What upset Reuven was that all hell broke loose in the news in our first week on the air, and we lacked the facilities to cover it. On that weekend, Israeli troops attacked the Suez Canal, Britain and France threatened retaliation, Adlai Stevenson, campaigning for president, attacked Eisenhower. Russian tanks rolled out to put down the Hungarian uprising. The Hungarian Red Cross asked the world for help in caring for fifty thousand wounded. We did a poor job getting all that on the air. NBC had not yet built much of a television news department and had few bureaus with correspondents and cameras in foreign capitals and was still discovering, reluctantly, that television news was far more expensive and far more difficult than radio.

For several months, the new program did poorly. The audience remained small, the advertisers few.

This went on until NBC began to think the pairing of the two of us had been a mistake, and there was talk of dropping Huntley. Since he was by nature a cowboy, he had often told us his ambition was to retire and buy a ranch in Montana, his home state, stock it with cattle, and pass the late afternoons sitting on the front porch of his ranch house, his feet up on the railing, looking out over a mile or two of his own land, his cattle standing around in placid quiet while he watched. When he began to worry that our program was a failure, he went as far toward that goal as he could. He bought farmland across the Hudson River from New York and stocked it with cattle. He had a farm machine that dried hay while keeping it green, therefore bringing a premium price. He was selling his hay to horse trainers at the racetracks. He seemed happy there with his wife, Tippy.

She was the beautiful young weather girl when television still had weather girls, and she did her number each night on the local Washington NBC station. One night, as she was walking through the studio on her way out to the parking lot, Huntley was in his studio in New York and I was in mine in Washington. Each of us had a television monitor that let us see and talk to each other before we went on the air. Tippy walked through and stopped to chat with me for a moment. Huntley stood in his New York studio and watched.

When she left, he asked me, "Who was that?"

"That's Tippy Stringer, the weather girl here on our local station."

"She married?"

"No."

End of conversation. A few days later I heard Huntley had been flying down to Washington and asking Tippy Stringer out. Next, within a month or so, we were invited to a dinner to celebrate their marriage. And the only time I ever visited his New Jersey farm she was there with him, and they happily remained together as long as he lived.

The Huntley-Brinkley Report continued to limp along, hardly successful but not a total failure. Until one happy day when we got the news the program was catching on, the mail was becoming highly positive, the ratings were rising, advertisers were clamoring to come on, until Augustus C. Long, chairman of Texaco, called NBC and said he wanted to buy all the advertising time on the entire program every night of the week. Success. Slow in coming, but success.

There remained a detail, important and difficult to settle. How would we end the program? Some word or series of words—very short—to sign off, something in the nature of a trademark. I've always thought the greatest of all television closers was Jimmy Durante's. He ended his program by walking in near darkness toward the backstage, through one brilliant spotlit pool of light after another, stopping in each one to raise his hat and say, ''Good night, Mrs. Calabash, wherever you are.'' No one ever knew what it meant, but no one ever forgot it.

We could never match that, but Reuven suggested that we end the program by my saying, ''Good night, Chet,'' and with Huntley saying, ''Good night, David.''

We both hated it. Huntley thought it was sissified. I argued we should say good night to the audience, not to each other, and I thought it sounded contrived, artificial and slightly silly. We lost. We used it. It worked. It caught the public's fancy quickly. I knew it was a success when people in friendly fashion began shouting ''Good night, David'' to me in the streets, as now, years later, they still do.

IV

On November 14, 1908, a baby boy born in Grand Chute, Wisconsin, was given the name Joseph McCarthy. In forty years of sustained effort he made the name stand for (1) a United States senator and (2) the Grand Champion American Liar. In Washington, a city already well supplied with your ordinary, everyday liars, nobody could lie like McCarthy. While he was deeply unimpressive in manner, appearance and speech, he lied with an energy and determination so intense that some otherwise skeptical people were led to believe him.

His story was a simple one: the United States was in danger of being undermined by a rabid gang of devoted Communists, paid by and reporting to Moscow. Some skeptics were unwilling to believe McCarthy until the highly publicized arrest, trial and execution of Julius and Ethel Rosenberg for stealing American nuclear secrets and sending them to Moscow and the discovery that Klaus Fuchs, a scientist working on the atomic bomb in New Mexico, was found to have sent Moscow every detail of the bomb's design and construction and managed to escape to East Germany before the FBI could seize him. All this was true. And since three known Communist spies had actually been caught, could anyone say with confidence there were no others still at large in this country and secretly serving Moscow? McCarthy found a willing, credulous audience when he said the U.S. government was crawling with them.

Along the way, somebody I did not know introduced McCarthy to my sister, Mary Brinkley Driscoll. She was a bright, pretty and highly experienced legal secretary working somewhere in the Capitol building. McCarthy hired her and put her on the U.S. Senate payroll as his executive secretary.

During McCarthy's life Mary and I were unable to discuss her work because I so detested McCarthy that whenever his name came up in our conversations I routinely pronounced him to be what he was, a loudmouthed liar. Out of loyalty to her employer and in her belief that there was some small truth in what he was saying, Mary tried to defend McCarthy, and this always led to an angry, shouting argument. In time we had to agree that to avoid ugly fights we could never mention his name. Our agreement held until he died. Only then was she willing to tell me the truth.

When McCarthy first arrived in Washington, he said his prime interest as a senator would be to promote decent housing for veterans returned from the war. And Joseph Alsop, a friend of mine later and then a respected newspaper columnist, said he "had known McCarthy first as the big, raw-boned pride and joy of the real estate lobby, which is where he found his friends when he first came to Washington. . . . McCarthy adored attention and as a politician had tried to get it several different ways.''

In 1950 he found the attention he hungered for when he said in a speech to the Wheeling, West Virginia, Republican Women's Club, ''I have here in my hand a list of two hundred and five—a list of names that are known to the secretary of state as being members of the Communist party and who nevertheless are still working and shaping the policy in the State Department.'' (This number kept changing.) Here McCarthy began calling Alsop ''All Slop.''

After his death, I asked Mary: ''What did he have in his hand?''

''He had a few scribbled notes to use in his speech. Nothing about Communists. Mostly about housing for war veterans. That was his big interest when he first came to Washington.''

''Did he have two hundred and five names?''

''No.''

''Where did he get that number?''

''He made it up.''

She told me that when he saw the headlines in the press about his Wheeling speech, McCarthy was nearly insane with excitement. He clutched the newspapers and ran around the Senate office shouting, ''I've got it, I've got it!''

''Got what? What did he think he had?''

"He thought he had the issue he needed to make him into a great political figure and to guarantee his Senate seat forever."

While it did not make him into a great political figure, it did satisfy one of his unwholesome urges. In the 1950s it made him the center of attention in Washington—on the front pages of the papers every day, in the flickering, bluish pictures on John Cameron Swayze's television news at night. People stopped him on the street to shake his hand and urge him to carry on with his great work of saving the country before the Communists swallowed it whole. Washington hostesses eager to snare celebrities for their dinner tables invited him to places he had never been before. The post office needed a special truck to deliver his mail. Not all of it supportive, but he did not care. That people were paying attention to him—talking about him, writing to him— was more than enough, and it did not matter whether they were for him or against him. For a junior senator from a small town in Wisconsin, it was a heady time, and his exuberance swept him near to delirium and occasionally beyond.

Had McCarthy been truthful, had it been true that Communists, like termites, were eating away the foundations of the U.S. government, he actually would have been seen as a great political figure, fighting a lonely battle to rescue the Republic by exposing its enemies. But it was only one lie after another, and almost everyone in Washington knew it, including most of his colleagues in the Senate, but they were so afraid of him and of his noisy band of supporters that they had long since run for cover, protecting their precious seats. When I invited a senator or two to be interviewed on the air, they either declined out of hand or agreed to come only if I promised not to ask questions about McCarthy. We could not allow a guest to dictate what questions could be asked, and so in McCarthy's time we seldom had senators as guests. Instead, they stood in cold, sweating fear of him, in fear of endangering their own careers by annoying him, in fear of unpredictable and unwelcome reactions in their home states, in fear that a senator attacking him might lose his seat.

For a time, he allowed his admirers to call him Tail-Gunner Joe, suggesting but never quite saying he had served in the war as a tail gunner in an Army Air Corps bomber. Another lie, though one of his smaller ones. He was a member of the Army Air Corps but never a tail gunner.

And as Mary described it later, he spent the afternoons in his Senate office drinking whiskey, reading his press clippings over and over in tones of reverence, fondling them in an almost sensual way and discussing them in great detail and often finishing the day down on his knees, shooting dice on the carpet.

Slowly, slowly, American democracy worked. As layer after layer of McCarthy's lies were peeled away like an onion, revealing one outrage after another, his friends in the Senate, including Senator Taft of Ohio, began to see that they had been deceived, lied to, and McCarthy's support started to fade. Eventually, the Senate found the courage to censure him, not for his lies but for another of his nasty habits—holding one-man-committee hearings with no one present but himself and maybe a staff member. In these ugly sessions, staged for the press and having no legislative purpose, McCarthy played the role of Torquemada avenging sins nobody had committed while enjoying hounding, abusing and insulting witnesses sitting in terror before him in a depressing scene out of the Middle Ages.

What finally brought him to his knees was a resolution introduced by the quiet, mild-mannered Senator Ralph Flanders, Republican of Vermont. He asked that McCarthy be condemned for only a few of his accumulated sins, not including his five-foot shelf of lies. Instead, the Senate chose to punish him for sins more easily described and more easily proved—his abuse of witnesses before his committee. Lies? Trying to prove a senator guilty of lies was to drag the investigators into muddy, murky territory. When was a senator a liar? When he promised in an election campaign what he knew perfectly well he could not deliver? Was that a lie? Was there a senator who had not done this?

The Senate responded to Flanders by appointing a six-member committee to consider the sins he enumerated. During the committee's hearings I sat in the press area and Mary sat in the elevated section behind the senators, there to run errands for McCarthy if asked. We both carefully avoided noticing each other, staying apart and never to be seen talking to each other. I was afraid one of the reporters from a paper feverishly supporting McCarthy, perhaps the Washington *Times-Herald*, might find it amusing to discover that a brother and a sister were on opposite sides in McCarthy's ridiculous campaign. McCarthy and some others knew, but no one said anything and it never came to public attention.

The committee decided "condemned" was too strong a word, since it called up nasty visions of sending McCarthy off to a Dantean purgatory and on beyond into hell, and so they toned it down to a motion of "censure," roughly equivalent to a fine for exceeding the speed limit but with a high possibility of damage in the next election. But, put simply, the Senate of the United States barely remembered how to use its power to punish or discipline its members because the power was so rarely used, and it was unwelcome and embarrassing when it was used. They saw the Senate, after all, as a gentlemen's club with the highest admission standards. Everyone here, they told themselves, was elected by the people of one of the states, and if punishment was called for it should be imposed in the next election. But McCarthy was not abusing people in his home state who had the power to vote him out. He was abusing, among many others, people brought in to testify before a committee of the United States Senate.

As the committee assembled, McCarthy said in a speech: "Now the Communists have extended their tentacles into the United States Senate to make these committee members their unwitting handmaidens."

No one could recall a member talking of the Senate in these bitter terms. But then no one had ever before been threatened with censure and been called to account before a committee including Judge and Senator Samuel Ervin, Democrat of Morganton, North Carolina. A grand old gent, World War I veteran, born in 1896 and still living in the house he was born in, with his wife who was born in the house immediately next door, still occupied by her family.

In response to McCarthy's nasty remark about the senators acting as communism's handmaidens, Ervin said: "Senator McCarthy flees now to his customary refuge—his claim that he is the symbol of resistance to Communist subversion and any senator who fails to bow and scrape to him is doing the work of the Communist party."

That was Sam Ervin, an elder in the Presbyterian church, a Mason, a Knight of Pythias, trustee of the University of North Carolina, a member of the American Legion, Veterans of Foreign Wars, Disabled American Veterans, the Army and Navy Legion of Valor, the Kiwanis Club and the North Carolina Society of Mayflower Descendants, who still insisted on being called Sam.

Of course the motion for censure carried in the Senate and it destroyed McCarthy. Roy Cohn, his top legal assistant, said later, "Joe McCarthy bought Communism as a political issue the same way other people buy an automobile."

In the end, McCarthy having never, ever found even one Communist not already known, the whiskey got to him and he died of cirrhosis of the liver.

My sister turned down several book offers and retired.

Some time later, I went to Morganton for a talk with Judge Sam Ervin, now retired. He was still practicing law but not breaking his back about it. We sat in the high-ceilinged library in his house, and I commented on the shelves running up fourteen feet high and all lined with legal tomes.

I asked, "Judge, what happens if you get a legal case that requires you to use a book from that very top shelf?"

He answered, "I wouldn't take the case."

FOR A TIME in the 1950s I was doing a weekly radio program on NBC that may have been the most boring half hour ever broadcast. The participants' wives and children may have listened to it, but hardly anyone else did. My own wife refused. It was more than boring. It was stultifying. It was titled *America United*, and mostly it showed that America was not. The idea was to bring together each week four spokesmen—one each for labor, business, agriculture and government, and with me as the so-called moderator. The four of them were asked to discuss their work and their differences and to look for solutions while the American people listened and, presumably, were encouraged to see that the country's problems were being attended to by men of goodwill. But there was not much goodwill to be found. The business spokesmen complained every week that taxes were too high and the country was turning socialist. They may have been right, but after about the fortieth hearing this became a little tiresome.

The farm spokesmen favored us each week with the same litany of complaints—that farm subsidies were far too low, followed by an almost operatic soliloquy about the evils of "suitcase farmers." That is, people who owned and operated farms but did not live on them, who instead hired managers to run them while they themselves lolled in upholstered luxury in the cities, well away from the muddy pastures and the barnyard odors. The absentee owner occasionally visited his farm, carrying a suitcase, but was not dependent on it and so had an unfair advantage over real farmers who lived and worked on the land for a living. Not only that, he brought all that big-city money out to the country-side and bought fancy machinery the real farmers could not afford. And since, of course, it was well known to everyone that the farmers were the back-bone of America, the only ones still addicted to the Protestant work ethic, the suitcase farmer, we were assured repeatedly, was a hungry rat in the corncrib of democracy.

But that was as nothing compared to the uproar down on the dairy farm when Congress considered allowing oleomargarine to be colored yellow to make it look like butter. Public relations operatives swarmed all over town—roughly half from the food industry touting yellow margarine and the rest from the dairy lobby saying that butter made by good old Bessie the cow should never be imitated. One said to me on the phone, "We've all heard the political leaders talking in wartime about guns versus butter. Ever hear one talk about guns versus margarine?"

The farm spokesman kept shouting that we would soon see the supermarkets selling "filled milk." I asked him what that was. What was filled milk? He continued spluttering in rage and never answered. I never found out.

Few will remember now that when margarine first appeared in the grocery stores it was white and highly unappetizing. It looked like lard. A law the dairy farmers had pushed through Congress years earlier did not allow the manufacturers to color it yellow because they were afraid it would hurt the market for butter, and some might even sell the cheaper margarine to customers who thought they were buying butter. It came in the shape of a brick, and packed separately inside each carton was a small capsule containing yellow coloring in powder form. This, laboriously, had to be poured over the white margarine and then mixed in with a fork until it produced a suitable yellow color. This took about half an hour to mix, and it wound up with orange streaks.

Congress, responding to pressure from the food industry and consumer groups, finally voted to stop this nonsense. If people wanted their margarine yellow, how did that come to be the business of the United States Congress? Obviously, this was a question that needed to be treated on *America United.* I invited our usual group plus a congressman from a dairy state, Wisconsin, and asked him the question. His answer was that selling yellow margarine was a fraud on the American people. "It's fake butter is what it is." He spluttered angrily about city people who knew nothing, who thought all their food grew on the supermarket shelves and gave no thought to the farmers who produced it. Incredible as it may seem now, this was a Washington sensation for more than a month. In time, Congress voted to allow margarine to be colored yellow at the factory, and another threat to the survival of democratic government was met and surmounted; margarine turned from white to yellow, even though I obviously was too thickheaded to see how the color of margarine was any of government's business. I still don't.

Almost nothing said on *America United* was worth listening to. The union spokesmen delivered their familiar discourses on the selfishness and greed of your typical employer lining his own pockets while paying his employees so poorly their children were threatened with the ancient scourges of malnutrition such as pellagra and ringworm. One Sunday the leader of one of the electrical unions said American employers should be investigated for their clear and obvious Communist sympathies because they much preferred to negotiate with Communist unions. When I asked why, he said because Communist unions were more interested in making political points and serving Moscow's interests than in looking after their own members. That ridiculous statement stood unchallenged, hung in the air like a gas-filled balloon waiting to be punctured. Nobody did.

Again, in several years almost nothing said on the program was worth repeating here, but there was one line, just one, that I thought deserved to be chiseled on a granite slab. It was a clear and forceful expression of a particular point of view, spoken with great verve and economy of language by William C. Doherty, president of the Letter Carriers Union. In the middle of our plodding conversation about how to preserve peace in the world after the war was over, he blurted out:

"How you gonna have world peace if the letter carriers don't get a pay raise?"

LATER, on a topic perhaps of greater public concern, at Doherty's urging I invited a guest we had not had on the air before and had never met—a newly elected and almost unknown congressman from Massachusetts named John F. Kennedy. A veteran of the Pacific war, he was sallow, skinny, and since he was still recovering from a case of jaundice or malaria, he was yellow and entirely unprepossessing.

He had survived the war, and then, a few years later when he had acquired the Kennedy family's taste for politics, he was lucky enough to survive the 1956 Democratic convention in Chicago, where the nominee, Adlai Stevenson, was girding himself for a second run against Dwight Eisenhower, the same war hero who had beaten him four years ago and was now waiting calmly to do it again. He flirted with Kennedy as a candidate for vice president, but the convention chose Senator Estes Kefauver of Tennessee. Senator Albert Gore of Tennessee, father of President Clinton's vice president, took the lead in dumping Kennedy. Unintentionally, he did Kennedy a great favor. Had he been nominated to run with Stevenson, he would have gone down to defeat with him. Instead, he was saved for the next election year, 1960.

Eisenhower was unbeatable in 1956 because in his own way he was the most successful president in modern politics. He came to office at a time when people were profoundly weary of war and murderous wartime tax rates up to 92 percent, shortages of almost everything and constant government importunings to save this and collect that to help win the war. After four years of automobile dealerships with nothing to sell, heavily bechromed new cars now gleamed and glittered in the showrooms and a Cadillac could be had for a little more than fifteen hundred dollars and gasoline for its tank cost fourteen cents a gallon. Golf and tennis balls were back. The United States stood astride the world in peace and prosperity, the only country to come out of the war without a scratch. The stores were piled high with merchandise not seen since in years. The cities were peaceful and not yet ravaged by crime. There were few muggers in the shadows, hardly any drugs and no firearms in the schoolrooms. Eisenhower presided over this special time in American history— a time many think the happiest this country ever had—and he stood off to the side and let the good times roll. Everything had fallen in place for him, making him an enormously popular president.

Twice, I assume at press secretary James C. Hagerty's suggestion, Ike invited me to the White

House, once for dinner and once for a talk, his talk, a rambling discourse about the fact that, after World War I, he had an office in the Old Executive Office Building, then called State-War-Navy, immediately next door to the White House. Since the Army had been almost totally demobilized and barely had enough money to feed its few troops, it had almost nothing for training. Eisenhower described his deep boredom sitting at a desk in the old State-War-Navy building about a hundred yards from his presidential desk with nothing whatever to do. Even General George C. Marshall, who commanded the U.S. Army, what there was of it, before World War II, was far away and the commanding officer at Fort Leavenworth, Kansas, where there was very little to command. Later, he and the president commiserated in recalling these drab, boring years when the Army was so small and so strapped for money a captain waited twelve years for promotion to major.

Now, one war later, he was our national father figure, the great general who had won the war and who also had a nice smile. But several times he was heard to say, "As president I made two mistakes, and both of them are on the Supreme Court." His two mistakes, he thought, were his appointments of Earl Warren and William Brennan to the Supreme Court. Warren was never noticeably liberal until he was appointed to the court, and Brennan was never noticeably anything else. In the president's view, expressed one night in my hearing, both of them

habitually overstepped their judicial authority. Instead of deciding if new laws passed in Congress
and the states were constitutional, he thought the
two of them wrote new laws to reflect their personal
views in the guise of interpreting the Constitution.

Warren, as attorney general of California, had aggressively demanded after Pearl Harbor that American citizens of Japanese descent be rounded up and
put into gangs doing farmwork and their property
seized. As I write this, my dentist for twenty years
in Washington, Raymond Murakami, an American
citizen, was born into a second-generation California family of Japanese origins. In December 1941,
he was seized, forced to work on somebody's farm;
his family's own nursery business was seized and
never returned. He and his family were sent to live
temporarily in the stables at Santa Anita racetrack.
Later he did farmwork in segregated areas of the
South, where in some places he was told to use the
water fountains labeled WHITE and in other places
those labeled COLORED. Rural southerners did not
know who or what he was and did not know what
to do with him.

There were pressures on Earl Warren to do this
—from an enraged and frightened public and from
General DeWitt, the Army's West Coast commander. Whatever the pressures, his eagerness to
lock up peaceful, productive American citizens won
him no cheers from the liberals. And so when he
was perceived in Washington to be turning the Su-

preme Court leftward, the city's political classes propounded a theory often heard—that some western politicians, being thousands of miles from the national political action, believed the Washington–New York axis, and particularly the press, to be a writhing nest of left-wingers and assorted radicals. And when West Coast politicians moved to the East, to Washington, they tended to believe that a liberal stance, real or contrived, would earn them more favorable notice. And that, they said over cognac on Georgetown nights, explained the behavior of Earl Warren. Whether that was true or not, Eisenhower thought Brennan and Warren were his two big mistakes; his third biggest was to choose Richard Nixon as his nominee for vice president, giving him a start toward his unhappy career in the White House.

Before Nixon was forced to resign the presidency, he chose Spiro Agnew as his vice president, only to begin still another degrading and humiliating episode in American presidential politics.

In November 1969, Nixon made a speech about this country's unhealing sore called Vietnam. He went on the television networks saying he had agreed with the South Vietnamese on "an orderly schedule for complete withdrawal of American forces from the war." His speech was carried live on ABC, CBS and NBC. Since he spoke longer than expected, he spilled over into the networks' next half-hour time period. Since network time is always divided into blocks of half hours and hours, this meant the networks had to fill whatever part of the half hour Nixon left. We filled it in the only way we knew—by assembling a few of our own correspondents and an outsider or two to discuss the speech the audience had just heard. On this night, following Nixon, I and a few others got the somewhat unpleasant duty to discuss his speech until the beginning of the next hour. I can remember nothing of it now and no transcript exists, but I assume there were a few critical remarks about a war that threatened to tear the country apart. Nobody, including us, really liked filling time this way, but no one knew any alternative. How else on short notice, or no notice, could we fill network airtime? Organ music?

Ten days later, Spiro Agnew spoke to a Republican dinner in Des Moines, Iowa, complaining angrily about what we had said on the networks about Nixon's speech. "Why?" he asked. "Why can't the president of the United States make a speech without the networks following it with instant analysis and querulous criticism?"

It was a good question, but Agnew did not want the answer. He wanted the politician's soul-satisfying pleasure of publicly slandering his enemies in a place where none of them could answer back. And "David Brinkley," he said, "was the worst of them."

I wish I could remember what I said, but I can't.

And I hope I may be excused here long enough to note with some pride that I was the first one Agnew attacked by name, and on three networks in prime time—an honor not awarded to many of us who work for a living in the news trade. Normally venom and invective like Agnew's were directed at ax murderers, child molesters, drug dealers selling near the high school and politicians advocating higher taxes.

The applause for Agnew was loud, prolonged, and the mail was ugly. A man on a downtown sidewalk two days later actually tried to spit on me, but he didn't have sufficient lung power.

Not long after, Agnew was driven out of office by accusations he was accepting cash bribes delivered to his vice-presidential office, and I cannot guarantee that none of my colleagues was guilty of a little schadenfreude—secret, malicious pleasure.

Despite Agnew's whining, television was becoming the box that entertained America. And among the first to see its political potential was James C. Hagerty, Eisenhower's press secretary, on loan to him from Thomas E. Dewey. His staff had long and tedious negotiations with the networks about allowing the president's press conferences to be broadcast on television. Not broadcast live; that was never even considered. Too risky. The president of the United States talking to the nations and people of the world, talking without notes or prior discussions? Impossible. Suppose he made a mistake? It would embarrass him and the country, reverberating as it would down the corridors of the world's foreign offices. Parsed and analyzed by foreign secretaries around the world looking for hidden meaning and inventing what they could not find? Looking for some benefit for themselves from the only country still able to confer a benefit? No, not live television, ever. Bill McAndrew and Julian Goodman, negotiating for NBC along with others from CBS and ABC, finally agreed to cover the press conferences on film with the understanding that—as Hagerty insisted—the White House reserved the right to say this answer or that answer could not be broadcast. Since the network negotiators were sloshing in a muddy swamp never traversed before anywhere with any president, it was Hagerty's deal or nothing. We took his deal.

The next problem was that the film cameras we then used—magnetic tape was still new and slow and cumbersome—were a little noisy, motors running and pulling film through their gates and unwinding it from one reel and rewinding it on another. Too distracting, Hagerty said. It would upset the president to have to talk over the whirring sound. Actually, I doubted that at his age he could even hear it, but the networks were in no position to argue. So they brought in blimps—heavily quilted and padded covers to be hung over the cameras to muffle the noise. Thus for the first time ever, the president of the United States answered press conference questions on almost but not quite live television.

It was less than a great success. Eisenhower made no news that day, and even if he had, it would have been difficult for us to figure out what it was. His ad-libbed sentences bounced around like Dodgem cars at a carnival, bumper cars that bounced off one wall, swung around, hit another wall and another car and then bounced somewhere else and wound up—as Eisenhower's sentences did—in the middle of nowhere, with nobody quite sure what he said. Then it dawned on us that this was the first time we had ever heard him ad-libbing. Theretofore, we had only heard him reading prepared remarks, usually with mimeographed copies handed out to reporters. That was easy. Covering his press conference on film was not. Running his film back and forth through the editing machine, the Moviola, we kept looking for a few sentences that started with a thought and moved coherently through it and came to a clear end. There weren't any.

Hagerty and the president were agreeable enough. I don't recall that they ever asked us to edit out a line. Good. But that was not the problem. The problem was going through the film and finding something, anything, that the television audience—or anyone else—could understand.

Some thought Eisenhower did this deliberately, that he did not really want to make any clear statements off-the-cuff at a press conference. Maybe so.

There was even a story around the White House that once when a press conference was about to begin and some particularly difficult and complicated issue was to come up, Eisenhower said to his staff, "Don't worry. Send the press in to me and I'll confuse them." Intentionally or not, he did.

IN AUGUST 1956, when the Democratic party's convention opened in Chicago, Adlai Stevenson was nominated for president and then announced what he thought was the properly liberal and democratic way to choose his running mate for vice president. Normally, the presidential candidate announced his choice for vice president, and the convention dutifully ratified him. But Stevenson said he would state no preference. He wanted the convention to choose a nominee to run with him. The delegates, having never seen this before, were confused. On the first ballot the votes were scattered among thirteen candidates. Estes Kefauver, riding a wave of publicity from his Senate investigation of big-city criminality, was first with 483. He might have swept the convention and won the presidential nomination for himself but for one mistake. His mistake was that when he exposed the workings of organized crime he also exposed its connections with some of the big-city Democratic political machines and seemed to take a little too much pleasure in embarrassing his own party. The bosses now sitting in the convention hall smoking their cigars remembered. And while Kefauver came first it was a weak first. John F. Kennedy, a new face and a product of a settled and reliable political family, was second with 304. On the second ballot, Kennedy moved into the lead but did not have a majority. He was 40 votes short. There he was stopped. Who stopped him? Senator Albert Gore, Sr., father of Clinton's vice president, who withdrew from the race and threw his votes to Kefauver, his fellow Tennesseean. Then the bandwagon rolled and it rolled to Kefauver and gave him 755 votes and the nomination. Kennedy was second with 618, and the pols noticed that even in losing, he showed impressive strength, and they remembered that in 1960.

During the 1956 campaign I traveled with Kefauver for a few days to see what he was about and found him to have some amusing habits. One was that he shook so many hands he wound up with blisters and the skin around his thumb worn raw with six or eight small stick-on bandages on the sore spots. He said he had shaken twenty-five thousand hands. Then as he was being driven along the highway toward the next political rally, he always slept in the backseat with a cigar in his mouth, unlit and with the cellophane still on it. And late in the day when he was about to finish campaigning and he was giving his last speech from some platform, his eye roamed over the crowd looking for an attractive woman who appeared to be alone. When he saw one who looked promising, he whispered out of the corner of his mouth to a campaign aide and said something like "The red-striped dress." A staffer quietly went down to speak to the woman in the red-striped dress and to invite her to join the senator after his speech for a drink or dinner or more. Of those I saw invited, many accepted.

No doubt Kefauver enjoyed his evening frolics in hotel and motel rooms on the road while Stevenson enjoyed making his polished and poetic speeches, but their fun and games ended on Election Day when Eisenhower beat them by 10 million votes. The only Democratic winner in 1956 was John Kennedy. All he had to do was wait four years. He did, and on January 2, 1960, he announced himself a candidate for president.

Yes, a very nice boy, they all said, but he was Catholic and no Catholic had ever been elected president of the United States. Look at the last one to run for president, Al Smith, in 1928. He couldn't even beat a stiff, colorless wooden figure called Herbert Hoover. True, yes, but that was another age. How far back did Kennedy's critics want to go? Back to William the Conqueror in 1066? How to reassure the Democrats who worried about Kennedy's Catholicism? Easy. Run him in the forthcoming primary in West Virginia, one of the most Protestant states in the Union. The Kennedy crowd said they would do that, go to West Virginia and prove to the doubters that a Catholic could win Protestant votes. His only real opponent was Hubert Humphrey, and he had too little money for a campaign.

I went to West Virginia early in the spring of 1960 and asked questions about Kennedy and Protestant-Catholic politics. And beyond the politics, I was struck by the state's natural beauty of rivers, mountains, forests. It could easily be and perhaps should be the American Switzerland, I thought. The beauty was there. So were pleasant, friendly and hospitable people. But there were ugly holes in the ground where a century of coal mining had defaced vast areas, dug out the coal, sold it all over the world and then sent the money to Cleveland and Chicago, not to West Virginia. Why didn't the people of the state get some benefit from all the coal getting dug out of their ground and hauled away? The local journalists told me it was because so much of the state legislature long ago sold out to the mining companies and blocked any tax on coal. The result was that a state with mineral riches surpassing those of the Middle East oil potentates allowed outsiders to come in, dig out its mineral wealth and haul it away, leaving behind little more than holes in the ground and a culture of poverty.

I put all this on the air in the days leading up to the Kennedy-Humphrey primary and heard from a great many local people who said it was even worse than I reported and that the world seemed not to know that in their view their beautful state was almost literally being raped. I recalled Tennessee Ernie Ford's song "You dig sixteen tons and what do you get? Another day older and deeper in debt." I called the local United Mine Workers union office and asked if a pick and shovel miner could actually have dug sixteen tons in a day. No, they said. Nowhere near that much. The song went on to say a miner had to sell his soul to the company store, the only place he could buy groceries on credit.

The next day, in traveling around the state, we drove one of NBC's vehicles into a rural gasoline station and asked the attendant to fill it up. Several middle-aged men loafing around the station, sitting on stacks of tires and empty oil drums, got up, and out of curiosity I watched them as they strolled over to watch the gas pumped into the car. The attendant looked at me looking at them and volunteered, "They haven't worked and had money in so long they never hear anybody telling me to fill it up. They want to see how much it takes and how much it costs." Watching the numbers spinning on the gasoline pump was the only amusement in town.

The next day I got a message from West Virginia's governor, Cecil Underwood, asking if I would come by his office to see him. I went; we had a nice chat; he said my reporting on the state's problems was accurate and he and others were trying to correct this historic crime. Then he said he wanted to give me a gift with the thanks of the people of West

Virginia. He said, "I'm going to give you a small-loan license."

"A what?"

"A small-loan license. It allows you to operate a small financial business in the state, legally."

Having no idea what he was offering, I declined politely and then went over to the NBC affiliate's newsroom and asked, "What on earth was Underwood offering to give me?"

"He was offering to make you a millionaire. To get a small-loan license in this state is almost worth your life. All kinds of bureaucratic restrictions. A little bribery is said to be helpful. It takes months or years. He was offering to hand it to you today."

"What would I do with it if he handed it to me?"

"You could open a money-lending operation in a poor state where people are always struggling, always eager to borrow twenty dollars to feed their families today and pay back thirty dollars on payday in two weeks. With interest rates like that, I believe it comes to thirteen hundred percent, I know people who claim to have run a hundred dollars into a million in a year or so. What did you tell the governor?"

"I thanked him and declined."

"First time that's ever happened."

Right up to a few days before the West Virginia primary, all the polling showed Kennedy losing. There were stories, never proved, of old Joe Kennedy's money being passed around in a state so poor that in past years votes had been bought for as little as a half-pint of off-brand whiskey. We even managed to get some of these vote-buying deals on news film and show them on the air. No-body complained.

It was in this place at this time we began to hear Kennedy's father's famous remark: ''I will pay for a victory but I will not buy a landslide.'' True or not, it became a Democratic party legend.

Whatever the reason, Kennedy the Catholic won the primary in Protestant West Virginia, and the religious issue died a natural death there in the state's hills and hollows. And he was duly nominated on the first ballot in Los Angeles, defeating a formidable list of opponents: Lyndon Johnson of Texas, Adlai Stevenson of Illinois, Stuart Symington of Missouri, Ross Barnett of Mississippi, George Smathers of Florida, Hubert Humphrey of Minnesota, Robert Meyner of New Jersey, Herschel Loveless of Iowa, Orval Faubus of Alabama and Edmund G. Brown of California. His only active opponent in the primaries, Hubert Humphrey, never had a chance. Along the way Kennedy had enlisted the help of a lot of clean-cut young men and women to do the telephoning, to go out for hamburgers, to pass around bumper stickers and to keep the voter files on three-by-five-inch cards stacked in shoe boxes. One election later, when the computer had arrived, this kind of filing system would have been ludicrous, but when the help was young enough, numerous enough, eager enough and energetic enough, it worked. And Kennedy's staffers were all of that. Enthusiastic, optimistic and an entirely impressive crowd of young people mostly in their twenties. They were ready and willing to do anything they were asked, anything at all. And it was these devoted young people who three years later suffered the profoundest and most grinding agony when they were forced to face a tragedy they could not understand.

In early November 1960, Chet Huntley and I and about a hundred others in studio 8H at NBC in New York were ready for election night but without file cards in shoe boxes. Multimillion-dollar mainframe computers bigger than four-door Buicks had replaced the shoe boxes and taken over the job of counting the votes coming in from fifty states.

Also coming in, before we even said a word on the air, were complaints that the networks with their fancy computers were ruining election nights. Sacks full of letters described the election night scene at home as it used to be—a cozy gathering on a cold November night with friends, families, beer, snacks and election returns that drifted in slowly, a few numbers at a time. Depending on what states were counted first, the lead could change and one candidate could pull ahead of another and then back again. ''These election nights were exciting,'' viewers wrote. ''Now what is it? You damned smart

alecks with your computers call the winner even
before I get home from work. Why do you do
that?''

The question is easy to answer, but the answer is
not satisfying. The answer is that we do it because
we *can* do it. We can do it because we have made
the effort and done the work and spent the money
to arrange for hundreds of people across the country
to wait at the polls and call us with the results the
instant they are counted. And then by matching
the numbers from carefully chosen precincts against
the same precincts in past elections and running it
all through massive computers programmed specifically to do this and do it fast, we know the winners
quickly. And the last figure I saw showed an accuracy rating close to 100 percent. But accuracy is
not the point here. Nobody complains about the accuracy. What they complain about is that we have
taken the fun out of election nights, and I think we
have. But I see no way to go back to the old slow
and easy and comfortable election nights and their
atmosphere of early American country villages.

I might say, if it matters, that Huntley and I and
others like us at the other networks have no role
whatever in all of this. We wait for the statisticians
and the computers to do their work, and we merely
pass along the numbers they hand us. I could not
program a mainframe computer to save my life.
Even so, he and I got all the letters of complaint,
thousands of them.

Not only viewers at home complained. So did the politicians. The chairman of the House Ways and Means Committee, Representative Al Ullman of Oregon, complained angrily that the networks caused his defeat, the loss of his seat in Congress and the loss of his hugely coveted committee chairmanship. Why? Because, he said, the networks called the winner so early that in the West Coast time zone people waiting in line to vote heard that television had said the presidential election was already decided, so they stepped out of line and went home without waiting around to vote for the local candidates for Congress. Ullman argued that enough of those who went home without voting, if they had stayed and voted, would have reelected him. Could he prove that happened? No. Could we prove it did not happen? No. But long after Ullman's complaint, political candidates remained wary, dubious and suspicious of our computerized vote counting. The counting formerly done by hand and out in the open in county courthouses, firehouses and other public polling places was now being done invisibly, inside a machine that just sat there humming softly, clicking a little, some red lights glowing and pretty soon spewing out columns of figures. Presumably the figures were always correct. But were they? Who knew? How could anyone know? Political bosses had long since been caught rigging their own local voting machines, manipulating the voting rolls and conveniently losing the votes from unfriendly areas of the state. In a Texas election, some precincts in the Hispanic areas of the state gave Lyndon Johnson 100 percent of their votes, inducing laughter across the state, but no challenges.

Attorney General Nicholas Katzenbach asked me to come to his office in the Justice Department and explain to him why the networks with their computers could not easily rig a presidential election. Why couldn't they decide among themselves, in private, which candidate they preferred and simply report on the air that their computers said he was the winner? Why couldn't they do that? he wanted to know. Katzenbach was and is a good lawyer, but this one he simply had not thought through, perhaps because it was too simple for a quick and suspicious mind to grasp. The simple answer was and is that nobody is elected by the figures we put on the air. They are elected by their own state governments on the basis of their own vote counts, not ours. Our only service, actually, is to count the votes and announce the winners faster than the states can do it.

Even when that is explained, people still ask us, "Why is that kind of speed so important? People waited days to learn that Abraham Lincoln had been elected. In 1932 Franklin Roosevelt was elected with paper ballots, and we had to wait for them to be counted. What's the great value in telling us the winner in a few minutes?"

It's a good question, and I can't answer it. It is

pointless to say that in the modern world there is always pressure to move fast, learn fast, act fast, think fast. Maybe we felt pressured to move faster because our new computers did. And there is, of course, the competitive pressure among the networks, each hoping to be able to boast the next day that it had the news first, not that this ever matters much. A "scoop," a word nobody uses anymore, is something else. It is news you have uncovered through diligence, skill or luck that your competitors in journalism do not have, and there is some satisfaction in that. But there are no scoops to be had on election nights. Every network winds up with the same numbers, and there is no excitement in that. And it is not very exciting to hear who was elected in a congressional district eight states and a thousand miles away. It was not very exciting for me to announce that Strom Thurmond, in the Senate from South Carolina since not too long after Columbus landed, had been elected one more time. Or, until he died, it was not exciting that Senator Carl Hayden of Arizona, in Congress since his state joined the Union in 1912, had been elected again.

What is useful and worth the expense and effort is to bring in the election figures reasonably early while people are still awake and to put them on the screen clearly, legibly and in some pleasing and understandable form. I've always liked the huge map twenty feet high and lighted from behind we used one year with great success. When a state went Democratic, it was lighted up in red. Republican, lighted in blue. It was successful not because our numbers were any faster than the other networks' but because they were easy to see and quick and easy to read.

As for the complaints about announcing winners while people in the western states are still voting, the sensible answer would be to close all the polls across the country at the same time. Something like 10:00 p.m. in the eastern time zone and 7:00 in the West or some variation of those hours. In Congress, the House of Representatives has voted to approve this idea several times, but the Senate, time after time, has refused. It recalls a silly little joke from an old song, "The Arkansas Traveler": A wife says to her husband on a rainy day that the roof is leaking and asks him to please climb up and fix it. He says he can't go up on the roof today because it's raining. On the next dry day she asks him again, and he says there's no need to fix the roof because it's not raining. The Senate's arguments about the poll-closing hours every four years are about as nonsensical. It discusses the question and then stalls around until the election is over and there is no need to do anything and so it does nothing. Perhaps there are still some lingering suspicions hanging over from the days when a politician's life and future career were determined by the counting of small slips of paper, usually honestly but not always. I guess it is that to a member of Congress, his seat is his life, the only life he has, his heart's blood, and he is simply unwilling to entrust it to anyone he cannot control, including the networks and their computers. It may be on the edge of nuttiness, but I believe it is true.

Our competition among the networks to get election returns in quickly is about exhausted. Any future improvement will have to be modest. It is really not possible to count votes any faster than the American people cast them. That is the natural, immovable limit, and we have already come close to it. Certainly close enough.

A newer development is actually far more useful than the computerized vote counting—the exit polls. The networks on their own began asking people leaving the voting booths how they voted and why. No one has to answer, of course, but most people do answer, freely and openly. They cheerfully stand in line, waiting to be questioned. The result is a far more detailed look inside the heads of the American voter than we have ever had before. This proved to be so interesting, not to say fascinating, that the news media in general joined in, and now we all share the work and the cost and the results. On election nights we can tell who won and by how much and, most interesting, why. Then we give out the information never available before

—why the winners won. It seems to me this is a substantial contribution to democratic government.

KENNEDY and Richard Nixon, the two parties' candidates for president in 1960, had a debate, or something loosely called a debate. It settled nothing much but created a lot of conversation now passed into folklore. Some thought Nixon lost the debate because he needed a shave, but they were not aware he always looked that way. People in the White House swore, half seriously, that Nixon kept an electric razor in his desk drawer in the Oval Office and used it off and on through the day trying to keep his whiskers down. The truth was that he had a very heavy, very black beard, so black it was almost purple, and no amount of makeup could completely hide it. And on television then, as now, dark beards were accentuated and made to look even darker and heavier than they were.

While eight years later Nixon was one of the most intelligent presidents of modern times, he never seemed happy or seemed to enjoy what he was doing, whatever it was. He always looked lugubrious, heavy, mournful, unsmiling. In the picture files it is difficult to find a photo of him with a smile on his face. Why? Nobody could say, exactly. But when he was in his presidential office about to receive a visitor he did not know, he began to perspire, and looking fearful and uncomfortable, he usually called in Henry Kissinger, his chief adviser, and grilled him at length before the visitor was let in. For half an hour, while making notes on a yellow legal pad, he asked questions about every detail of the visitor's personal history, his political views, and why, exactly, was he coming in today? And what could Nixon expect to hear from him, and what should he say in return? It was as if he were girding himself for an unpleasant encounter, possibly dangerous. He seemed to feel his cronies— H. R. Haldeman, John Ehrlichman and that gang— were his only friends, and everyone else was an enemy, and probably out to get him. To my knowledge, no one ever heard Nixon tell a joke or laugh at one. Highly intelligent but socially a total bust.

Kennedy, on the other hand, joined in the debate looking clean, neat, and in a couple of television shots he was smiling and seemed to be laughing at Nixon. They spent their airtime, or wasted it, arguing about two essentially worthless and almost meaningless dots of land twelve miles off the coast of China. Two islands called Quemoy and Matsu, claimed by both Taiwan and mainland China, but hardly worth claiming by either. China was asserting its claim by firing artillery shells at the two islands. In an inscrutable Oriental decision, it announced it would fire the shells only at certain hours of the day. That allowed the islands' residents to watch the clock and wait for the firing to stop at the scheduled time and then to go out with their carts to collect the scrap metal left by the artillery shells and sell it. Two candidates for president of the United States used most of their time for this, no doubt the silliest argument ever mounted in a presidential debate. Nobody was hurt or politically bruised, but the consensus was not so much that Kennedy won as it was that Nixon lost.

On election night when the vote numbers began rolling in and the computers began chewing on them and pouring out columns of figures, Kennedy was ahead, but not by much. Then Nixon gained. Kennedy still ahead, but by even less. Hour after hour we stayed on the air waiting. At 3:00 a.m. Nixon said if the trends continued Kennedy would be president, and he would support him. It was not much of a trend, and it did not continue. At 4:30 a.m. Kennedy was one electoral vote short of victory. The numbers hung there. Kennedy's lead dropped to below seven hundred thousand votes. Those of us who had been on the air all night were beginning to drag. Tuesday was gone, and the Wednesday sun was beginning to light the streets of New York City. Still no decision. The *Today* show, then with Dave Garroway, was due to take over the network at 7:00 a.m. Finally, at 7:20 somebody—I don't know who, and everyone denied it—decided that California had gone to Kennedy, and so the election was over, Huntley and I and all of us could go home, and the *Today* show could take over. But some hours later we found that somebody had made a mistake. Kennedy had not won California. Nixon had. It was so close it came down to counting of absentee ballots, to be done without computers, and so those numbers came in eight days later. But Nixon conceded at 12:45 on Wednesday afternoon, and the election night program signed off after eighteen hours.

ON INAUGURATION DAY, Kennedy's speech asked his listeners to ask not what their country could do for them but to ask instead what they could do for their country, a sentiment well received across the country. That night the family all went to two of the ten inaugural balls taking place around town. Even with sirens and police escorts struggling through the crowds and the gridlocked hired limousines it was difficult to get to even two. Nobody has ever been known to attend all of them.

Then to the White House, where Kennedy found himself alone with about sixteen friends, the staff now in bed and the building dark. Later he told friends he could not find a drink and could not find where to turn on the lights. The presidential limousine was gone, he thought of going back to his own house in Georgetown but was told the police had sealed off the whole neighborhood, infuriating the residents. The new president of the United States had nowhere to go, with no lights, no food, no drink. So they walked through the streets to the residence of Joseph C. Alsop, a friend and newspaper columnist, and stayed there talking and laughing until 2:00 a.m.

Reuven Frank wrote later: "Memories of the Kennedy days are memories of television. From its beginning to its end we remember less what happened than how it looked on television."

He looked on television like what he was, a younger, livelier, handsomer president than Americans were accustomed to seeing after years of older, more settled, statelier gentlemen named Hoover, Roosevelt, Truman, Eisenhower.

And wittier. When he was criticized for appointing his younger brother, Robert Kennedy, to be attorney general of the United States, he said, "I can't see that it's wrong to give him a little legal experience before he goes out to practice law."

Kennedy's father had had a stroke and was not well enough to travel much, and so he sat home and watched his son's campaign on television, trying to see him every time he appeared in the news and carefully noting which programs, in his view, treated his son fairly, meaning favorably, and which did not. I liked Kennedy a little more than Huntley did, but neither of us bowed and scraped before him. And when I look back on the campaign all these years later, my recollection is that the news program with by far the largest audience in television, ours, dutifully reported Kennedy's campaign successes as well as his troubles, reported what he said about himself and what his opponent said about him. Richard Nixon, it seems to me now, felt all along that he was outshone by his young and handsome opponent's personality and speaking ability and probably concluded early that he would lose. As it turned out, when Kennedy won by only a handful of votes the talk in Washington was that he won only because his candidate for vice president, Lyndon Johnson, somehow manipulated a victory in Texas, and his friend Mayor Richard J. Daley did the same in Chicago. Nixon was certain there was some corruption in the vote count in Chicago, but said he would not make an issue of it, and he did not. In any case, Kennedy's father watched it all on television at home and told his son that somehow my treatment of him on the air had been so effective that I had elected him president. Although I had several talks with Joseph Kennedy, he never said that to me, and I would not have believed it if he had. But he did say it to his son, the president, and other family members told me about it. If his son believed it, he didn't mention it to me, and it would have been awkward and inappropriate if he had. It was never brought up again by anyone.

Unlike Eisenhower, who had grown up without television, Kennedy had grown up with it, took it for granted and assumed from the beginning that his

news conferences would be on live television, carried around the world, and there was hardly any
negotiation with us since none was needed. He
would move his news conferences out of the Indian
Treaty Room in the Old Executive Office Building
next door to the White House and hold them in the
much larger State Department auditorium several
blocks away. There, as during the campaign, we reporters found him to be quick, witty and prepared
for any question. It was a triumph partly because he
was good at it and partly because it was new and
different from what we had seen for the eight years
of Eisenhower—extreme caution, unwillingness to
discuss what was in the news that day and a preference for waiting until the issue, whatever it was,
was settled and no longer likely to change. Presidents had always preferred to talk about history instead of news. History is finished and it is easy to
be wise when the results are already known and the
issues settled. But news changes so fast today's wisdom may turn out to be tomorrow's embarrassing
mistake. But not Kennedy. He dealt with any question, any at all, a new experience for the reporters,
and we loved it.

About then, a new and vastly popular restaurant
opened in Washington—the Jockey Club, in what
is now the Ritz Carlton Hotel—and it quickly became a hangout, or mess hall, for politicians and
reporters involved in big-time politics. It was where
any one of us could drop in any time and be sure

to find someone we knew—the Kennedy gang, their retinue, odd politicians looking for company or sometimes for a date. And it was where we discovered the Kennedys declined ever to pay a check. One night my wife and I went there for dinner and sat where the restaurant had a number of small, square tables arranged in a straight line. We were looking for a little quiet time for just the two of us, for once inviting nobody else, and finding a quiet time could not be had. First arrived Bobby and Ethel, giving the usual salutation, ''Hello! How are you? Nice to see you!'' And they sat at a table adjoining ours. Then came Arthur Schlesinger and his then wife, Ruth. Teddy Kennedy and his then wife, Joan. Others and then others. Shortly there were twenty of us seated at a row of small tables. Food, wine, champagne, jokes and laughs and gossip and for two hours. When the check came, the waiter handed it to me, since I was the first to arrive. First to arrive, yes, but I had not invited any of this crowd, did not see myself as their host, all of them far richer than I was, and did not feel called on to pay a check they had run up close to two thousand dollars. What to do? I picked up the check in gingerly fashion, tried to be unobtrusive in holding it out where everyone could see it. I waited for Teddy or any of the rich Kennedys to offer to pay it. No one did. I really could not take the check and work my way down the row of tables asking who ordered the champagne and who had the asparagus. I waited. Nobody moved. Seeing no way out, I paid the check.

KENNEDY'S private life, the Marilyn Monroe stories, the Judith Campbell stories, his premarital activities, eventually became the subject of public gossip, but not during his lifetime. I have been asked at least a hundred times, if we publicized Gary Hart's private affairs and Bill Clinton's private affairs, as we did, why were the press and television silent about Kennedy's?

There are two answers. The first, honestly, is that I did not know about them until later, and I never knew of any newsperson who did. What a president does in the privacy of the White House, surrounded and guarded by police and Secret Service agents, is simply never available to the news agencies. Of course, we all knew that before he was president, Kennedy was extremely active in Washington social life, often with attractive women, but since then he was just another senator, we all thought that was none of our business. Rightly, I think.

The second answer is more complex. In the early days of television, the rules were tight and explicit. For example, I was not allowed to say the word "rape" on the air. A rape had to be called a criminal assault, a code word then widely understood. I was not permitted to say the word "abortion" on the air. It had to be called an "illegal operation."

As everyone is aware, since Kennedy's time, the sixties, there has been a more or less dramatic change in the unspoken, unwritten rules or habits in public communication, helped along by various court rulings. Look at movies insisting on at least one bedroom scene with nudity, even when it serves no dramatic purpose but is put in only to avoid a G rating. It seems Hollywood fears that a G rating means to the public that the movie is about cute children, kittens and puppies. Look at the supermarket tabloids, at the array of sex magazines on the newsstands. None of this was true in Kennedy's time. It would all be made public if he were to become president now. It simply was that a communications device, television, with a circulation so massive and so indiscriminate, going everywhere at home and abroad, was reluctant to join in the trend toward sexual candor and openness, restrained by its own intrinsic massiveness and its managers' fears of giving offense, fears of losing their new and valuable broadcast licenses. What finally ushered in the new licentiousness were the rulings of the Supreme Court of the United States saying pornography was speech, and under the Constitution speech must be free. But during Kennedy's lifetime his numerous boudoir exploits remained out of public view. Since so many have asked me about this over the years I have come to wonder if their questions were rooted in envy.

Before he was sworn in as president on January

20, 1961, Kennedy began choosing his cabinet, and the U.S. Senate cooperated by confirming all of them the following day and all were sworn in two hours later, with only one negative vote. Senator Gordon Allott, Colorado Republican, voted against the president's brother, Robert Kennedy, appointed to be attorney general, saying he did not "have the legal experience to qualify him for the office." And so the new administration began.

EARLY IN 1961 fourteen Washington newsmen and I were invited to contribute essays to a small book called *The Kennedy Circle*, giving our thoughts about the new and very different government taking shape in Washington. We wrote at a time when we were seeing President Kennedy and his new cabinet close up almost every day and while the time, the people, the atmosphere, were fresh in our minds and have since slid sidewise from the news pages and news broadcasts into the historical archives. Here are some edited excerpts from my contribution, called "The New Men," written thirty-odd years ago:

> A new member of the President's Cabinet arriving in Washington first sends his wife out to look for a house big enough for the entertaining soon to be demanded of him, and then he goes down to his office and bravely and hopefully enters into American history. He also enters a government

department that is well aware it was there before he came and and will be there when he is gone, where oil portraits of great secretaries from the past look queruously out from gilt frames seeing him sitting there behind a ponderous desk and chromium water pitcher, wondering how to get control of an agency filled with people who know more about it than he does.

While he reflects on this, his wife telephones to say the really suitable houses are in Spring Valley and Wesley Heights, but they have racial covenants—legally binding restrictions listing about eight races, religions and various minorities forbidden by law to own the houses or live in them. In Washington in 1961 there were covenants on almost all the attractive neighborhoods in the city. While nothing really had been said, it is somehow understood that nobody in the new Kennedy administration may sign a covenant. He asks his wife to look in Georgetown. A lot of the new fellows are moving in there where the houses are quaint, historic, expensive and cramped, and while those with three small bedrooms begin (in 1961) around $60,000, many of them are too old to have covenants.

Now to try to see just what this agency he has been appointed to run is all about. One of Kennedy's appointees tried to learn this by calling in all his bureau heads and asking each one, ''What do you do and why do you do it?'' The answers may boggle him. For example, the new Secretary of Commerce, Luther Hodges, finds he has been put in charge of trade fairs, public roads, charting navigable waters, issuing patents, collecting business statistics, exports and imports, inland waterways, taking the census, supporting the merchant marine and predicting the weather.

So there it is. While he is indeed the secretary, his is not the privilege of deciding what the institution he heads is expected to do. That was decided for him long before he came here—by Congress, in densely printed volumes of statutes, by the encrustation of habit and tradition, by the orders of presidents long dead, sheer habit and leaden bureaucratic routine and by Congressional insistence on writing rules and orders to micromanage the agency's every move, however trivial.

The new secretary then finds that within these suffocatingly tight boundaries of law, tradition and ancient habit, his agency does have policies and objectives, or will have when the new administration has had time to choose them, but it will take months to see precisely what they are and how to direct them. (''I am not aware of any school for cabinet officers, or Presidents either.'' —President Kennedy.)

Along about the sixth month, when he is settled and cramped in Georgetown, he is perhaps spending a fourth of his time testifying before Congress or preparing to, another fourth in meetings with people in his own agency and from others, and the rest of his time handling paper, reading and writing reports, including those brought home in his brief case. He finds that the only time he has for undisturbed thinking is when he is shaving, and he will wonder if he has taken over the agency or if it is the other way around.

The first responsibility facing a new President is to find ten people for these cabinet agencies who can do the work and survive the frustrations. The ten must also be able to stay out of trouble and out of embarrassing stories in the papers, contribute something to the success of the administration, collectively represent a suitable geographic, religious and ideological spectrum and furthermore to demonstrate a devotion to the principles stated or implied in the party's platform. In this, John Kennedy, even in the judgments of his enemies, succeeded brilliantly. With the exception of two or three, he got every cabinet officer he went after. And the ten finally chosen make up what many here believe is the most talented cabinet in modern times.

The level of ability found along the White House corridors and in the high-ceilinged warrens of the Executive Office Building next door is also impressive. Theodore Sorensen is there. He is no Sherman Adams in terms of power but he is the foremost of the Presidential assistants. At any moment he may be found looking over the papers on a contested airline route, on some convict who wants a pardon, or something on the wheat surplus. Or he may be writing the President's next speech in prose clear and lucid if slightly wordy.

Lawrence O'Brien may not be in his office, since his job is Congressional liaison. That is to say, his job is to roam the Capitol and talk to people, see what is happening or about to, and occasionally try to persuade some member of Congress to do something—much like a routeman for a line of household cleaners. He is more politician than anything else, talks with pure pleasure, great expertise and total recall about the last campaign and seems impatient to begin the next one.

Walter Heller, of the Council of Economic Advisers, a talkative, high-strung ectomorph, may be heard saying exultantly that he sent the President a twelve-page memorandum on some complex economic problem and discovered at a cabinet meeting an hour later, "he had *read* it and was *quoting* from it."

What kind of people did Kennedy choose to fill his cabinet and his White House secretariat? Contrary to some pre-election forecasts, they are not New Dealers. Franklin Roosevelt came here in 1933 at the head of a noisy column of hot-eyed reformers, intent on making over the basic institutions of this country, determined to end the depression and to change our class structure while they were about it. They brought with them the passions and the zeal that always go with immoderate loves and hatreds. They were tinkerers, experimenters, social workers and agrarian reformers. They were geniuses and an occasional crackpot. They fell on Washington with zestful shouts of pure joy and looked around for things and places they thought needed reform.

There is nothing nearly so gaudy as that in Washington now. In New Deal days, a good idea was a good idea, period. If it failed to work, it was because not enough money had been spent on it or because no alphabetical agency had been created with an adequate budget to administer it. But in Washington now, a good idea is an idea that works. And the best idea is the one that works fastest with the least fuss while irritating the fewest people. Pragmatism probably is the word. It is heard so often around Washington now it must be. At a party on one of the first few dozen nights, the wife of a government official was heard to circulate the room asking each guest in turn, "Are you pragmatic?" Had Treasury Secretary Douglas Dillon been asked, he might well have given the answer he gave later: "I believe in doing things the orthodox way when the orthodox way works. When you run into places where the orthodox won't work, then you try something else." Or had he had more time, he might simply have said, "Yes."

Pragmatism (the word literally was invented at Harvard) has an honorable history. It has engaged the attention of such philosophers as William James, who proclaimed it to be "the attitude of looking away from first things, principles, supposed necessities, and of looking toward last things, fruits, consequences, facts." And, he said, "meaning, other than practical, there is for us none."

For nearly a century, then, the word and the philosophy have rolled off tongue and pen, but not until now, I believe, have they been applied to the governing of the United States, not until Kennedy. As I and a hundred other correspondents questioned and listened to him at his press conferences and noted his insistence on the practical and the result-oriented. He knew what he wanted even though he did not always get it.

Another example came from Secretary of State Dean Rusk who in his 1960 Elihu Root lectures made a formidable, almost unassailable case against summit conferences. He declared them to be unproductive, a waste of time and Presidential energy, and even dangerous. But pragmatic to the last, he still refused to rule them out entirely. Instead, his conclusion was that as worthless as summit conferences were, there might nevertheless be times when they could be useful to us and might therefore be used sparingly with suitable precautions to prevent them from becoming a habit. Rusk's little spiel recalled the ancient vaudevillian's firm statement, ''I hate that son of a bitch and I won't have him in my act unless I need him.''

Whatever the results of the Pragmatic System, or government by the Palmer method, large numbers of people in the early months of the Kennedy administration, in mail to me at NBC and in the polls, professed astonishment that it was not more radical than it was. A small-town Republican businessman listened to a visiting lecturer in the high school auditorium discoursing about Kennedy's doings and blurted out, ''You know, that fellow hasn't done anything Eisenhower wouldn't have done.''

That judgment may not be pleasing to the New Frontiersmen but it is nevertheless one honest reaction to the careful, unemotional mood that now fills Washington as smoke fills a room. It flows from the President himself and is further thickened by the men he chose to staff his government. Some of Kennedy's taste and attitude can be seen in all of them. Those of advanced liberal views wound up in secondary jobs. For example, G. Mennen Williams, the very liberal former Governor of Michigan now known as "Soapy," was appointed to a steamy post in Africa, causing Senator Barry Goldwater to opine, "I'm glad they sent Soapy to Africa. If we'd been elected that's where we'd have sent him."

The same pragmatic trend could have been seen even earlier when Kennedy chose Lyndon Johnson for his nominee for Vice President, to the intense distress of Walter Reuther of the United Automobile Workers union. Critics offered the feverish prediction that when Kennedy took office Reuther would get a gold pass key to the White House. Here Goldwater said, "The Kennedy people go to Walter Reuther for votes, to Joe Kennedy for money and to London for their clothes." As it turned out, in the early months, Reuther was not seen anywhere near the White House. On the contrary, he was telling Congress more in sorrow than anger that Kennedy's views on labor matters were not good enough.

The liberal view is there but it is concealed behind a concern for the possible. In his first months, when the President needed southern Congressmen's votes to open the New Frontier, there was not a word or a line from him about the new civil rights legislation. He came, like no other member before him, directly from Congress, bringing with him a close knowledge of its ways and means, its members, its rules written and unwritten, and a conviction that the thing to ask of Congress was what it was willing to give, or perhaps a shade more. Anything beyond that could be had, if at all, at a political cost too great to pay.

There is another factor: Franklin Roosevelt came here at a time of urgency so great that in his first week he could have seized and national- ized the country's banking system had he cared to. John Kennedy has no such power. If the ur- gency is that great, the American people are not aware of it. Neither is Congress.

Kennedy, therefore, staffed his administration with people who share his own style, who eagerly welcome new ideas but who insist first on can- dling them like eggs held to a light.

Those of us who were hired and paid to watch the new administration and to tell the American people about it could see characteristics generally new to Washington. The Manchester *Guardian* commented that ''There can be few governments on earth equal to it in energy, youth . . . its new sense of dedication, its preoccupation with Asia and Africa, its correspondence courses in quick reading, Swahili and the diffuse nebulae . . .'' The concentration of campus intellectuals in soft jack- ets and easy shoes is perhaps unequaled in Amer- ican history. Roosevelt never ran so heavily to men like this. He preferred experts in consumer economics, labor organizing, hybrid corn and egg marketing. But now, those who were enchanted with Adlai Stevenson and his eggheadedness find that in the new administration he has joined he is just one of the crowd. One of the news magazines briskly went around counting the Phi Beta Kappas among Kennedy's appointees, finding sixteen. It also found four Rhodes scholars and one Nobel prize winner, and printed their names in a box with the caption: "In the new administration, the accent is on scholarship as well as on youth." The cabinet and other government officers usually were depicted in the form of an organizational chart, made of many boxes connected by many lines, looking a little like the plumbing diagram for a twelve-room house. But when I asked Kennedy about this, he said he preferred a diagram in the form of a wheel and spokes with himself at the hub.

"One of the problems of any President," he said, "is that his sources of information are limited. I sit in the White House and what I read in the newspapers and magazines and memoranda and things I see—like you and Huntley—is the sum total of what I hear and learn. So the more people I can see, the wider I can be exposed to different ideas, the more effective I can be as President. So, therefore, it is a mistake to have one person working on one subject because then you don't get any clash of ideas and therefore have no opportunity for choice."

The Harun al-Rashid method of roaming the streets incognito and questioning the citizenry is not available to the President. As he says, the only information he can get is whatever is brought to him. His brother, Attorney General Robert F. Kennedy, did try walking in his shirtsleeves around the streets of New York and questioning juvenile gang members. The President therefore has cast aside President Eisenhower's method of having his chief of staff Sherman Adams bring information to him after running it through his own fine-screen filter.

THE WHITE HOUSE was my first regular beat when I arrived in Washington in 1943 and over the years since I have watched the organization of the White House staff change to reflect the personalities of one President after another. At one extreme, before my time, was Calvin Coolidge, who liked the government quiet. He had an adviser named Frank Stearns, who occasionally was summoned to the President's office, there to sit, the two of them, in a haze of cigar smoke for an hour or more in total silence. Hoover, believing the government should be small, kept his staff down to three secretaries, military and naval aides and forty clerks. Roosevelt vastly enlarged it but never organized it, preferring to keep it in a cheerful sort of confusion, with Harry Hopkins upstairs working at a card table set up in the Lincoln bedroom. In 1945 Harry Truman found the White House offices so overcrowded and disorganized that one of his advisers, George Allen, was unable to get a desk or a telephone and so he chose to walk down Pennsylvania Avenue to a drug store and transact his business in a telephone booth.

There is a federal law Congress never passed. The Law is that whenever two or more government officials meet more than once a month to say or do or plan anything whatever, their meetings quickly become institutionalized. This process begins with the employment of a coordinator to insure that whatever decisions are made are carried out. The coordinator gradually acquires a deputy, a staff of assistants, a secretary for each, a wall or two of file cabinets, desks, chairs, glass-fronted bookshelves and then begins the complaint that the institution, not yet named, needs more staff and more budget. The complaints grow and there, without anyone really intending it, an entirely new government institution has been formed, now with a name, a payroll and a letterhead all its own.

As The Law has worked over the years at the White House, Hoover's staff of forty-five people has grown into The Executive Office of the President with more than a thousand people and an annual budget in the millions. And its functions, as listed in the United States Government Manual run heavily to mobilizing, advising and coordinating.

The resulting bureaucracy has come to be, in the view of several political scientists, an Institutionalized Presidency—a vast accumulation of people and agencies concerned in one way or another with using the powers the Constitution gives him. Benjamin Franklin feared presidents without advisers and counselors would be "subject to caprice and intrigues of favorites and mistresses, etc." But so great was the prestige of George Washington that the writers of the Constitution left it entirely to him to choose his own advisers in whatever numbers he chose. So the President's secretariat, in the years of my own reporting on the White House, and indeed the cabinet itself, have grown to the towering dimensions of today entirely through individual and widely spaced acts of Congress, Presidential decisions and through the inexorable workings of The Law.

Kennedy, on moving into this Institutionalized Presidency, has begun to change it to suit his own preferences so far as change is possible to him. Congress can be nasty when a President declines to follow its precise instructions. He has abolished a few bodies that exist mainly on letterheads and nowhere else, has put in his wheel and spokes with himself at the hub. The spokes are, by general consent, men of outstanding ability and intelligence whose pragmatic planning and careful candling may or may not please the American people. The application of the scholar's intelligence to institutions that often grew up without it will inevitably cause distress, outcry and perhaps blunders, as in the early attempts to undermine Cuba's Castro. A Kennedy staffer quotes Schopenhauer, "Great intellectual gifts mean an activity pre-eminently nervous in character and consequently a very high degree of susceptibility to pain in every form."

They did.

A year or so into his presidency and now feeling pretty sure of himself, he began to use his new political power in interesting ways. Kennedy the cigar smoker called in his press secretary, Pierre Salinger, also a cigar smoker.

"Pierre," he said. "Get a White House car and driver, more than one if you need them, go around Washington to all the good tobacco stores and buy up every top grade Cuban cigar they have in stock and bring them all back here."

Pierre did and told Kennedy he had brought every good Cuban cigar in town to the White House. Whereupon Kennedy issued his order banning all imports of cigars from Cuba.

ROBERT KENNEDY and my wife and I had shared many personal friends in Washington, a friendship cemented one night when George Stevens of the movie industry pushed Arthur Schlesinger the historian into our swimming pool. That had become the new party prank among the Kennedy friends, begun at Bobby and Ethel's house in Virginia, Hickory Hill, and spread around from there and seen as an act of carelessly amusing abandon when times were good and the country was prosperous and everyone could afford dry clothes. Dry shoes were more difficult, and late in an evening it was not unusual to see several guests wandering around fully clothed but barefoot. Those days were energy and jokes and touch football on the lawn. One player was a former college football star named Byron "Whizzer" White, who delivered his Colorado delegation to Kennedy at the Los Angeles convention and was rewarded with a seat on the Supreme Court at a time when the Senate Judiciary Committee was not so heavily politicized as it was to become and when candidates for the court were more lightly and casually cross-examined. And on Easter it was Art Buchwald in a white fur rabbit suit and heavy black glasses, smoking a cigar and entertaining the kids out on the Kennedys' lawn. One was John F. Kennedy, Jr., visiting his Uncle Robert and Aunt Ethel on a Sunday. My recollection is that one Sunday he sat beside me at the table for lunch, eating a drippy grape Popsicle and, when he finished it, reaching over to dry his hands on my new white pants. The sugary purple came out in the wash. In these, the Kennedys' happy two and a half years, almost everything came out in the wash, in their big houses with manicured lawns, along with political success and fun and games in the Cape Cod summers at Hyannisport that Edith Wharton and Scott Fitzgerald would have found familiar and the endless supply of old Joe Kennedy's money.

Always in summer on the lawns at Hickory Hill and at Hyannisport, there was touch football. It seemed to be required. And here, for the record, I would like to incorporate my news script from *The*

Huntley-Brinkley Report on February 28, 1961, as I find it in my files:

Some of the energy that used to be, and may again be, used up in playing touch football is now being burned up in the presidency with a result unlike any Washington has ever seen.

Through most of our history the president has been a remote and sometimes even shadowy figure who might occasionally come out in public to lay a cornerstone, who maybe once a year would make a speech to Congress, but who otherwise spent his time in the White House.

Mr. Eisenhower's traveling changed that a little. But when he was here in Washington he was nearly always inside the White House and was seen around town very little.

When he left office he was seventy. President Kennedy is forty-three and turns up everywhere.

A cabinet officer sitting around in his office having a quiet and decorous little gathering of his staff looked up to see there was the president, walking in to sit in on the meeting and see what was happening.

The other night, people in a downtown movie theater looked up and there was the president coming in to see a movie called *Spartacus.* He wanted to see it. He went.

Several other times, people on quiet neighborhood streets have found the president coming in for a private dinner with some of his friends who live there.

Just after inauguration day, when Mr. Kennedy was swearing in his cabinet, it was possible to see what was coming. In the past, this was always a fairly solemn ceremony with everyone embarking on his new duties in a setting of quiet gravity. But not this time. This time it looked like Parents' Day at a grade school.

(INSERT SOUND ON FILM KENNEDY
AND KIDS: 38 SECONDS)

As it turned out there were so many cabinet children they never could get them all lined up for a group photograph and after a lot of milling around they gave up trying.

Instead, the children were turned loose in the White House, where they ran and whooped and shrieked up and down the hallways and slid down the balusters in a scene of nearly total chaos and confusion. They did finally get the cabinet sworn in.

Another little episode occurred in Palm Beach when Senator Fulbright, chairman of the Senate Foreign Relations Committee, went down to talk with the president about the state of the world. They had their talk and then a news conference on a terrace outside. The president was standing there . . .

(SILENT FILM KENNEDY AT THE MICROPHONE)

. . . talking about foreign policy and his thoughts about it, when there was a clacking noise in the background. They tried at first to ignore it, but it was impossible to ignore a three-year-old girl clattering across a flagstone terrace, in the glare of the photographers' lights, wearing her mother's high heel shoes.

(FILM, KENNEDY LEADING CAROLINE AWAY)

He had to leave the problems of NATO and the Congo and the balance of payments long enough to lead Caroline, still wearing the shoes, back inside.

(HOLD FILM TO JFK LEADING HER THROUGH THE DOOR)

It was her bedtime anyway. And not only that, she was stealing the scene.

(FILM OUT)

Beyond this, not long after the election it became apparent that Mrs. Kennedy, too, was attracting the kind of attention not usually given to first ladies.

(TAKE FILM, PIX OF JACKIE)

The drawings in the newspaper ads selling women's fashions began at first tentatively and hesitantly, and then openly, to look exactly like her. They even began making mannequins for window displays that looked like her, wearing hats like hers. The women's clothing trade was enraptured by all this, quickly seeing that whatever Mrs. Kennedy wore they could then sell to other women. It also worked out pretty well for those skinny girls in New York who model clothes. Several of them told NBC that since they more or less looked like Mrs. Kennedy their professional careers were advanced. A woman who runs a model agency told us, "If Mrs. Kennedy came to New York she could get a job as a model because she looks like us."

(FILM OUT)

So, the president is all over town going to meetings and in his spare time to parties and movies. The children are in and out of the White House ceremonies. Mrs. Kennedy has become something like a twentieth-century Empress Eugenie with the women copying her hats.

And the old-time politicians with the cigar ashes on their vests don't know what to make of it.

ON FRIDAY, November 22, 1963, I was in my office at NBC on Nebraska Avenue in Washington thinking about that night's *Huntley-Brinkley Report* and what news to put on it. There wasn't much. Some NATO business in Europe with Charles de Gaulle objecting as he usually did. President John Kennedy, a day or two before, when asked about some recent scandals in Washington, said he thought the ethical climate there was about the same as in other places. And now, on this Friday, he had gone to Texas at the invitation and urging of Vice President Lyndon Johnson. Since Kennedy's first term would end in about a year and since he had barely carried Texas in the 1960 election, it seemed a little politicking down there would not hurt. We decided to lead that night's news program with Kennedy's trip to Texas. Not because it was such a big story. It wasn't. But because that day there was nothing else.

It was a quiet Friday, and we were all looking forward to two days off, and my wife and I were planning to spend two days with friends in a pretty little country town in Virginia.

Robert MacNeil, then an NBC correspondent, went to Texas for NBC and rode along in an open-top car in a motorcade behind the president. He heard shots fired up ahead. He was young enough and fleet of foot enough to get to a telephone ahead of some dozen other newspeople desperately grasping for the few telephones available around Dealey Plaza in Dallas. MacNeil dialed the news desk at NBC in New York, somebody answered, he screamed, "This is MacNeil in Dallas!" Before he could get the terrible news out, the voice in New York said, "Just a minute," put the phone down and *never came back* leaving MacNeil with the agony of having the biggest news story of his life and unable to get it out. These were the most agonizing moments he ever knew. Merriman Smith of United Press International was riding in a Secret Service car with a built-in phone. He grabbed it and dictated to UPI one of the two shortest news stories ever written: "JFK shot." The only other news flash this short was moved on the INS wire in 1945 when Franklin Roosevelt died, "FDR dead."

At NBC, whoever answered the phone and then left MacNeil hanging was tracked down and fired the next morning, his crime so hideous the network would never say who he was. In the meantime, Huntley and I were told to get into our New York and Washington studios and keep the news going. Before we could reach the studios, an NBC staff announcer gave the news, his voice trembling so severely he could hardly get the words out: "President Kennedy was shot in Dallas today. Blood was seen on the President's head as they rushed him to a hospital. Mrs. Kennedy was heard to exclaim, 'Oh, no!' "

At that hour, 1:45 in the afternoon, the network normally is not busy and the affiliate stations are running local programs, but in less than two minutes it was all pulled together and stayed together for seventy hours and twenty-seven minutes, all day and all night, giving the American people the horrible news and showing them everything as fast as we could bring it in. From that Friday afternoon we went, as all the networks did, without a halt until 1:16 a.m. the following Tuesday morning with no entertainment programs and no commercials. Such wretchedly terrible news was frightening to people who already were afraid the country was coming apart, and in times of such stress we all knew as everyone knew that ugly rumors begin and spread rapidly. We stayed on the air to show the new president being sworn in, showing that our constitutional processes were continuing as usual and giving President Johnson the microphone to speak some reassuring words to a people who desperately needed them. All of us in television believed or hoped that in these three days we had helped the American people get through one of the most difficult and frightening times in their history.

Even so, there were rumors that this was a part of a plot emanating from Communist Cuba or the Soviet Union or some other dangerous place. In the first hours we did not know for sure which of the rumors, if any, were true, and so we all decided we could do nothing but report the news as we got it and deliver it without histrionics or emotional displays.

In the years after, speculation and guesswork about the Kennedy murder became somewhere close to a heavy industry. More than two hundred books and one very bad movie tried, or pretended to try, to prove who shot Kennedy, why, who else was involved and what the motive was. Many of them were nonsensical. For example, a very silly book by Edward Jay Epstein argued tediously that Earl Warren and the other famous members of his commission did very little of its work, leaving most of it to the staff. Of course they did. That was how it was, and is, always done. The chief justice and the other respected public figures were appointed to give the commission a weight and seriousness and to encourage public acceptance of its report when it came. They could not be expected to spend months studying reports from the FBI, the CIA, the Dallas police, the Zapruder film, ballistics experts, the surgeons, the pathologists and hundreds of eye-witnesses. They were not equipped for this kind of work anyway, so the controversy was unending. In late summer 1993, there was one more book, *Case Closed*, by Gerald Posner, that seemed to me and to some others to finally settle it all. I think Posner's book proved that Lee Harvey Oswald alone killed Kennedy and that no other country nor any other person or group was involved, and the motive, if it can be called that, was a product of madness. Which is what I had always believed. Others still argue there was some evil conspiracy. I doubt all the questions will ever be answered.

The networks stayed on the air throughout, down to the funeral, Kennedy's young son saluting his father's coffin, and the American flag being folded into a triangle. I believe it was television's finest hour.

A few days later, Robert Kennedy and Ethel, along with Teddy and Joan and a couple of others, drained and tired and in need of a little company outside the family and in need of picking up their lives again, came over to our house in Chevy Chase, Maryland, for lunch and a little talk, the first time any of them had been out since the funeral. It was strained and difficult. We sat around and tried to speak about something else, something other than violent death. When the head of a family has been murdered in a horrifying public spectacle, what can you say to the surviving members? Once the expressions of sympathy have been offered, the flowers sent, the obsequies spoken, and once the tears have dried, the English language offers no vocabulary.

Teddy Kennedy knew that since I liked to play with stereo and musical gadgets, I had all kinds of sound equipment, and he brought with him a reel-to-reel tape of a recitation by one of their Boston friends, a witty Irish character and a lifetime friend of the family. Since the Kennedys did not have this kind of tape recorder at home, they asked if I would play it for them.

I put it on. We heard funny stories and amusingly recorded recollections and reminiscences of summer days in Hyannisport with children, boats, dogs and fish chowder. About two minutes of this was all they could take. Ethel asked me to stop the tape. They left, in tears.

V

DURING EISENHOWER'S eight years in the White House the Republican conservatives and moderates stopped their North/South, urban/rural, East/West trench warfare to avoid embarrassing the party's first president in twenty years, and to show the voters that they actually could do more than complain about their most feverish hatreds—high taxes, fumbling bureaucrats and the welfare state. And to show at their 1964 convention in San Francisco that they could nominate the hard-line conservative Barry Goldwater and even agree on a party platform, yes, and without a lot of tedious argument and without a lot of pointless, unstructured debate. On that point, they were wrong. Senator Hugh Scott of Pennsylvania offered an amendment to denounce the John Birch Society, an even harder-line right-wing fringe group, along with the Ku Klux Klan and the Communist party. All of these, he said, were trying to infiltrate the Republican party. Governor Nelson Rockefeller of New York, a candidate, spoke in support of Scott's amendment. He was booed and the delegates rejected the amendment by a margin of two to one. Governor George Romney of Michigan suggested an amendment to reject all extremist groups without naming any of them, leaving each delegate free to decide for himself who was extremist and who was not. Rejected two to one. Scott offered another amendment calling for ''faithful execution of the 1964 Civil Rights Act,'' but saying this was ''a matter of heart, conscience and education as well as equal rights under the law.'' Defeated two to one. Romney proposed another promising ''action at state and local levels to eliminate discrimination everywhere.'' Defeated two to one.

All of that settled to the right wing's satisfaction, the party did what it came to San Francisco to do —first, nominate Senator Barry Goldwater, and, second, drag the news media through a political gristmill of insults and unconcealed loathing. The delegates detested those involved with reporting news—print, television, radio, magazines—they did not discriminate. They hated all of us.

NBC put up its people in the Mark Hopkins Hotel, where each morning coming down the elevator and each night going up, I was threatened with bodily harm. Once there was a conversation in the back of the elevator between two men pretending to discuss the news media's sins, crimes and failures with their remarks pointedly aimed at me.

One said, ''You know these nighttime news shows sound to me like they're being broadcast from Moscow.''

Then, on cue, the other presented his view. "Why can't we find Americans to do the television news?"

Chet and I agreed never to say anything, since a fistfight in an elevator would resemble a scene from the Marx Brothers.

In these days, San Francisco was uglier but less violent than Selma, Alabama, ever was. The whole scene was ludicrous, but no more ludicrous than some of these delegates in their asininity. After a few more of these elevator scenes, I worked out a little exchange with Huntley when we were riding up and down together, saying to him, "The security squad waiting downstairs?"

"Yes. All of them."

I had no idea what this meant, but neither did they, and for a time it shut them up. But soon they continued the sneering insults on the elevators, on the streets, in bars and restaurants. It went no further than this until President Eisenhower rose to the speaker's rostrum to endorse Goldwater and to defend him against the "sensation-seeking columnists and commentators."

The convention hall exploded into a deep, hoarse roar of hatred. The delegates left their chairs and rushed over to the edge of the convention floor just below where Huntley and I and the other network newspeople were working high up in glass booths over the floor, several of them in their anger and haste stumbling past the chairs, looking up at us, shouting at us and waving their fists. Eisenhower appeared bewildered, seeming to wonder what ugly primeval force he had set loose. Now that the delegates' hatred of us had the official support and sanction of the former president and war hero, we were quite happy to be in our booths high up and out of their reach. I don't know what they would have accomplished had they been able to get to us, but they were furious enough to do anything.

Oddly enough, I liked Senator Goldwater. I thought some of his political views were extreme and excessive, but it seemed to me he was saying only what he figured an Air Force general from the Arizona desert country was expected to say. There was little or no meanness in him. On the contrary there was a real friendliness and generosity in him and he was always good company when he was not surrounded by those of his followers who behaved like political banshees.

WHEN the Democrats that same year arrived to hold their convention in Atlantic City, the delegates were greeted with the work of Newton Minow, a Chicago lawyer in Adlai Stevenson's firm and President Kennedy's appointee as Chairman of the Federal Communications Commission, who is remembered for his complaint that American television was a "vast wasteland." The Republicans had erected a huge billboard thirty or forty feet above the famous boardwalk. It was an advertisement for the Republican nominee, put there to rub Goldwater's image in the Democrats' faces during their convention. The sign carried a very large and flattering portrait of Goldwater, and just below it his campaign slogan for that year spelled out in Cheltenham, an old-fashioned typeface: IN YOUR HEART YOU KNOW HE'S RIGHT. Minow found a sign painter and arranged for him to add another line just below Goldwater's sign and in the same antique typeface, saying: YES, <u>EXTREME</u> RIGHT. It was there to greet the Democrats on their first morning in Atlantic City. Within a few hours of that first morning Minow's sign was removed, but not until the Democrats had laughed at it, and it had appeared all over the newspapers and the television news programs.

When the convention opened, it was almost as if a box of faded and crumbling valentines had been brought down from the attic. The Democrats went through one more series of floor fights about their old and contentious issue of race, one I thought both sides secretly enjoyed, and specifically about the all-white delegation from Mississippi challenged on the convention floor by a racially mixed group called the Mississippi Freedom Democratic party, demanding to be seated. Hubert Humphrey, about to be nominated for vice president, worked out a compromise, asking the delegates to pledge to support the regular Democrats and to agree that future conventions would accept no delegation from a state allowing racial discrimination in voting. The convention itself voted to accept this, but the Freedom Democrats walked out of the convention. Then nearly all the regular Mississippi Democrats walked out right behind them. Having settled that issue by not settling it, by leaving it hanging in midair, repetitious, the Democrats nominated Lyndon Johnson for president and Hubert Humphrey for vice president and went home, mostly angry.

It was a routine, predictable few days for the Democrats, but not routine at all for Huntley and me. For reasons neither of us ever knew, even though we continued to report the convention about the same as we had described others in the past, this time the ratings were so lopsided, placing NBC so far ahead of CBS, they were hard to believe. NBC checked and rechecked to see if they could possibly be right. They were. At one point in the evening, they showed we had 84 percent of the audience. So far as I am aware, that was the highest share and rating for any one network ever in broadcasting history. How to account for it? I have no idea. Neither did anyone else.

These numbers were so distressing to CBS it reacted quite foolishly by pulling Walter Cronkite off the air and replacing him with Roger Mudd and Bob Trout. There was no improvement. It was embarrassing to Cronkite and to his old friends, including me. I have always known him to be a solid, straight, reliable news broadcaster and in private a likable, pleasant person and a friend. He deserved better.

When the convention was over and NBC had won as no television program had ever won before, and we were all a little puffed up with ourselves, packing papers and preparing to leave Atlantic City and go home, I was told Robert E. Kintner, president of the network, wanted to see me. I went to his office somewhere in the back of the convention hall. He was short, stooped, no neck, slits for eyes, gravelly voice, half blind, bow ties and a taste for the bottle. But he had built a news department as good or better than any in broadcasting. I had barely ever met him. So I wondered what he wanted with me. Give me a raise? Time off? A word of thanks for our spectacular ratings? Or maybe a walnut plywood plaque like those you get from the Rotary Club for perfect attendance? Nothing, as it turned out. He was alone in his office, holding a Scotch and water. He gave me a handshake, his hand wet from his whiskey glass, asked if I wanted a drink, apologized for having no ice. I said no, thanks. And that was it. The highest rating in the history of television and that was it? Yes, that was it. I left. We went back to Washington and prepared for the election night when Lyndon Johnson beat Goldwater by 15 million votes.

BY THE 1950s television was bumping along, growing and coming to be about old enough and rich enough to afford to have its first real scandal. It came.

An old radio program from the war years called *Doctor IQ* had done pretty well in building an audience. Its producer took the program from city to city, in each place broadcasting from a local movie theater. His assistants moved among the seats, choosing members of the audience at random and when one was selected saying to the announcer up on the stage something like "I have a lady in the balcony, Doctor." The doctor, so-called, asked a series of questions, and if the woman answered them he said, "Give that lady two silver dollars." Then, another question, the payoff doubling with each correct answer—two, four, eight, sixteen, thirty-two dollars, and then Doctor IQ said, "Now for the sixty-four-dollar question." Or, if the woman missed, he said, "Give that lady a box of Milky Ways and two tickets to next week's production here at the Palace Theater."

It was strictly low budget—a few dollars to the winners and twenty-four nickel candy bars to the losers—but it drew a substantial audience, and the term "sixty-four-dollar question" became and remained a part of the language. Whereupon several showbiz sharpies saw the possibilities. With commercials from Revlon, they took over the quiz show idea, moved it from radio to CBS television and raised the cash prizes, dropped the candy bars and came up with a program called *$64,000 Question*. It succeeded quickly, since it was a new idea and it was entertaining. It was such a success that it made prosperous heroes of an Italian shoemaker who could answer any question about opera and several others whose heads were crammed with useful and useless knowledge.

NBC felt it had to have its own quiz program, and it came up with one similar to the casino gamblers' card game twenty-one, or blackjack. If a player answered a question correctly, he or she could take the winnings or have another turn, and if right again, double the winnings. Seeking an appealing person who could answer a lot of questions, they found Charles Van Doren, a young lecturer at Columbia University and a member of an esteemed family of authors, teachers and poets. He became a star by answering one difficult-to-impossible question after another and running up huge cash winnings. Like the other contestants before him, he was placed in a glass "isolation booth" where he could hear the questions but could not hear the answers when they were given to the television audience. Van Doren squirmed, wrung his hands, perspired, mopped his brow and suffered as he tried to remember such fairly obscure facts as the name of the king of Belgium. But week after week he came up with the answers, the studio audience clapping and cheering and shouting at Van Doren, "Go for it! Go for it. Go! Go!" The program was a great success and the audience ratings rose to new heights. *Time* magazine ran a cover story on Van Doren, praising him as a new kind of American intellectual who was making the life of the mind fashionable again.

Then it all collapsed in scandal, corruption and embarrassment. It was publicly discovered that Van Doren and the program's producers were cheating all the way. He had been given the answers in advance. The squirming and struggling to recall the answers were all faked. For the program's producers, he was an attractive figure, a young scholar who carried a great many miscellaneous facts in his head and was able to recall them, an intellectual athlete performing before audiences in fifty states. It was very good television. It also was a total fraud.

No congressional committee could pass up this chance to play the role of outraged defender of the truth, champion of the American people's right to know that when Van Doren had known the name of the king of Belgium the answer had secretly been fed to him in advance. The congressional committee chairman, Representative Oren Harris of Arkansas, duly expressed his deep sadness on camera and his crushing disappointment, whereupon Van Doren confessed in the witness chair that he was a cheater.

The producers of the program argued that they had done nothing wrong, that they were only in the entertainment business, that their program's one and only purpose was to amuse the audience and not to teach a college course in obscure facts.

Did their argument wash? Was it true that the program's only purpose was to entertain the audience and therefore no harm had been done anyone? I thought I knew the answer to this question, that the audience had accepted the program in good faith, impressed by what appeared to be Van Doren's encyclopedic knowledge, and was entitled to be upset to find it had been deceived. That's what I thought. And that was the opinion of editorial writers, of hundreds of Sunday sermons from the pulpits. But as I traveled around the country a little that year, I had an unexpected and unsettling experience. One person after another—over time, perhaps a hundred—stopped me in airports, in the streets and hotel lobbies, and with the same little greeting, "Aren't you Charles Van Doren?"

"No."

"You don't need to deny it. I know who you are. And I want to tell you that I don't think you did anything wrong. You put on an entertaining performance and made a lot of money. Nothing wrong with that."

Why did they think I was Van Doren? Because we looked very much alike. We both had the same sort of nondescript face and hair. And for several months, this happened everywhere I went—people insisting that I was Van Doren in spite of my denials and telling me they thought I had done nothing wrong and they, given the chance, would have done the same.

A professional pollster would not accept this as a scientifically selected cross section of American opinion and would say that nothing could be deduced from these random comments to me in public places. True, no doubt. But in several months the opinions offered to me by people I did not know made about the same point: What was wrong with entertaining people and making money out of it? Wasn't that what show business was all about? Offering us entertainment in the form of fiction we were asked to accept as fact? Why else would anyone cry in the movies? Isn't that what the movie industry does? Isn't a quiz show on television pure show business? Yes. True, all of it. But a television program that says or clearly implies it is factual, surely must be what it says it is. Still, the fact that the audience was led to believe Van Doren was relying on feats of memory only to learn the answers were given to him in advance did not seem to bother people. The only polite answer I could offer while avoiding tedious debate and argument in the streets was ''You may be right.''

I HAVE NEVER understood my literary friends' and others' fascination with prizefighting—Norman Mailer, A. J. Liebling, my producer Stuart Schulberg and many others. Stuart was the brother of author Budd Schulberg and the son of B. P. Schulberg, one of Hollywood's godlike figures when he was president of Paramount. As we traveled the world in the mid-1970s making documentary films for my program *David Brinkley's Journal* on NBC, he entertained us at night with tales of the old Hollywood, including this one: Every Christmas morning, the two Schulberg boys, then teenaged, awoke to find one huge room in their house piled clear to the ceiling with gifts from Hollywood's famous names who were seeking their father's favor—gifts with name tags from Norma Shearer, Clark Gable, Gloria Swanson, a hundred others. The boys spent weeks unwrapping them. Then one day Stuart's father was forced out as president of Paramount, and in true Hollywood style, the gifts stopped instantly. He was too ashamed and embarrassed to tell his sons. Instead, he again filled the same room to the ceiling with gifts with the same movie stars' name tags on them. Stuart told us this one night with tears in his eyes.

I learned he liked prizefighting when he told us another Hollywood story. One of the studios hired a German actor named Conrad Veidt. He arrived in Hollywood from Germany on the night people from his studio were going in a group to a prizefight.

They invited Veidt to go with them. As they walked into the arena, the celebrities in the thousand-dollar ringside seats were being introduced, and the audience was applauding them. Veidt did not know what was going on, and he thought they were applauding him. He responded, smiling, bowing and waving to the crowd. He was a little annoyed, Stuart said, when somebody knew enough German to suggest to Veidt that he should sit down.

Then Stuart got to his point. In about a month in Las Vegas there was to be a fight for the world heavyweight championship with Sonny Liston, the champion, fighting Floyd Patterson, a former champion trying to take his title back. He thought this would be a time to do a story on the fight in Vegas and move on from it into the modern history of boxing and its corruption, a history of fighters with 250 pounds of muscle but a good deal less in brain cells, who typically fought for huge purses, millions, only to find that in retirement they had brain damage and no money—their millions having disappeared in unexplained expenses, travel, training fees and legal fees and outright swindles. Stuart knew of a boxer who at one time was world champion and had earned millions and now was shining shoes in a Vegas hotel.

We went to Vegas and spent a week shooting Liston and Patterson training, rising in the beautiful desert dawns to run for miles. Back in Washington our film editors were assembling film footage from past fights and interviews with boxers who had won titles and then found out their money had disappeared. There were many of these, all of them physically powerful but in many cases suffering mentally from blows to their heads roughly equal to being kicked by a horse. Pathetic, all of them. But I thought it would make a powerful half hour on television and might possibly, conceivably, lead to some improvement in the financial abuse of prizefighters who could barely add or subtract.

I was staying in a ground-level room in a Vegas hotel, half asleep one night when the door opened, even though I had locked it and had the key inside. In walked a powerfully attractive young woman wearing very little. She sat on the side of my bed. I was awake enough to remember that the mob, the financial descendants of Bugsy Siegal, were still powerful here in Vegas in 1963, and I was afraid of a trap, photographs, blackmail or God knew what. It soon was made clear. The woman, now nearly naked, said, "Relax. Nobody's going to hurt you. I came here to deliver a message."

"What's the message?"

"The people who run this place sent me to offer you anything you want and to tell you they do not want any bad publicity about this town."

I said, "Tell your friends we are doing a film about boxing, not about this town and Vegas will only get a brief mention. No more."

And, still fearful of embarrassing photographs,

perhaps through a peephole in a room they may have had built just for this purpose, I said to her, "Tell them that and now get out." She did.

Sonny Liston knocked out Floyd Patterson in the first round and it did, indeed, make a powerful half hour.

WHEN George Washington campaigned for election to the Virginia House of Burgesses, before the American Revolution, he offered voters the inducements of 160 gallons, or about four barrels, of rum, beer and hard cider. His alcoholic blandishments worked and thus started one of the great political careers of all history. And thus started one of the more enduring American campaign tactics—offering the voters food and drink. Over more recent years, other Washington reporters and I have watched as candidates tried to persuade the voters with blandishments of chili, barbecue, watermelon, clambakes, baked beans, crabs, crawfish, hot dogs, hamburgers, pancakes, down to and including—on tables set up in campaign headquarters on election night—Ritz crackers, Velveeta and cheap jug wine. And so by this standard when Lyndon Johnson defeated Barry Goldwater in the 1964 chili-and-watermelon election, he said to me, "You know what beat Goldwater? A ton and a half of chili." Amusing, but what beat Goldwater was Goldwater.

Johnson had acquired a ranch and substantial land

near Austin, Texas, and he also owned—in his wife's name—the only television station then on the air in the city. The Federal Communications Commission had authorized three TV broadcast licenses for Austin, a city big enough to support three channels, but somehow, somehow, if broadcasters applied for the other two licenses, they were never found to be qualified. Johnson's surviving intimates, Jack Valenti, among others, assure me to this day that for several years no one applied for the other TV licenses. Austin was not then big enough to support more television stations, they said. But of course there was talk that Johnson used his political power in Washington to see to it that no applicant could get the other two licenses and end his profitable monopoly in Austin television. This talk never stopped, but nobody ever proved anything, and the Johnsons coined money with their one and only station. The deal then was that in cities with only one channel, its owner could arrange to carry programs from any or all of the three networks. And a station owner in this highly profitable situation, choosing carefully, could broadcast only the most popular and highest-rated program from any network in each time period, day and night—as if it were the only bookstore in town and able to fill its shelves with nothing but best-sellers. Every two or three weeks, Johnson called me at Washington's NBC studios to ramble around, saying nothing much, until he worked his way around to remind me that for his evening news program in Austin, he could choose either CBS's Walter Cronkite, ABC's John Charles Daly or NBC's Huntley and Brinkley. He picked us, he said, "Because you boys have the biggest audience and Bird likes your program." Bird was his wife, Lady Bird.

Some of the cynics at NBC wondered why he called me about this. Was he reminding me that he was doing me a favor and maybe in return expecting more generous treatment in my news broadcasts? I never thought so. With our program carried on NBC's powerhouse stations in New York, Chicago and Los Angeles and in more than two hundred other cities and towns, his one smallish station in Austin was not enough to make much difference. As for generous treatment, the Vietnam War was raging then; I thought it was a total abomination that should be stopped immediately, that every life lost there was a life wasted for no purpose, and that Johnson was to blame because he lacked the political courage to halt a pointless, endless, bloody war that could not be won. When we talked, he never mentioned a word about that.

On a Sunday afternoon in 1966, my wife and I were in Poolesville, Maryland, visiting our friends the Kephardts for a picnic beside a little stream on their farm. We were cooling the beer in the water, grilling hamburgers and lying around on the grass. Off to the east we heard the roaring, beating sound of a helicopter. Where's it going? we wondered. It was coming toward us. It landed nearby, the whirl-wind from its rotors mussing the women's hair, scattering paper plates, cups and napkins over ten acres and blowing sparks from the charcoal out of the grill and starting a fire in the grass. We put it out by pouring beer over it. The pilot climbed out and said he was "looking for the Brinkleys."

I asked, "What do you want with us?"

"President Johnson is at Camp David. Couldn't get you on the phone. Sent me to tell you he wants you to come up there for dinner and a movie and spend the night. He's got pajamas and a razor and toothbrushes for you and I'll fly you home in the morning. Or leave your car here and I'll fly you back here in the morning to pick it up and drive home. Or I'll have a Secret Service agent drive your car up to Camp David and in the morning you can drive yourself home. It's only an hour."

That crazy Lyndon Johnson had tracked us down deep in the Maryland countryside, ordered one-size-fits-all pajamas for the two of us, had one of his daughters call our house and say we wouldn't be home until the next morning.

We protested to our hosts that we didn't want to leave the picnic. But they said, "Go! Go! When will this ever happen again?"

Never, maybe. We went.

Camp David was built by the Civilian Conservation Corps in the 1930s. During the depression the CCC put unemployed men to work in the outdoors, mostly in the national parks building roads, bridges, drainage ditches and other facilities. It was one of the most successful, most useful of Franklin Roosevelt's New Deal agencies. Its work can be seen and admired today in a hundred places across this country. For its own workmen, the CCC built a camp on a mountaintop in the Maryland mountains about an hour from Washington. It was leafy, green, breezy and altogether beautiful. So private and so pleasing that Roosevelt seized it for his own use and called it Shangri-La, a name he took from James Hilton's 1933 novel *Lost Horizon*, an imaginary, remote paradise on earth. As for the scenery, it nearly was that. Shangri-La it remained until President Eisenhower began using the place and changed the name to Camp David, for his grandson.

By Johnson's time, and the more so after a president was murdered in public, it was surrounded by fences and alarms and armed guards. Inside there were tiny cottages scattered among the trees like vastly cleaned-up and modernized versions of the 1930s roadside "tourist cabins," later called motels, each cottage named for a flower or a tree. My wife and I were assigned to the Dogwood. A bed and bath and nothing more, but pleasant and immaculate.

Around the clipped and manicured camp were a swimming pool, tennis courts, a bowling alley, a helicopter pad, parking spaces and a very large lodge built of logs with a terrace overlooking a broad Catoctin Mountain valley. It is one of the most pleasing of the perks and privileges that come with being president of the United States. By helicopter it is about ten minutes from the White House. My house in the Maryland suburbs lies directly under the helicopter route from the White House to Camp David, and on Friday afternoons in the summer around three o'clock, particularly during the George Bush presidency, we heard the helicopter pass over, taking the president, and sometimes guests, off to the cool and splendid mountaintop. And late on Sunday afternoons we heard them coming back.

The place is maintained by the U.S. Navy. When Roosevelt took it over and made it his own in the 1930s he thought, probably rightly, that the Navy had the best cooks, and so it still remains a naval facility perfectly manicured.

At dinner, Johnson ate a steak and mused on his view that he knew he was highly unpopular among the Washington intellectuals. To another of his guests, Jack Valenti, and then to me, he directed his question, "Why do they dislike me? And what is an intellectual anyway?"

Jack and I both floundered around for a definition that would satisfy but not insult him. To say to him that the intellectuals among his critics and enemies were those who used their minds instead of their muscles, suggesting that he did not or could not do this, would have annoyed him. In fact, Johnson was an intellectual of his own sort, quite capable of reasoning his way from the abstract to the particular and back again, a talent he used freely for years to become the most effective majority leader of the U.S. Senate in modern times. His great ability, more or less intellectual, was to study and assess the limitless arrogance in the politicians he dealt with every day, observe their habits, listen to their speech, learn their background, to search around inside of them to find and contemplate whatever weaknesses were there and then decide how to turn the weaknesses to his own purposes and make them like being used. He was so good at this that one day I overheard two senators talking about a bill about to come to a vote in the Senate and certain to pass. One of them said, "What is the bill? What's it about?"

The other said, "I don't know a damned thing about it."

"Then why are we going to pass it?"

"Lyndon wants it."

If intellectualism is described as creative use of the mind, as expressed in abstract thought, study and highly developed artistic and literary tastes, then Johnson would not qualify. But such a person would never make it to the top levels of American politics. That requires cunning, a cold cynicism, deep knowledge of the occasion and the people involved in it, the ability to join wholeheartedly in the general conviviality when work is done and the bottles are uncorked and the gossip and the jokes begun, and above all the ability to suffer fools gladly, since the U.S. Senate has at least its fair share of them.

For maybe twenty minutes Johnson held forth on one of his favorite hatreds, the leaker—anyone who deals with him in confidence and then leaks it to the newspapers in the hope of some benefit for himself. Two or three times he had decided on an appointee for some cabinet-level job and discussed it with him in private with the understanding Johnson would announce the appointment when he was ready, only to find it in the newspapers the next morning. In each case, Johnson was so furious he withdrew the nomination. One who expected to be appointed secretary of something or other lost the appointment because he could not keep his mouth shut. Said Johnson at dinner: "If I can't trust him now, how can I trust him when he joins the government?"

Much as he hated it, he could never completely stop it. Nor could others. It was and is simply a Washington disease, seemingly incurable. An anecdote, possibly true, was that a general based in the Pentagon was so infuriated at leaks from his department he set a trap to catch the leaker. He wrote a memorandum on some important financial decision and gave a copy to each of his twelve staff members, but each copy had a different set of figures. And he kept his own copy in his desk drawer. He figured that if his memo leaked, whichever set of numbers appeared in the paper would reveal who leaked them. His memo did leak, and the numbers in the paper were those from the copy in his desk drawer.

After dinner, it was time for a movie, Johnson said. The chairs were arranged facing a screen set up on aluminum legs in the living room, a sixteen-millimeter projector rolled in. For Johnson, a Bar-calounger allowing him to halfway lie down, his head back and his feet up. Jack Valenti presided at the projector and started a nice, easy and amusing little movie called *The Russians Are Coming! The Russians Are Coming!*

In about ten minutes, Johnson had stretched out on his lounger and fallen asleep while we all tried not to notice. But then suddenly he awoke with a start, sat up, looked at the screen for a minute and shouted at Valenti, ''Jack, I don't understand it. Wind it back.''

He didn't understand it because he had slept through the first ten minutes of the film. Valenti laboriously unthreaded the projector, rolled the film back to the opening titles and then threaded it again and started it again. Johnson did this twice before we all got into our cabins and to bed.

Even though the keys to my car were in my pocket, the next morning I found somebody had gone down to Poolesville, picked up my car where I had left it the day before and driven it up to the camp, where it was parked and waiting for us the next morning. Johnson simply wanted company, and he had the means to find it and have it brought to him.

He took to calling us from the White House at midnight or later and saying something like, "Bird and I are sitting around here in the upstairs quarters having a drink. Why don't you all come on down here and join us?"

We went a few times. On these occasions, Mrs. Johnson usually did not appear. She was in her nightgown looking at television. Her favorite program, Johnson said, was *Gunsmoke*. But LBJ was still up and dressed and looking not for conversation but for listeners. He rambled and reminisced about himself and the Senate and how he maintained his power over it—by the complex but simple system of delivering serious, politically valuable favors to the members while demanding their loyalty and support in return, and getting it. He controlled the Senate with a power not seen since the days of Senator Walter George of Georgia in the 1940s. I once saw him rise on the floor and say: "The vote on this will be this afternoon and the Senate will pass it." The Senate did as it was instructed. Senator George carried himself with such granite dignity that even his wife of more than thirty years called him Mr. George. And so I always wondered about the story I heard about him, that each morning he shaved with a parakeet sitting on his head.

A story told a hundred times and having, for Washington, the unusual virtue of being true: Senator Frank Church, a Democrat from Idaho, kept asking for federal money to build a dam on a river in his state. At the same time, he was constantly making speeches in the Senate opposing the Vietnam War, blaming Johnson for it and quoting Walter Lippmann's newspaper columns bitterly attacking the war and the president himself. When Johnson held a White House reception for the senators and Church moved through the receiving line to shake his hand, Johnson said to him, ''Frank, that dam you want in Idaho? Ask Walter Lippmann to build it for you,'' and turned to the next senator in line.

And a story Johnson liked so much he told it to me at least three times:

When he ran for the Senate in Texas for the first time he gathered a group of friends one night and led them all into a graveyard to take names off the tombstones and to enter them on the voting rolls and, on election night, show them as having voted for Johnson. They moved down the rows of tombstones copying off the names until they came to a stone so old and overgrown with moss it was difficult to read. A member of the group said to Johnson, ''This one is hard to read. I'm going to skip it.''

Johnson responded, ''You will *not* skip it. He's

got as much right to vote as anybody in this cemetery.''

DURING Johnson's presidency, early in 1965, NBC's London bureau sent us confidential reports that the great statesman Winston Churchill, ninety years old, was seriously ill and nearing his death. Twenty years after the war, during which the prime minister of Britain's brilliant oratory had held his country together in the face of threatened defeat by Hitler's Germans, Churchill was still the most admired, even revered, statesman in the world. And so without hesitation NBC resolved, if Churchill died, to devote all its resources to bringing the event to the world. So did the other networks. It was an obvious decision for us, since we were all young enough then to remember and admire Churchill's great and glorious wartime days. On January 24, he died.

NBC chartered from TWA a four-engine airliner, removed the seats, installed processing and editing equipment in the plane and sent me to London with instructions to cover the funeral on radio to America as it happened and then to fly off for New York immediately, bringing along with me a crew to edit the film while I was writing the details during the flight home, the news to be broadcast directly from Kennedy airport to save the hour or so it would take to get through the city traffic into the city and to our studios in Rockefeller Center.

We arrived in London to learn that Churchill had planned his funeral in great detail. Rehearsals had begun three years earlier when he fell and broke his hip and it was feared he would not recover. Power cables, never needed or wanted before, had been laid in the marble floor of the cathedral for television lights. But he recovered and the arrangements for his funeral were filed away to be used when called for, along with notes from interviews with Churchill describing, in his words, exactly how he wanted his funeral to be arranged. He asked among much else that, as a former first lord of the Admiralty, his casket be placed on a gun carriage to be pulled by British sailors—two white ropes in front for drawing the carriage, two white ropes in the rear to hold it back when rolling downhill. Eight guardsmen who would be the pallbearers had rehearsed this duty by lifting a lead-lined five-hundred-pound coffin, heavier than the one to be used in the funeral. The funeral planners had to make sure they could carry the coffin without breaking down. Of all the military bands in Britain, Churchill had chosen the ten he wanted to march and play in the procession. He chose the hymns to be sung with a choir during the funeral service. As a tribute to his American mother, Jeanette Jerome, he picked a hymn from the time of the American Civil War composed in downtown Washington's Willard Hotel by Julia Ward Howe: "Battle Hymn of the Republic." The service would be in St. Paul's Cathedral, designed by Sir Christopher Wren, and overlooking London from the top of Ludgate Hill. The dean of the cathedral in the seventeenth century was the poet John Donne, and a few lines of one of his poems were much quoted in London on this day because they seemed to sum up the meaning of the death of a great leader: "No man is an island, entire of itself; every man is a piece of the continent, a part of the main; . . . any man's death diminishes me, because I am involved in mankind; and therefore never send to know for whom the bell tolls; it tolls for thee."

So many foreign leaders asked to attend the funeral, 111 in all, they could not all be seated in St. Paul's. Only Communist China rejected Britain's invitation outright. And the ambassador of Mongolia was sick. From the United States, President Lyndon Johnson had a head cold and was told he could not fly. And so did the secretary of state, Dean Rusk. The American delegation, then, consisted of Chief Justice Earl Warren and David K. E. Bruce, the American ambassador to Britain.

The current prime minister, Harold Wilson, delivered his eulogy in the House of Commons, Churchill's old home: "The noise of hooves thundering across the veldt, the clamor of the hustings in a score of contests, the shots in Sidney Street, the angry guns of Gallipoli and Flanders, Coronel and the Falkland Islands, the sullen feet of marching men in Tonypandy, the urgent warnings of the Nazi threat, the whine of the sirens and the dawn bombardment of the Normandy beaches—all these are silent. There is a stillness.''

Big Ben sounded the hour at 9:45 a.m. and was silenced for the rest of the day. The funeral procession began with the world's most magnificent display of military and civilian dress dating to medieval times, the splendor and pageantry of Shakespearean brilliance only the British could produce. The most affecting for me, standing on Ludgate Hill and watching all of this, was a group of about forty middle-aged men, survivors of the Battle of Britain—the vastly outnumbered and truly, truly brave men in tiny fighter planes who turned back Hermann Goering's entire Luftwaffe when it tried for months to bomb Britain into submission and prepare it for a German invasion. The British fighter pilots succeeded in this, God knew how, mostly at the cost of their own lives. After the war the survivors were so revered as public heroes that whatever public nuisance they committed, and a few were known to drink too much and start fights in the pubs, the police refused to touch them.

Churchill's coffin, made of oak from a tree on the grounds of Blenheim Palace where he was born, passed crowds of hundreds of thousands. I was assigned to an elevated stand on the route of the procession and from there I described the scene on radio to the United States. NBC had on its staff a young Englishman, John Lord, who had served in the British Army and who knew the details that I and other Americans did not. He told me about the military units, the history of the medals lying on top of the coffin, and I passed this on to our audience in the United States.

The cortege left London by barge on its way to the village of Bladon, where Churchill would be buried beside his parents. As it moved up the Thames River past the docks and the cranes used for loading and unloading ships, there was a strangely emotional moment, unexpectedly inducing tears in those around me, when the gigantic cranes a hundred feet high, normally the machinery of commerce, were made to bow slowly and deeply as Churchill's barge sailed northward toward the grave.

The entire world had seen, I thought, the end of a great statesman and the last romantic figure surviving from the Victorian era.

Hoping to be first on the air with the pictures and to be able to boast about it, NBC arranged with the Royal Air Force to have a plane leave London instantly when the ceremonies were nearing an end and fly our film nonstop straight to New York, ahead of everyone else. But partway across the Atlantic, the plane developed problems with its fuel pump and had to turn back. With the TWA jet we had hired, we would still be first, we thought. But CBS sent its first pictures to Canada, much closer than New York, and fed them to its American stations from there. Their plan to be first worked. Ours did not. We were second. But we told ourselves that while we were not first we were better. In any case, the American viewing public had been extremely well served.

It was an odd and interesting fact that twelve years earlier, in 1953, for the coronation of Queen Elizabeth II, NBC had a strikingly similar experience. The new young successor to the British throne was seen in the United States, as President Harry Truman called her, as a "fairy queen," and the American public's interest was enormous. On that occasion, NBC had hired a fast British military plane to fly the first film to the United States. And, again, it developed fuel problems over the Atlantic and had to turn back. Some in our crew believed the British were lying, that the fuel pump problem was nonexistent and simply an excuse to delay the arrival of our pictures in the United States until, again, they were broadcast in Canada first. After all, Queen Elizabeth II and Winston Churchill were both theirs, not ours.

Some time later, the queen visited Washington, and as she traveled around the streets in a convertible limousine with the top down I was assigned to do a little descriptive commentary. A remark of mine that infuriated the British, but not the Americans, was that as the queen rode around the city two or three times I referred to her in the third person —"the queen arrives in her car," and so on. I guess I knew then but did not remember that in public at any rate one never refers to the queen as "her," but only as "Her Majesty." I thought nothing of this until I began to hear from Canada, where American broadcasts are easily heard. A Canadian newspaper carried an eight-column headline in 144-point type, RESENT SLURS ON QUEEN, quoting from a group called the League of Empire Loyalists. And beyond that I was editorially dismembered and dismissed as a crude, insensitive American boor. Probably I should have learned this from my mother, who always demanded that she be referred to in the same way.

To this day I am glad I started in television so early that I committed my many blunders before there was much of an audience to see and hear them.

BY 1967, *The Huntley-Brinkley Report* was flying high, winning awards and audiences, and NBC reveled in its great success in news, believing that at last it had bested its old rival, CBS. And it had. Along the highways there were huge billboards advertising hotels, and in letters six feet high the words GOOD NIGHT, DAVID, & GOOD NIGHT, CHET. People shouted those words at us in the streets.

They entered the language. Became the punch line in jokes. All this was success as I never imagined it and still don't fully understand. Perhaps strangely, none of this has ever meant much to me. Of course it was better to be a success than a failure, as these terms were understood. But it sticks in my mind that I or anyone can write a sentence or two with a pencil, a pen, a typewriter or word processor, and do it entirely alone. But television? It is a mass—and massive, and massively technical—medium requiring a mass of transmitters, cables, amplifiers, cameras, lights, enough electric power to light a small city and battalions of technicians who understand and operate all this, as I cannot. So I live with the thought that when I do a little something on the air, good or bad, have I done it? Or have they?

In any case, it seems to me now that Huntley's and my success lay mainly in the fact that we were new, as television was new, and we had few competitors. I wrote pretty well and Huntley looked good and had a great voice. Nearly everything we did had never been done before because it had never been possible before. As when within a few years we were able to show people the back side of the moon and the bottom of the sea and about everything in between. What is now commonplace was in its beginning a grand and glorious adventure for the people of our country and the world, a vicarious balloon ride into the stars, and Huntley and I—happening to be in the right place at the right time—

were able to grab hold and ride it up. To where? I don't know.

IN 1968 Nelson Rockefeller, no longer satisfied merely to be governor of New York, or to spend his time supervising the building of the country's largest and most expensive array of state office buildings and college campuses, announced he would run for president, the only political job bigger and grander than the one he already had. He set forth across the country to campaign, and it appeared to me that when his clothes were being packed for travel, he or his valet rummaged around in the voluminous Rockefeller closets and dresser drawers looking for shirts frayed at the collars and cuffs, suits and overcoats a generation or two out of style, all of it in luggage that looked as if it might have been carried on a sweating mule train through the Indian Wars. So this was how a man famous for being rich pursued the presidency and tried to avoid flaunting his wealth, tried to appear to be concerned about paying next month's rent? Thus equipped, he set off in pursuit of the no doubt sensual pleasures of political power, accompanied on his travels by a small retinue of reporters, including me. Small because the newspapers and networks did not regard the Rockefeller candidacy as a serious campaign for the White House, but more like the self-indulgence of a multimillionaire who had seen, bought, had, done, experienced everything the world offered and was now pursuing new excitements of unknown nature. No one I knew thought he had any chance to win. Pleasant, friendly, likable man that he was, would a political party nominate for president a man whose very name stood for inherited wealth and great privilege? Probably not, since it was taken as a fact of life that in American politics envy and resentment were synonymous, an enduring hangover through ten generations dating from the seventeenth-century arrival of the Puritans, arrogant and overbearing in their conviction that all wealth and pleasure were corrupting and sinful. It is deeply astonishing to realize how this attitude has persisted down through the years and to some degree still exists today. It remains expected that a person of wealth will not flaunt it. Even Nelson Rockefeller's family, no doubt the most generous of all the American rich—financing national parks, hospitals, medical research, libraries, universities, historical preservation—continues to feel the need to keep its money out of sight.

In contemplating this dichotomy—voters resenting accumulated wealth even while trying to acquire it for themselves—and watching Rockefeller campaigning and hearing what the pols were saying behind his back (''too rich''), I thought of Emory Folmar. He once ran for governor of Alabama, making this point in his speeches: ''God has been good to me. I have made some money, and so I have no need to steal.'' I thought, too, of the day I spent following West Germany's chancellor Ludwig Erhard as he traveled around his country in an election campaign. As I watched one of his appearances in a small German town square, a band began playing a half hour ahead of time to draw a crowd. Functionaries arrived to raise flags, pennants and campaign banners. Then Erhard rolled into the square in a Mercedes slightly shorter than a battleship, looking like what it was, a two-hundred-thousand-dollar car in gleaming black. A hatch in the rear roof silently glided open and the candidate's head came up through the opening, like a turtle emerging from its shell. When Erhard stood and talked from the backseat, he was seen to be plump and extremely well fed, wearing a black homburg, expensive and dressy clothes and more than enough gold jewelry, and smoking one of Fidel Castro's best five-dollar cigars, an entrance dripping with wealth and self-satisfaction.

In small-town America a candidate arriving in this luxurious fashion would be laughed at. But a German journalist traveling with us said this was what the local voters expected: ''They want political leaders who are not failures in life, leaders who have got through the postwar hard time and come out of it successfully.'' And, as he did not bother to say, Germans have never had any tradition of equality, often believing instead that equality is an obsession almost entirely American. The campaigning Nelson Rockefeller knew better than most the American voter's dislike of great wealth publicly flaunted, and so he traveled in what sometimes looked like his grandfather's clothes.

But his problem was not his clothes. It was that the reporters traveling with him, along with those from the local news media who appeared at every stop, always expected some sort of press conference, a few questions and preferably some answers not already heard a dozen times, if that was still possible. For reasons I did not understand at the time, Rockefeller handled these little events very poorly. Even though the questions were nearly always predictable, he often had difficulty answering. He appeared to be uninformed, giving halting and even stumbling answers to factual questions about public affairs he should have dealt with quickly and easily. Not until much later did I learn that Rockefeller was dyslexic and had difficulty reading. In one of its forms this neurological disorder causes printed letters and words to appear backward, making a "b" look like a "d," and the word "governor" might appear to a severe dyslexic as "ron-revog" and unreadable. This problem made him sound sometimes as if he were a bit slow in recalling facts, when in fact he was highly intelligent, and once information was put into a form he could use he grasped it quickly. And he could afford to have staff people around him—Henry Kissinger, for one—who verbally helped him acquire the information he needed without having to struggle to read it.

Since for him I was a visual image, a product of television requiring no reading, he found me easy to deal with. He enjoyed joking with me about a nonrelative of mine, Dr. John Brinkley of Little Rock, Arkansas, a famous old medical fraud who became a millionaire by promising to rejuvenate elderly men's sexual powers. He accomplished this, he claimed, by removing the sex glands from a goat and surgically implanting them somewhere in a man's sexual apparatus. The medical profession attacked him for quackery and tried to have his medical license revoked but never could prosecute him because his elderly patients swore his surgery was so effective their sexual lives were like those of randy teenagers. Few believed that, but it was and is believed that if a man thinks he is sexually stimulated, he is. Rockefeller found this whole story hilarious, and he kept mentioning it to me and kept joking about it, even though his personal history suggests he never had any need for Doctor Brinkley's assistance.

After a week or two, I had to leave the Rockefeller political road show for reasons that perhaps should be flattering but in fact were embarrassing. The Huntley-Brinkley news program by now had made the two of us as familiar to Americans in fifty states as their kitchen wallpaper. As we traveled around the country we became objects of public curiosity, television then being more of a novelty than it later became. And it was still new enough that many people did not see much difference between television's actors and actresses, who often were sexy and exciting, and newspeople like us, usually bland and boring. And so at Rockefeller's appearances in smaller cities I tried to stay out of sight but could not avoid drawing bigger crowds than he did. It was embarrassing to him and to me and so I left and went back to Washington, where no one pays much attention to anyone, and I have not traveled with a presidential candidate since. I'm sorry. It used to be fun.

For their 1968 nominating convention, the Republicans met in Miami Beach and found they had eight candidates, including one Stassen and two Rockefellers—Nelson and his brother Winthrop—and it was all very tame. Winthrop had moved to Arkansas so he could run for governor where he would not have to be involved in the aches and pains of the big cities and where he could campaign out of sight of the New York and Washington press.

Before I dropped out, I joined the pack of reporters traveling around the country, trailing the candidates for president, reporting the minutiae of political campaign and the news when there was any and becoming a little cranky when there wasn't. Each day, like a traveling minstrel show, the candidate delivered his stock speech with occasional embellishments, depending on what his campaign headquarters had telephoned to him about political developments he needed to know and depending on what was on the front pages of the big-city newspapers and on the television news programs. In small towns the candidate's arrival was big news. One year Richard Nixon carried his campaign into the small town of Alexandria, Minnesota, where he spoke standing on a box in the high school gymnasium just under the basketball net. All around were little tufts of colored crepe paper held in place by thumbtacks, left over from decorations tacked to the walls, and signs proclaiming the urgent necessity to BEAT TECH. Nixon was introduced by the principal, a man of great dignity who behaved with suitable gravity for what he saw as a great occasion.

"We are honored," he said. "The last time anyone on a presidential ticket passed near our town was in 1912 when Theodore Roosevelt rode through on a train fifty miles to the north."

At the Republican convention in Miami Beach it was Nixon all the way. Rockefeller was simply too liberal for the delegates. On the first ballot, it was Nixon, 692; Rockefeller, 277; Ronald Reagan, 182. Nixon chose Spiro Agnew for his vice president. That was about it. Essentially, nothing happened at the convention. The only fight was over a move to throw Representative H. R. Gross, a hardheaded Republican from Iowa, out of the convention hall. He was a Neanderthal always intent on saving money but never having saved enough to notice. On that issue, he was seen as boring but harmless. He antagonized both parties, however, during the funeral arrangements for President John F. Kennedy. As a burial place was being prepared for him in Arlington cemetery, across the Potomac from Washington, it was announced that Kennedy's widow wanted the grave designed as a memorial to include a flame fed by natural gas, never to be extinguished and to be known as the Eternal Flame. At a time when Americans' emotions had been assaulted and bruised, this seemed reasonable enough. But H. R. Gross rose in the House and testily demanded to know how much the Eternal Flame would cost. For that and other reasons, the Republicans tried to kick him out of their convention and replace him with a Des Moines housewife. People were seen wearing buttons reading H. R. GROSS CERTAINLY IS. The move to force him out failed on a tie vote. Not long after, Iowans voted him out of office.

LATER in August of 1968, the Democrats were planning to meet in Chicago and looked forward to it with no pleasure whatever. The opposition to the Vietnam War was seething, and the anger and hatred were directed at Lyndon Johnson. He was squirming and sweating and deeply unhappy to be the object of such public hatred. In what he later confirmed was a last, desperate attempt to bail himself out, he told Vice President Humphrey he wanted him to tour Western Europe, talk to its leaders and try to persuade them to send at least a token military force to Vietnam. If they did, it would no longer be strictly an American war but an international force fighting the Vietnamese Communists, and, Johnson thought, it would take some of the heat off him, since he would no longer be the lone battler standing alone and taking all the abuse.

Humphrey, always loyal and true and faithfully obedient to the president, set out for Europe in a White House airplane. As he boarded, a letter from the State Department was awaiting him. It urged him to go first to Paris, talk to President Charles de Gaulle and remind him of the many great deeds the United States had done for France—helping out in World War I, rescuing France from the Nazis in World War II. This, said the letter from State, should move de Gaulle to be more accommodating. Humphrey read the letter, tore it up and dropped it in the trash. He thought that to ask de Gaulle for a favor while reminding him of our past favors would be too heavy-handed and likely to produce a reaction exactly the opposite of what Johnson wanted. When he met de Gaulle, he recalled his conversation this way: "Mr. President, I am here to thank you for all France has done for my country. In our revolution you sent the Marquis de Lafayette to help George Washington fight the British. Later, you sent the French fleet to Yorktown to help the Americans defeat General Cornwallis in their final battle and win their independence. You were the first country to recognize our thirteen colonies as an independent nation. And in the nineteenth century you gave our country the Statue of Liberty. We are grateful.''

Humphrey looked across the desk and saw President Charles de Gaulle, a man of great dignity, crying like a baby.

De Gaulle was touched, yes. Moved to tears, yes. But was he willing to commit French troops to Vietnam again? No.

In the poisonous political atmosphere of August 1968, the Democrats came to Chicago for their convention and soon wished they hadn't. It was less a convention than a riot. The Vietnam War was losing public support, and the polls were showing 60 to 70 percent of the public had turned against the war as unwinnable, too costly in lives, and had already forced Lyndon Johnson to admit the antiwar pressure was too strong, he could not win in November, and so he had withdrawn from the race for president, throwing his support to Hubert Humphrey. When Walter Cronkite on CBS turned against the war and said it was unwinnable and should be ended, Johnson told me on one of those late nights in the White House, that settled it for him. And he thought that settled it for millions of Americans. I thought it had been settled long before that.

The candidates, then, were Humphrey, who under Johnson's pressure claimed that yes, folks, he really did support the war, difficult as that was for any of us to believe, and Senators Eugene McCarthy of Minnesota and George McGovern of South Dakota, both of whom agreed the war was an abomination. They arrived in Chicago to find the area around the convention hall, the International Amphitheater, resembled a concentration camp—surrounded on all sides by chain-link fencing, barbed wire, 11,900 Chicago policemen, 7,500 U.S. Army troops, 7,500 Illinois National Guardsmen and 1,000 agents from the FBI and the Secret Service. The mayor, Richard J. Daley, proclaimed that he would not allow the young antiwar demonstrators now coming into the city to agitate for violence.

Now, thousands of anti-Humphrey, pro-McCarthy young people, mostly in their twenties and mostly white, arrived in the city, calling for demonstrations, marches and sleep-ins in the city's parks. They crowded around the entrances to the convention hall and tried to stop the delegates from entering. The delegates resisted. Police and military forces intervened. There were fights. At night, when the protesters gathered and said they wanted to sleep in the city parks, the police ordered them out and attacked them with clubs. Tear-gas shells were fired. In the stately lobby of the Conrad Hilton, there were the choking fumes of gas seeping in from the park across the street.

Huntley and I in our glass booth watched the turmoil. Mayor Daley ordered the city's sewer and other workers to appear inside the hall at night carrying posters printed WE LOVE MAYOR DALEY. Senator Abraham Ribicoff of Connecticut rose to the rostrum for a speech in support of McGovern, and it was not easy. On the convention floor directly in front of him about five rows back sat Mayor Daley himself. When Ribicoff spoke to nominate McGovern for president he said, "With George McGovern as president of the United States we would not have Gestapo tactics in the streets of Chicago." The mayor rose to his feet, cupped his hands around his mouth and shouted at Ribicoff over and over: "Fuck you. Fuck you. Fuck you."

Ribicoff was and is a good friend of mine, and while I sat in our booth with Huntley looking down on this sordid little scene, he continued his nominating speech, ignoring Daley's shouted vulgarities, and I said to no one in particular, thinking my microphone was closed, "Atta boy, Abe." I didn't know until later it had gone out on the air—didn't know until the mail, mostly favorable, began to arrive. NBC never said a word.

The Chicago police announced at the end of the week that 589 persons had been arrested and 100 demonstrators injured, with injuries to 119 policemen.

The Democrats nominated Humphrey for president and Senator Edmund Muskie of Maine for vice president. Muskie was well remembered by members of the press corps because in the New Hampshire primary he, like many candidates, had earned the hatred of William Loeb, the publisher of the local paper, the Manchester *Union Leader*. Loeb was the kind of man we all doubted even a mother could love. The only two adjectives that describe him accurately are (1) eccentric and (2) nasty. He denied the story I'd heard about him for years and am inclined to believe: One day a house cat he did not recognize strolled into his office at the newspaper. Loeb opened his desk drawer, took out a revolver and shot the cat dead.

Loeb's bad taste knew no bounds. When Muskie, running for president in 1972, appeared in New Hampshire, Loeb's paper attacked Muskie's wife, who was not involved in politics. Muskie reacted strangely. He stood in the snow outside of Loeb's office and burst into tears. We all agreed that if instead of crying in the snow he had walked inside and punched Loeb in the nose he would have won any election he entered and also earned our respect and gratitude.

SOON after Nixon won the presidency in 1968, he assembled a staff and began planning to go after his enemies, including me. For reasons I never quite understood, Nixon thought I was his number-one enemy. I never liked him much but never attacked him on the air. But as one of his henchmen, Jeb Stuart Magruder, described it later in his book, *An*

American Life: One Man's Road to Watergate, "Our enemies were always with us and there were many pressures to do something about them. I was involved in 1970 in efforts to counter criticisms by the NBC News team of Chet Huntley and David Brinkley. Brinkley was the one we felt was most actively and obviously opposed to us. We felt that even when his words were 'straight,' he would indicate his scorn for the President by a raised eyebrow or a note of irony in his voice. . . . Pat Buchanan had completed a six-month study of both the quantity and quality of the NBC television news coverage of our Administration."

H. R. Haldeman, an advertising man who promoted the sale of Black Flag insecticide until he joined the Nixon White House staff, wrote to Magruder and said, "I'm sure you have studied the TV summary done by Buchanan, which is a devastating indictment of NBC and especially of David Brinkley."

At this time Huntley either did or did not give *Life* magazine his view of Nixon: "The shallowness of the man overwhelms me; the fact he is President frightens me." *Life* printed this quote after an interview with Huntley, who later said he was misquoted. The truth? Who said what? Who knows now? But we do know the White House staff was in a frenzy to destroy Huntley and me. Magruder offered an eight-point plan to do this. He recommended:

That we have Haldeman's memo released by the Republican National Committee to indicate Brinkley's unfairness.

That we have a poll taken on Brinkley's credibility, as compared to Walter Cronkite's, and if it reflected a lack of credibility on Brinkley's part, get it out to the media.

That we have major businessmen who were friendly to the Administration and advertisers on television complain to NBC's owners about Brinkley's coverage.

What came of all this nonsense? Nothing. The only change I ever heard about was that during Haldeman's management of its advertising, sales of Black Flag declined.

ABOUT a year later, in June 1969, the spaceship *Apollo 11* was preparing to fly from Cape Canaveral, Florida, to land on the moon. While the flight was under discussion, I took a film crew to Florida and to Cocoa Beach, the town nearest the launchpad, to do a little sociology in a documentary. The subject: a small town about to explode into a big town, the first new community of the space age, growing rapidly with the arrival of people coming in to assemble rockets and launch them on their way into space, to the moon and beyond.

People and money were flooding in. The newest establishment was called the Satellite Motel. Everything in town was named Space Something or Rocket Something. Cocoa Beach was so new that poisonous snakes from the tropical undergrowth on the edge of town still slithered into the new shopping areas to warm themselves on the newly paved concrete parking lots, terrifying shoppers who, coming close to stepping on a snake, screamed in horror. In a new nightclub a woman comedian got laughs with jokes about how she became pregnant out on the sand in Cocoa Beach and the father was President Kennedy's press secretary, Pierre Salinger, who never was anywhere near the place. A hotel on the oceanfront was so busy and so crowded it hastily built an addition next door but failed to make sure it owned the land. It didn't. The true owner stood quietly watching the hotel going up on his property, waited for it to be finished and then stepped forward, showing his deed to the land and taking it over.

The town fathers, seeing that we were shooting film in their town, did all they could to persuade us to make their town look good, even including the old trick of the dry cleaner's trade—clean and press the customer's clothes and send them back with a dollar bill and a little change in the pocket, as if absentmindedly left there by the customer and then carefully and honestly returned by the dry cleaner. Cute.

Our documentary went on the air, showing Cocoa Beach for what it was—a rough and raw little frontier town with more than its share of hustlers and chiselers eager to get some kind of racket started while the town was growing too fast to notice what they were doing. Two or three of the hustlers were dumb enough and vain enough to sit before our camera and tell what they were doing. One even said he had already made a million in vaguely legal or illegal land deals and would be careful to get out of town before our program was broadcast. When all this sleazy stuff went on the air the town was infuriated. The first letter to reach me was brief: "You son of a bitch." Hundreds more letters were equally eloquent. Other slightly less abusive comments came from Sunday-morning sermons. The local paper suggested that I be hanged in effigy. I was. I had left town by then, but they sent pictures of a vaguely human form smoldering and flaming on the end of a rope.

None of them disputed the facts. They simply did not want to be seen as I showed them.

Several years later I went back there and found that Cocoa Beach had become a normal small town with lawns, shopping malls and PTAs. When I spent a few nights in a hotel, people, including the mayor, were a little dubious of me, but cordial. And when I sent a suit to the cleaner's, it came back with a dollar sixty-five in the pocket.

Apollo 11 was to be launched up the coast from Cocoa Beach, to fly to the moon and to land there. Two astronauts were to climb out and walk around, plant an American flag and send us earthlings our first television pictures from the surface of the moon. A first of any kind usually is news, but a first of this magnitude was just overwhelming. The flight plan was fiendishly complicated. When *Apollo 11* approached the moon a second and separate spacecraft with one astronaut in it would peel off and go into orbit around the moon, carrying what surely would be the loneliest man in the universe, Michael Collins, who for part of the time would be on the back, dark side of the moon and totally alone. While *Apollo 11* would land, and Neil Armstrong and Edwin Aldrin would get out and do what no human had ever done before, walk on the moon.

It was so complicated the director of NASA, knowing Huntley and I would put it all on the air for three or four days, asked to come to NBC for a meeting to explain it. He came, and we talked. I learned a good deal about space mechanics I had not known before, and I also heard a little about the Washington bureaucratic mind-set that I had, indeed, known before.

I asked the director, if all this worked as planned, history will have been made and what would be his thoughts about this great achievement? I was hoping for some poetic, romantic remark worthy of a truly historic occasion, of being taught to the next generation of schoolchildren, worthy of being chiseled in marble somewhere.

He thought about this for a moment and said,

''David, if this all works I can get Congress to raise my budget to twenty billion next year.''

There it was. The bureaucratic mind at work.

We knew we had to make a major effort to put the moon landing on television as effectively as possible, and Robert Kintner, then president of NBC, said he wanted our best efforts, and expense was no object. Television networks could talk that way back in the days when they had more than 90 percent of the viewing audience, before cable slowly began stealing much of it away. The difficulty was that after *Apollo 11* left the launching pad no part of this great event was within reach of our cameras. From the surface of the moon we could have only whatever picture NASA was willing and able to send back to earth. Until the astronauts actually stepped on the moon, during the flight from earth, there was nothing to be had but pictures of a big room filled with computers at NASA headquarters in Houston. Interesting, maybe, but not the story. We talked it through, and it seemed there was no way to report this effectively but with miniature models in the studio used to show what was happening between Cape Canaveral and the moon. There was a lot of interesting stuff, but most of it not visual. Easy to write, easy to talk about, but hard to show. For example, I found it fascinating when they explained to me that two astronauts standing on the moon only two or three feet apart could not talk to each other. Of course, speech is created by moving vocal cords vibrating the air and in turn causing vibrations of the listener's eardrum, making the sound of speech. But on the moon there is no air to vibrate and no way to talk except by sending out radio waves. And so Armstrong and Aldrin, two feet apart, could only talk to each other by radio, through small transmitters built into their pressurized spacesuits.

I suggested we ask the Walt Disney studios if they would make the models for us. They declined, saying they didn't do that kind of work. Somebody else produced them, they worked perfectly, and a complicated piece of engineering was made simple enough for anyone, including me, to understand. NBC's Frank McGee was superbly good at this, using the models in our studio to explain what was happening a quarter of a million miles away out in space.

In the easier times before we had to deal with the complexities of landing on the moon, NBC had built a television studio on the roof of a motel across the street from NASA headquarters in Houston, even though nothing much happened there. The action, when there was any, was at Cape Canaveral in Florida or in space, out of sight. So little work was done in Houston, but we were there in case something did happen. Nothing ever did. But we spent a good deal of time in that city awaiting the moon launch. One night we had a party outside, around the motel's pool; there was some drinking; the motel had a piano mounted on rollers, pushed it outside, whereupon Huntley rolled it into the swimming pool. I assume the piano was ruined, and NBC paid for it, but neither Huntley nor I ever heard a word about it.

At Cape Canaveral when we finally got some news, we came to see what we had understood before but never quite so relentlessly—that a television network is insatiable. We cannot write it or think it up as fast as it uses it up. Somebody at NBC calculated that at our usual rate of programming, we would use up everything William Shakespeare wrote in less than a week. There is not enough good and suitable material in the world to continuously program three networks day in and day out, week after week, year after year. Yet we fill the time and keep going, somehow.

When *Apollo 11* took off from Canaveral, I was standing as near as I could get to the launchpad without being incinerated by the rocket's exhaust. And I was stunned at the overwhelming noise, so loud it could not possibly be broadcast. If it had been sent out at full volume it would have destroyed NBC's transmitters and the listeners' television sets. The earth roared. The ground shook. The tail of flame was brighter than the sun, too bright for the eyes, even in daylight. And the air was vibrating with such tremendous power it seemed the very earth would come apart. I tried to describe all this on the air without too many mushy and fragrant adjectives and told the audience the sound was too loud to broadcast, the tail flame too bright for television cameras and standing there the vibration was so great that it rattled the coins in my pants pocket.

The story was pretty good, I thought, and so did NBC, because I kept getting messages from New York saying, ''That was wonderful. We need another like that in seven minutes and another in twelve minutes and then we're staying on the air all night.''

VI

IN THE FIFTIES and sixties, the Gulf Oil Company was NBC's practically perfect advertiser. Its deal was that when anything in the news was worth a special program we could go ahead on our own, put it on the air and send the bill to Gulf. And over the years of this relationship at meetings and lunches and chitchats with their staffers and ours, an anecdote they loved to tell about themselves was this: Gulf maintained a staff of inspectors who drove around the country and without identifying themselves stopped at their service stations along the highways to see if they were reasonably clean, including the rest rooms. In the women's room of a station in Ohio the inspector found a vending machine mounted on the wall offering condoms for sale at fifty cents each. Drop in two quarters, the sign said, and pull the handle. This in the years when even the word "condom" could be used only among giggling high school boys and in men's locker rooms. Drugstores hid them under the counters. And now it was discovered that the great Gulf Oil Company, heavily involved with the proper and fastidious Mellon family, was in the business of selling condoms? Intolerable. The inspector told the station manager the machine in the women's room had to be removed immediately because it was disgusting and unacceptable to Gulf. The manager responded, "Are you crazy? I get a hundred dollars a month out of that machine and it's never had a condom in it."

His pop psychology was that in the social climate of the 1960s no woman would be bold enough or crude enough to come charging out of the women's room to complain to the guys at the gas pumps that she had dropped fifty cents into the machine and did not get her condom. The machine stayed.

LATE WINTER of every election year and time for the quadrennial ritual all of us in the news world complain about while in fact loving it—the New Hampshire primary, the country's first real presidential votes cast by real people, and a chance to get out of the overheated studios and offices and out from behind the desks and typewriters. Until this primary, we all reported on the forthcoming election with few facts to go on except the numbers put out by the pollsters, the roving troubadours and minnesingers of American politics who create a little light entertainment for the public and the newspeople in election years. They and we and the presidential candidates travel all over this small New England state, asking questions and listening to the candidates' speeches at Rotary Club luncheons, waiting through the same speech over and over in the wan hope of hearing something new and interesting, and watching them shaking hands and dandling babies at the shopping centers. (Baby kissing disappeared from the political campaign repertoire somewhere around the 1960s when the new thinking was that it was dangerously unsanitary.)

In these early weeks of election years, the state and national parties brought in staff members and hired consultants to help their candidates run proper campaigns and avoid gaffes, training them to perform as traveling salesmen out on the road with a smile and a shoe shine, trying to move the line. It was they who called a stop to kissing babies in flu season. They held seminars in motel rooms describing the local political culture and listing points, people and places to avoid, beginning with the Manchester *Union Leader*. However nasty its editorials—and in the fifties and sixties they were breathtaking in their viciousness—candidates were warned never to respond. If they did, publisher William Loeb would charge out the next day with a poisonous personal attack and turn a political campaign into a back-alley brawl, and soon the voters would forget whatever the candidate had been trying to say. And they were taught how to deal with the difficult logistics of handshaking in a motel in one end of the state and having to dress for an evening event at the other end of the state. How? Change clothes in the men's room at a gasoline station. Once I watched as Estes Kefauver put on a clean shirt while he sat in the backseat of his car parked in a shopping center and a crowd gathered outside to watch. He went ahead with it.

During these months before the primaries, some family members accompanying the reporters to New Hampshire poked around during the day in this Early American state looking for antiques to take home—wooden butter churns, carved eagles, cross-stitched samplers saying GOD BLESS OUR HOME or other such impeccable sentiments as TIME WAITS FOR NO MAN and numbers of black iron or brass coal scuttles. A woman in an antiques shop said to my wife, ''A lot of them don't have fireplaces and can't use coal scuttles. So they plant petunias in them.''

Politically, New Hampshire is highly unrepresentative. It has less than one-half of 1 percent of the country's population, and its primary voters are fewer in number than the crowds at two or three Sunday-afternoon NFL football games. But when I suggested to an NBC producer that we might be giving too much attention and airtime to a state so small, he responded, ''In a political year, you got something better?'' So for a month or two every four years New Hampshire is overrun with print and broadcast reporters hungrily looking around for something that is or can be made to look like news to print or broadcast. Anything. One familiar story reported in detail every four years is the press's astonishment at finding the state has no income tax and no sales tax. We are accustomed to seeing that whatever a store's price tag says, the actual price will be more—5, 6, 8 percent more in sales taxes. And so in New Hampshire it is slightly startling to find that when the price tag says five dollars the final price is five dollars, period. Every four years we report all this one more time, always asking how New Hampshire does it. How does it maintain itself and deliver the usual services, including a reasonably good school system, without the usual array of taxes? A high school English teacher explained some of it to me. "It's the parents. If I want to take my classes to visit an art gallery, say, or the zoo or any kind of travel, I send word home with the students that on Tuesday morning at nine o'clock I need twelve cars and drivers to take them there and back. On Tuesday morning at nine o'clock there will be twelve parents waiting in twelve cars to take them wherever I want them to go. If the state is slow in providing them and I run short of supplies? Pencils and rulers. Notebooks. Whatever. Send the word home and they show up the next day. That's how we do it."

And they do it in other ways. For one, the four hundred members of the state legislature are paid one hundred dollars a year, and they get no office, staff or any perks whatever. A pampered and over-privileged member of the U.S. Congress seeing this would not know whether to laugh or cry. In either case this is a typically thrifty use of the public's money. Another is that in New Hampshire and in many small New England towns people are expected to dispose of their own trash by hauling it to the town dumps, where it is neatly collected under the supervision of the dump manager. He sees to it that aisles through the dump are kept open and that people line up and take turns leaving their trash neatly and in the right places. A couple of times I watched on weekends as the dumps became social centers where people brought thermoses of coffee and greeted their friends with informal chats and visits while awaiting their turns to dump trash. New Hampshire's former senator Gordon Humphrey, a retired airline pilot and hard-line conservative, ran for office promising to serve two terms only. He kept his promise and withdrew from the Senate in 1990, even though it appeared he could easily have won again. He retired, saying that some of his most successful and productive campaigning had been in the town dumps where people were unhurried and willing to take time to listen to him. The cost to the taxpayers of having people haul away their own trash? Next to nothing and one more reason their state taxes range from low to nonexistent.

In the late 1980s so many Americans were moving to New Hampshire looking for lower taxes, particularly people from Massachusetts, known locally as Taxachusetts, that, small as it was, for a time it grew faster and produced more new jobs than any state in the Union. New Hampshire residents seemed to have read and understood, as other states apparently had not or would not, that in poll after poll, year after year, the American people have said what they most want from their politicians is less government and lower taxes. Year after year in state after state and above all in Washington, D.C., this clear and simple message is ignored.

New Hampshire's primary has been held every presidential election year since 1920, but no one paid much attention to it until the fifties and the arrival of television's coverage of politics. Suddenly the candidates' faces and message were spread more widely than ever before, and at absolutely no cost to them. And since 80 to 90 percent of a politician's time is spent raising campaign money, the more alert managers saw that not only was this the first real, actual political event in an election year and in a tiny state, it could be the cheap and perfect way to promote a candidate. Soon the press and television discovered New Hampshire, and reporters, eager for some political action and hungry to get out of the studios and out on the road brandishing expense accounts, generated massive publicity and made it famous. Then, in 1952, Estes Kefauver used New Hampshire to beat Harry Truman and help him decide not to run for reelection. Dwight Eisenhower used it to beat Senator Robert Taft. Until Bill Clinton was defeated by Paul Tsongas in 1992, no one had been elected president without first winning in New Hampshire, since it offers, again, the first real votes cast by real people (as opposed to opinions given to pollsters); the news media from all over the world swarm over the state every fourth January and February for interviews at shopping centers, street corners and the town dumps.

It is nearly but not always accurate in predicting who eventually will be elected president, since anyone willing to pay a small fee and fill out a few forms can enter and have his name on the ballot. One year when Sam Yorty, mayor of Los Angeles, came all the way across our continental landmass to New Hampshire and entered the primary, we all wondered why. His reasons for filing were not entirely clear. We all thought he was wasting his time and had no chance. Oddly enough, all of us in the press and television were right for once. He did poorly. And so in checking in at the airport the morning after the primary, when many of us were going on to Florida for the next vote a week later, I happened to be in line behind Yorty at the airline counter, close enough to hear him telling the agent he wanted to cancel his ticket to Florida and take a flight home to Los Angeles. Few lines of work punish failure so quickly, publicly and even brutally as elective politics.

IN THE SUMMER after the primaries are finished, we cover both party conventions—each combining the worst features of a cattle auction, a clearance sale of damaged merchandise and a sheriff's auction of recovered stolen goods, and above all a social event and fund-raiser by and for the rich. At the 1984 Democratic meeting in San Francisco the party stopped barely short of setting up sales counters on the sidewalks like peddlers hawking fake wristwatches. They might as well have hung up signs reading CLEARANCE SALE, EVERYTHING MUST GO. They were offering to sell the following merchandise at the following prices: Membership in a shapeless, formless, meaningless group called the Democratic National Convention Club, five thousand dollars. That bought two seats in the convention hall, help with reservations at the better hotels, access to the VIP lounge and its free whiskey and tickets to several special programs. For ten thousand dollars, an invitation to a dinner for several hundred people, including the presidential and vice presidential candidates. For twenty-five thousand dollars, dinner and a reception with them in a small group. And for one hundred thousand dollars, your picture taken with both nominees, all of you together smiling into the lens, with the photos then to be autographed with suitable partisan sentiments. Those giving one hundred thousand dollars also got all of the above plus a list of the delegates and staff members and lobbyists and reporters attending the convention, all thirty thousand of us, with names and addresses, for what the Democrats called marketing purposes, presumably to be used in the future for trying to sell us something.

Beyond all this nonsense, a question often asked is this: What good are the nominating conventions? Increasingly, nominees for president are chosen in the state primaries, and the prospect is for more of this in the future. Some members of the political classes argue that this is the decent and democratic way to pick nominees anyway, not in a crowded convention hall filled with brass bands, hot-dog peddlers and balloons falling from the rafters. If any thought, reflection or discussion is needed, or any ideas generated, or serious decisions to be made, this is hardly the place for it. On the contrary, it has simply become the place for the parties' orgies of self-promotion in a boring four-day television commercial, the airtime supplied free by the networks. But in the late sixties we began to see in our ratings that Americans were losing interest in our convention coverage. It peaked in about 1964. In later years we began to see during convention sessions that some nonnetwork local stations around the country that were not carrying our coverage were drawing bigger audiences by showing old black-and-white movies. Accordingly, the networks began to cut back on the free airtime they were willing to give. They did this cautiously, trying not to antagonize the politicians too much, since television, after all, cannot broadcast without a license granted by government. But the coverage was decreased in response to the public's boredom and inattention, and the term "gavel to gavel" was heard no more. To our intense pleasure, no longer did Huntley and I or later Peter Jennings or any of the others have to stay on the air for fourteen straight hours until the very end of the end, when we were forced to sit there and describe such events as the convention's resolution of thanks to the fire department for keeping us all safe from harm. We broadcast through all these dreary hours because NBC's Robert Kintner ordered us, for competitive reasons, to keep going until thirty minutes after CBS signed off. "CBS plus thirty minutes," he said. And on the last night, executive producer Reuven Frank always rolled down the screen his probably famous closing credits listing the name of every one of the hundred or more NBC people involved in covering the convention, rolling them for what seemed half an hour over background music of "Stout-Hearted Men." Many of the stoutest hearts belonged to NBC's women directors and producers, but Sigmund Romberg never attended a political convention and was no longer writing lyrics for schmaltzy operettas.

By now we had covered a long and bumpy road since NBC sent John Cameron Swayze up into the rafters of the Philadelphia convention hall in 1948, when it was clear the politicians had no idea how to deal with television, some of them using it so poorly they nearly destroyed themselves. For example, it was painful to watch Governor Paul Dever of Massachusetts speaking to the Democratic convention and doing what then came naturally to him, doing what orating politicians always did. Knowing nothing of television, he ignored the cameras and talked only to the audience in the hall, waving his arms and shouting as he had always shouted from the speaker's platform when there were no microphones or amplifiers. On the air it looked ridiculous. A full-face close-up picture of Dever sweating and shouting, not yet knowing what all of us needed a little time to learn—that the television audience is not a sea of millions of people spread out at the speaker's feet. It is not an auditorium filled with millions waiting patiently to hear his golden words. It is millions of people, yes, but they are in small groups of one or two or so, each group in one room, mostly in their own homes, and to hold their attention it helps to talk to them in conversational tones, not shout at them. You are a candidate trying to win votes, not a hog caller. But it is difficult for a pol to remember to speak this way when he is on an elevated platform looking outward and downward over a crowd of twenty thousand or so people. He finds it hard to bear in mind that they are already members of his party and in no need of his persuasion. As a political reality, the delegates sitting in the hall do not matter anyway. If a party cannot count on winning the votes of delegates to its own convention, it is already too weak to win an election. What matters is the millions of television viewers. They will elect somebody in November. The delegates in the hall will not.

Hubert Humphrey, among the cleverest of politicians, preparing for one of his big convention speeches, looked for some way, some device, some gimmick, to help him hold the delegates' attention after they had already sat through days of tedious, repetitious oratory, a three-day warm shower of sleep-inducing platitudes. Most of them, by now, had simply stopped listening. Instead, they stood around in the aisles talking about farm prices, their hometown politics, how bad crime was getting to be and where they were going on vacation. This was the weary, bored audience Humphrey had to address, and he needed a way to wake them up. The plan he came up with worked, but not as he intended. He went through the script of the speech he was about to make and at each pertinent point, every few paragraphs, he wrote in "trumpets" and gave a copy of his speech, with instructions, to the bandleader up in the balcony. And so Humphrey's speech proceeded this way:

". . . and, fellow Democrats, this is a promise our party will *keep!*" (PAUSE)

At this point, eight trumpets, on Humphrey's cue, blasted across the hall with a two-note sting: *Da-dumm!*

" . . . our party offers the American people *experience!*" (PAUSE)

Da-dumm!

Two or three more *Da-dumm*s and the audience began to laugh, irritating Humphrey. He intended to stir their political hearts, not amuse them. He sent word to the bandleader to keep the trumpets quiet and to stop playing the two notes. But then each time he made an emphatic point, now the audience itself sang out, sounding like ten Mormon Tabernacle Choirs singing *Da-dumm!* I doubt anyone now remembers a word he said except *Da-dumm!* Humphrey was a bright, energetic, creative politician, but no one has tried that stunt again.

If eventually enough states hold primaries to choose presidential nominees themselves, as now appears likely, will there be any further need for conventions? The question is particularly pertinent now. In 1948 when they were broadcast on television for the first time, public interest was high and remained high for twenty years. This was, after all, the postwar time, when this country stood astride the world as the victor, the military powerhouse, wealthy beyond measure, the leader, the preserver of democracy for the world. The United States of America clearly had found the magic key to peace and happiness for all. We were the envy of the world. With all that power in our hands, it was fascinating to see what our politicians would do with it, to see what wonders lay ahead in a country awash in new and wonderful discoveries—the polio vaccine, color television, antibiotics, the jet airplane, stereo high fidelity and more. Life could be beautiful and was. For a time. Until a series of ugly events shook the American people's confidence in themselves and in their political leadership: the Vietnam War, the Watergate scandal and a president driven out of office, rampant inflation in the 1970s destroying personal savings, government debt rising dangerously and recklessly into the trillions, massive immigration changing the basic character of the country, sidewalks blocked by the homeless, streets owned by muggers and unsafe by day or night, rising illegitimacy among thirteen-year-old mothers, overcrowded jails, graduating high school students handed diplomas they could not read, taxes not only constantly higher but ever more complicated, demanding and intrusive.

Judging by my mail arriving by the sackful, thousands of letters from television viewers, here is what happened to the audiences for the conventions. People were angry and embittered, feeling their country was out of control and heading for disaster, and if somebody was to blame, it had to be the political leaders, didn't it? If not they, who? Weren't they the people who asked for power, were given it and then were seen to be more interested in protecting their power and perks than in protecting the country? Harsh judgments, yes, but with much truth in all of them. So many were so angry at their government they turned away from political issues and turned inward. One letter after another, commenting on the political conventions, said the identical words, ''I can no longer stand to look at them.'' Voting has declined in almost every election. (Future historians looking at our time will find thousands of my letters from listeners in the journalism archives at the University of Wisconsin in Madison.)

So, what now? Suppose the television audience for nominating presidential candidates is too small to justify the huge expense, the cost of delegates' hotels and air travel and restaurants in the big cities, the hours of network time. What is the alternative? No conventions at all?

Since they are as much social affairs as political, they give party members a chance to see each other, trade information, ideas and gossip, and to do what the delegates do at all kinds of conventions, political and commercial—eat in different restaurants, take time for shopping and sight-seeing. Is it possible to maintain and develop a political organization, a party, if its members never see each other? And never meet and talk in a pub? Never sit around talking and arguing for half the night? My guess is that in not many years candidates for president will be chosen entirely in primaries spaced out from midwinter through spring. They come closer to that now each election year. And it would be easy for the parties to decide that since future conventions would have little to do—nominate candidates already chosen in primaries, ratify a platform already written and soon to be totally ignored—what would be the need for conventions? Maybe none. The fact they have been a habit since 1832 when the Democrats met in Baltimore and nominated Andrew Jackson? And the Republicans in Baltimore in 1856 nominated John C. Frémont? Is that history weighty enough to keep the parties riding a tired old horse not dead yet but severely spavined and barely able to walk?

Beyond a habit a century old, there are some options.

As one who has attended and worked on a total of twenty-two conventions since 1952, I think this is a proposal worth trying, or at least worth studying: fifty primaries, one in each state. They could all be held on one day but probably should be spaced out over some weeks to give the candidates time to raise money and travel the country and campaign. Then the political parties meet in each state to choose three or four delegates to a small national convention, there to cast the state's votes for the winner of its primary and on the same day to ratify the nominee's choice for vice president, now already no more than a routine detail to be disposed of in ten minutes. That and the essentially meaningless approval of the platform already published days in advance and then ignored, all could be accomplished in one long evening session. Quick, largely painless and not long enough to be so boring as to drive the audience away. Quick because it would stop the parties' nonsense of trotting out a seemingly endless series of speeches by obscure candidates for obscure offices in the hope that television exposure will help elect them. Maybe it would if they actually got any television exposure. But they don't. The networks decline to put them on the air, preferring to cut away to something else they hope will be more interesting than a speech by an unknown candidate drooling a trickle of clichés. If all that were eliminated nothing would be lost, and that alone would shorten a convention by a third to a half. The new candidates could get television exposure in their home states. It was always quite silly to trot out somebody running for a seat in the House of Representatives and put him on national television. Silly because there are 435 congressional districts from coast to coast, and the parties often put on the air a politician running for office in only one of them, meaning that listeners in 434 of the districts across the country could not vote for him if they wanted to.

If this were done the candidate for president would then have full network coverage for his acceptance speech, probably the major speech of his life, minus the time-wasting distractions of minor candidates speaking endlessly and driving the delegates out to the bars and bathrooms and minus the delegates milling around in the aisles and chatting with each other. In a convention this small, people in their home states could see and identify their own delegates and could even watch their behavior.

The parties have already moved some distance in this direction, eliminating afternoon sessions and in that one stroke ending the thousands of peevish, querulous complaints from the devotees of afternoon soap operas, furious to find that in the soap based in a hospital the handsome doctor, instead of pawing the nurses in the linen room, has been wiped off the air by an overweight politician. This afternoon ritual is nearly religious, and a politician or anyone else disturbing it does so at his peril.

If this proposal suggests too little time for serious discussions and speeches on the issues, all of that surely would have been done already, during the primaries. Any politician remotely likely to be nominated for president could be seen and heard on dozens or scores of television programs across the country—press interviews, talk shows, paid politicals, news programs if and when he makes any. By now he could be Larry Kinged and *This Week*ed and *Met the Press* enough to satisfy any ego, however hungry for attention, and if anything is left unsaid, it would not be for lack of airtime. This would save a great deal of time, a great deal of money and certainly would be more interesting to the television audience than the present four days of endless, repetitive droning of platitudes from an out-of-date high school civics text. The parties would and should be preserved intact. In a country thousands of miles and many time zones wide, Washington and the president and the Congress are remote enough as it is, and we need the parties to help tie together this huge, sprawling nation. I believe this system would help build our parties into something more than the ninety-seven-pound weaklings they are now. All the world's developed countries have political parties in one form or another, and in my judgment we need them and need them to be stronger and more effective. And more responsive.

Throughout American public and political life there is a more or less continuous call, or low-level nonstop droning sound, asking for some kind of reform, for improvement, for more fairness and more attention to the people's real problems, or just for more, period. From time to time over the years Congress has responded, if feebly, by appointing one committee after another to study one reform after another, but the members have seldom been seen to reform anything. Why? Because all those appointed to study reform were members of Congress who had run for office and been elected and instinctively believed a system that sent them to Congress and kept them there was working perfectly and clearly did not need reform. Could not possibly be improved. If they were ever serious, members of Congress would be given the unlikely or impossible task of reforming themselves, since the reformers and the reformed would be the same people. So nothing happens. One sentence that ought to be engraved in copperplate Gothic in the political pantheon's sacred texts: ONLY LOSERS WANT REFORM.

This warm, soapy bath of sensual self-satisfaction is not shared by the public. Every poll I have seen showed about 70 percent or more disapproving of how Congress was doing its job and pessimism about the country's future and the federal government's ability to deal with it. Then why, it's often asked, do we keep electing and reelecting almost all of the same members to Congress year after year, 80 to 90 percent of them? The answer necessarily is speculative, but what we always hear is that yes, people do dislike Congress as an institution, but they like their own local members. If so, it must be because usually they only hear from their local members in friendly, chatty letters they mail out by the thousands, postage free, or in brief snippets or sound bites sent gratis to their local television stations, tapes of themselves recorded in their own television studio at the United States Capitol, built for their own use with the carefully contrived appearance and trappings of news pictures skillfully made to look like journalism, which they are not. Then the constituents see television pictures of them delivering speeches on the floor of the House of Representatives, appearing to be addressing the entire membership, when in fact they are speaking to an empty House chamber with the camera carefully aimed to show only the speaker and framing out the empty seats. With this deceptive trick and a dozen others the U.S. Congress conceals from the public what it really is doing and not doing. Voting themselves a pay raise in the middle of the night, as they have done, was only one of their stunts. They have many others. And as every member knows as well as he knows his own name, the first priority is to raise campaign money and to get reelected at all costs, anything whatever to hold on to a seat in Congress and oppose anything that threatens it, even remotely. Further, when intractable and politically dangerous issues such as rising illegitimacy, race, crime and abortion are forced on Congress's attention, whenever possible it declines to act and leaves these questions to the courts. Judges do not have to win elections.

Across fifty states massive numbers of people, politically active and inactive, are out and around every day talking and listening to each other in shopping malls, dime stores, coffee shops, bars, offices, factories and on front porches, where American life is lived. And where, ultimately, most political opinion slowly coagulates into some kind of form. I believe most political decisions are made by people who do not think of them as political at all. But collectively they create an upwelling of opinions, choices, likes and dislikes of the millions of Americans represented by the 535 members of Congress. In this huge country all this gradually evolves

into the American public's conventional wisdom. If
our parties were a little more developed they could
help tie together this huge, sprawling and complicated country.

HUNTLEY and I were required to belong to the
union called the American Federation of Television
and Radio Artists—AFTRA. The title gives most or
all of us members the benefit of considerable doubt
that we could claim to be artists. We could claim
to be journeymen reporters, newswriters, and pro-
fess a few other minor skills. But artists?

I never gave any thought to this and seldom paid
much attention to the union at all. Huntley and I
both had individual contracts with NBC spelling out
our terms of employment, and while the network's
contract with AFTRA required us to belong to the
union and pay dues to it and we did, it really had
little or nothing to do with us. That was so until the
word came that AFTRA was calling a strike at the
end of March in 1967. I had no grievance against
NBC, nothing to strike about, no demands to make,
and I really did not want to walk out, seeing no
sense in it. But my lawyer, Jack Katz, advised me
to refuse to work. "There's a lot of union members
in this country," he said, "and if you cross the
picket line it will antagonize them and it could damage your career."

So, I declined to work while Huntley declined to

strike. He showed up every day and carried on our news program without me, saying in private what he had said for years, that AFTRA was a union composed mostly of show-business people—"tap dancers and jugglers," as he put it—plus various office workers and elevator operators. Journalists, he thought, were or should be a kind of priesthood answerable only to their readers and viewers and should not belong to any union and should not join a strike, particularly one having nothing whatever to do with us. If journalists wanted a union they should have one of their own, he said. I generally agreed with him, even though all of that rhetoric sounded slightly snobbish. And Walter Cronkite dressed him down a bit and said, "Chet, if you don't like the Army you should have got out before the battle started, not now."

The New York *Daily News* carried a front-page headline in boxcar type: CHET TALKS, DAVE WALKS. In the first and only strike of my life, I learned this much: once it starts, it is impossible to find out why you are striking, and in fact impossible to find out anything at all. Meetings were being held, we were told, but what was discussed and what was accomplished, if anything, nobody knew. For the two weeks of our strike, I never learned anything about what was going on. Only after it was over did I find out the source of it was a small group of announcers at FM radio stations owned and operated by the three networks in New York, Chicago and Los Angeles, fighting over their fees for reading commercials. Since I was not working in radio, did not work in New York, Chicago or Los Angeles, had never read a commercial in my life and had never collected a commercial fee, I did wonder why I was striking. The issues, such as they were, had nothing to do with me. But I did not cross the picket line.

It soon began to appear that both Huntley and I had made a mistake. The mail from the television audience across America was hostile. The letter writers assumed I was striking for money and accused me of greed, trying to squeeze more money out of NBC when I was overpaid already, etc., etc. All of this was false but there was no way I could respond to it. Huntley's mail on the other side of the dispute was just as ugly. He was accused of being so rich and famous he cared nothing for the other and lowlier members of his union.

I thought when the strike was over and things returned to normal the audience's anger would fade away. I was wrong again. It did not fade away. Shortly, we began to notice a decline in our Nielsen ratings. They continued to drop, and soon we were in second place behind Walter Cronkite and CBS for the first time ever. We guessed—since we never knew—that I had antagonized the antiunion people in our audience while Huntley antagonized those who were pro-union, and that the two of us together had managed to antagonize both sides. True or not, after holding first place in the evening news broadcasts for eleven years, suddenly we lost it in late 1971. We were second and Cronkite was first.

We never got back the viewers we had lost. We were never sure why we lost them, but then—like everyone in broadcasting—we were never sure why we had them in the first place. Nielsen can tell us about how many people tune us in but cannot tell us why. In the strange, unreal, metaphysical and unexplainable relationship between television broadcasters and their audiences it was and is never possible to be sure of anything. What is here today can be gone tomorrow, leaving no message behind.

NBC was disturbed at our loss in the ratings but did not know what to do about it. Huntley took it in stride because he was ten years older than I and was looking forward to retirement anyway. He was the son of a station agent for the Great Northern Railway in East Point, Montana, where his father had worked at the traditional yellow oak rolltop desk with a telegraph key clicking and bringing in such messages as "Train 114 four minutes late." Huntley loved all this—huge steam locomotives powerful enough to pull strings of heavily loaded cars across the Rocky Mountains, roaring through his town without slowing down on their way to Chicago, whistle screaming, cinders flying, the ground shaking under the assault of their tremendous weight and power. Huntley had grown up with this and loved it and the West so much he always wanted to get back to it. For him it was a time when the American love affair with the railroads was still alive, if fading. The trains had opened the West and created a continent-wide country and then remained around long enough to see the airlines take away most of their passengers. Once I was traveling with Richard Nixon's campaign in some small town I can't remember but somewhere in the northern plains, a town of a thousand or two voters, where Nixon stood and shook hands for half an hour on the main street under the town's one traffic light. When he finished and went inside to use the bathroom, I noticed people were all drifting down the street in the same direction, intent on something. I asked what was happening. I was told, ''They're going down to the depot. The *Empire Builder* comes through here in seven minutes and they want to see it.'' That was the Great Northern's handsome, green-liveried luxury train from Chicago roaring through on its way to the Pacific Northwest, and I understood why Huntley loved it, and I understood why in 1970 he felt he had enough, retired from television at the age of sixty-one and headed back to the West. As a gift on his departure, NBC gave him a horse. Our saga ended, unhappily. I stayed on at NBC and wondered what would happen next. Huntley was always the friendly, open-shirted westerner who would have looked comfortable riding a quarter horse beside a herd of a hundred cattle, his leather saddlery squeaking and the chuck wagon rattling and bumping in the rear, driven by a cook looking and swearing like Walter Brennan. He lived in New York but never became a New Yorker. He refused to have his telephone unlisted, even though we warned him that keeping his name in the book would bring angry calls from viewers across the country awakening him at 3:00 a.m. to argue about something he said on the air.

He asked, "If they are nice enough to look at our program and want to talk about it, can't I be nice enough to listen to them?"

Well, yes, but not when they're drunk and calling in the middle of the night. One Sunday afternoon my wife and I were in New York, and we dropped by the Huntleys' house on the East Side for a drink and a visit. The phone rang. Huntley answered and described the conversation later:

"Hello."

"Is this Mr. Huntley?"

"Yes."

The caller said he was Judge Somebody or Other from Louisiana. He and his wife, Tillie, were in New York and didn't have anything to do, and he wondered if Huntley would have dinner with them tonight.

To our astonishment, Huntley said yes, he would love to come to dinner.

That was about as un–New Yorkish as it was possible to be. Who and what was this judge? How would Huntley even know if he was a judge at all? He could be some kind of con man. Most likely, he would run out of conversation before the shrimp cocktail was finished, and from there on Huntley would have to struggle to find something to talk about. He told me later that was exactly how it was.

In his office at NBC, Huntley began to notice that the twenty-four volumes of his *Encyclopaedia Britannica* were disappearing, one each day, from the shelves over his desk. The night cleaners were stealing them and taking them home. Huntley watched, halfway amused, for about a month, doing nothing. When only the last volume was left, the one with VASE-ZYGOTE stamped on the spine, he took it off the shelf and locked it in his desk, saying to me, ''Now they'll never get a complete set.''

He always looked at New York City's successes and failures as if seeing them from a distance, as if he were not actually here watching thieves at work, as if he were not actually walking through the city streets littered with candy wrappers, beer cans and empty pint bottles of Boone's Farm. He looked as if he were on a casual ride through town, reining his horse down to a slow amble and pointing him west.

ON THE LAST broadcast we did together, I recalled a little experience I had years earlier and had told in public a hundred times. It was this: I was walking through an airport terminal on my way somewhere when a pleasant gray-haired woman stopped me and said, "Excuse me. Aren't you Chet Huntley?"

I said yes. People often confused the two of us, it did not matter at all, and if I had said no, I was Brinkley, she would have been embarrassed and felt she had to apologize, which she did not, and during all this conversation I might have missed my airplane. So I said yes.

I still treasure her response: "Well, I like you on the news, but I can't stand that idiot Brinkley."

Huntley bought the ranch he had always dreamed of having. "I want a ranch," he always said, "where I can sit on the front porch and put my cowboy boots up on the railing and look out at my cattle standing around out there on my land a half mile away." He got what he wanted but had very little time to enjoy it. In about three years he was diagnosed as having cancer of the stomach and died quickly. And there was more bad news piled on bad news.

I became restless and irritable, away from home too much when my children were growing up; my marriage of more than twenty years fell apart and all the blame was mine. NBC, in one of the worst decisions it ever made, announced that since *The Huntley-Brinkley Report* obviously had to be called something else, it would become the *NBC Nightly News* (as it is still called), and the two of us would be replaced by a three-man news team. NBC decided and announced that John Chancellor, Frank McGee and I would rotate the nightly news program—Chancellor and Brinkley one night, Chancellor and McGee the next night, McGee and Brinkley the next, and so on. It was an immediate flop. We never knew exactly why. Chancellor was extremely good and so was McGee. Both top-level professionals. But we told ourselves, maybe rightly, that the audience disliked the constant changes, that at 6:30 each evening they wanted to see a familiar face or faces as they had for years, and that Walter Cronkite, capable and reliable, was more appealing than a group that changed every night. Right or wrong, the three-man team was a failure. Their next change was to move McGee to the *Today* program and put Chancellor and me on together for a time, still looking for something, anything, that worked as it had in the past.

Nothing did. Then they asked me to revive a weekly program I had done in the past, television's first magazine program, called *David Brinkley's Journal*, fairly successful but nothing sensational. The idea of a television magazine did become a sensation later when Don Hewitt at CBS borrowed my idea (I didn't own it and he was welcome to it) and produced *60 Minutes*, which became the most successful public affairs program in television history. It still is, today.

ON APRIL 4, 1968, about forty of us in the press and television were ready to fly with President Johnson to Honolulu where he was to attend a meeting of American diplomats and others in the Pacific area to discuss a peace offer to the South Vietnamese. This had been so long in coming, the American people's support for a bloody and pointless war had turned so sour, he was ready to negotiate.

In the early evening, we sat in our plane parked at Andrews Air Force Base outside of Washington, waiting. The departure time given us by the White House came and went. We wondered. Then the news came: Doctor Martin Luther King had been shot and killed in Memphis, Tennessee, where he had been trying to settle a strike of garbage collectors. One shot by a sniper and he was dead on the balcony of the Lorraine Motel. God only knew what that meant, but it certainly meant Lyndon Johnson was not flying to Honolulu tonight. We scrambled off the airplane and took taxis back downtown. Before we got there we saw the skies turning red, the flames rising ever higher. And soon we were close enough to see that Fourteenth Street was a two-mile stream of fire. H Street Northeast was another. Both had in the past been commercial streets with restaurants, movie theaters, jazz clubs, including one called the Kavakos Grill, where Washington people of my generation were introduced to something variously called progressive jazz, or bop, or something else. Now there was no music, and looting was rampant. We saw men and women climbing out through broken store windows stealing whiskey and television sets—then and thereafter to be the prizes of choice for those free to steal anything they wanted. Lyndon Johnson ordered the U.S. Army to take over the city and stop the looting. As I roamed around through the smoldering buildings a soldier, looking younger than one of my sons, told me to get out. I showed him my White House pass. He said, ''This is not the White House. Get out.''

His orders, he said, were to clear the area of looters. The fact I was carrying no whiskey and no television set proved nothing, he said. ''Just get out.''

Two days later King's widow, Coretta Scott King, led a march in mourning and spoke at the end, urging the crowd to ''carry on because this is the way he would have wanted it.'' And, choking on her tears, she asked the crowd, ''How many men must die before we can have a really free and true and peaceful society? How long will it take?''

I put all this on television, including her questions that are still unanswered and now, a generation later, many of the burned-out buildings are still burned out.

IN the 1968 political season in June, we moved all of NBC's political circus to California for the last big primary. My friend Bobby Kennedy, carrying on at the head of a now broken and suffering family, campaigned all the way across the country, wound up in Los Angeles at the Ambassador Hotel to hear the political news. He won. There was the usual celebration, a speech offering thanks to all those who had helped, worked in the campaign, put out the Ritz crackers and the jug wine and who now looked forward to the campaign for president. Bobby finished his little speech and pushed through the crowd, looking for breathing space and a drink and a chat with his friends. The nearest door opened into the kitchen. As he moved toward it, we thought we were about through for the evening, and Robert ("Shad") Northshield, the director, said in my earpiece we probably would get off the air in five minutes or so. Bobby walked into the kitchen. A man named Sirhan Sirhan was waiting with a gun concealed in his shirt. He pulled it out and shot Bobby Kennedy in the head. Roosevelt Grier, formerly a great football star and now two-hundred-odd pounds of muscle, quickly threw Sirhan to the floor, disarmed him and held him down. Shouts, screams, sirens. My God! Another Kennedy shot? Yes, another Kennedy shot. We forgot any plan to sign off the air and stayed on, waiting for news. We did not broadcast it, but the news looked bad. Frank Mankiewicz, doing press work for Bobby, came out and in a sort of press conference said the doctors had just arrived and did not yet know how serious a wound it was. But they soon found out the brain was involved. Mankiewicz, asking me not to use it on the air, told me privately the doctors said there was no hope. A matter of hours. A family barely recovered from a tragedy in Dealey Plaza in Dallas now had to face another one. At least, for the smallest of small favors, the identity of the killer was clear, and there would not have to be an endless and highly publicized and highly rancorous argument about grassy knolls, Cuban conspirators, and so on. Bobby died that night.

BUT LIFE in television went on as we traveled the country and the world with *NBC Magazine with David Brinkley*. Stuart Schulberg was one of our producers and an extremely good one. One day he came in accompanied by two very neat-looking young men in their twenties. He said they were two hitchhikers he had seen on a highway outside of Washington. He picked them up because he was intrigued by a large handmade sign they were holding up to passing motorists. It read: WE ARE BRITISH. Stuart interviewed them and thought we might put them on the air to tell their story. It was not news, but it might be an interesting feature for our magazine program. Their story was this: They were English college students spending the entire summer hitchhiking across the United States and had been given free rides all the way to California and back, each day keeping meticulous records of every person, nearly two hundred, who gave them rides, where they got in and got out and records of their conversations as they rode along, intending to use them for a dissertation when they returned to school in England in the autumn. Each driver picking them up was, not surprisingly, attracted by their sign saying they were British. But the most stunning and unsettling fact was that their notes showed 92 percent of those who picked them up sooner or later said to them, "If you were Americans I would not have picked you up." What has crime done to our country?

ON JULY 4, 1976, the bicentennial of our country's existence, television and every other communications medium made complicated plans to cover perhaps a thousand events on patriotic themes in fifty states, beginning in New York's harbor with one of the most splendid sights ever seen by anyone anywhere—a procession of great and magnificent sailing ships, four-masted square-rigged schooners and others, their immaculate white sails gleaming in the July sun, sailing majestically up the Hudson River. About every maritime country in the world sent its most beautiful ship to join the parade, a floating display of respect and affection for our country. NBC put me and its cameras on the roof of the World Trade Center, 110 stories high and overlooking the river. Visually, the most striking for me was Italy's ship, the *Cristoforo Columbo*. Not only was it splendidly handsome itself, but all the way up to the top of the rigging, two hundred feet above the water, I guessed, on every horizontal spar, standing at attention in immaculate white uniforms, were perhaps a hundred young Italian naval cadets, shoulder to shoulder—a stunning sight. I had always halfway thought in any question of taste, artistry, devotion to creativeness and beauty, the Italians did it better than anyone else. On this day they did. It was an event of such emotional power that New York City, for the only time in my experience, nearly came to a halt, was almost quiet, and on that day there was next to no crime.

Standing beside our cameras high over the river and looking down at the ships, I was expected to do some narration in the usual style of television. That is, a little light chatter, more or less in the style of the baseball announcer on radio who keeps talking about something or nothing even when the game is stopped and the home team is changing pitchers. Listeners are used to it and unconsciously expect it. If it stops they lay aside their knitting, look up and wonder why they are not hearing anything. Broadcasters are used to it. Without some kind of sound coming from somewhere they reflexively, a little nervously, begin checking their knobs and switches and VU meters. Their slight uneasiness lies in the fact that one small knob on the engineers' audio panel, a black plastic knob an inch and a half in diameter, stops and starts and controls sounds that originate more than a hundred floors in the air over New York City, are sent down to the ground through a million tiny wires, heavy cables, fifty thousand soldered joints, each one crucial, through underground vaults to NBC's control center at Rockefeller Center and then up twenty thousand miles in space to a satellite hanging there and waiting, receiving the sound and finally sending it twenty thousand miles back down to earth and around the entire world. It is no wonder they are always at least a little uneasy. This is not a great place for technical blunders. Even after a lifetime in broadcasting it continues to seem to me astonishing that it all works, and I still do not know how or why. But it is a miracle that occurs every day.

Looking down at the beautiful ships, I saw very little need to say anything and I almost didn't. When one of them filled the screen, I told its name and what country it came from and that was about all. By now I had acquired a reputation at NBC for being a professional talker who did not talk much. On a television program like this one, almost entirely visual, its purpose obvious to the viewer and with no need for explanation or clarification, I always shut up. Every once in a while when I was on top of the Trade Center, Shad Northshield, the director and a good friend, said in my ear, ''Are you there? Are you alive? Are you okay?'' He knew I was, since in his control room he could see me in the pictures flooding in from six or eight cameras, but he had the same tic affecting everyone in broadcasting—an involuntary muscular tension and the subconscious feeling during a period of silence among people accustomed to constant chatter that with or without any ideas or information somebody should say something. How else could they be sure everything was working? That all those soldered joints were holding together? But they all worked and it was magnificent.

IN THE MONTHS before our country's bicentennial year, NBC asked me to do a series of documentaries about the flow of immigration into the United States in the late nineteenth and early twentieth centuries, the countries the American people came from and how they got here. Northshield and I went to work on it. The records told us that a great many of the English, Irish, Scottish, German, Polish and Russian immigrants sailed to America through the English port of Liverpool. We found the docks there looking to be frozen in amber, as if nothing had changed in a century. The same docks, the same gangplanks with their woven wire enclosures, used by only God knew how many European immigrants walking up their wooden floors and leaving for new lives in America. Somebody's estimate was that the ancestors of maybe a third of the American people walked aboard ships up these same gangplanks at these same docks.

Nineteenth-century emigrants sailing to America, traveling as cheaply as they could, carried their own food aboard the ships, and along the Liverpool docks stood a line of small grocery shops that sold food to fill the emigrants' baskets. Almost incredibly, in 1976 many of them were still there. One still had on its front a polished brass plaque reading EM-IGRANTS SUPPLIED. The sign had been polished so many times for so many years that the lettering was barely legible, and with all the reflections in the polished brass it was impossible for our cameras to get a picture of it. I saw it as a splendid little artifact of American and European history that belonged in some museum in this country. I offered to buy it and to have a new and identical sign made to replace it. But the shopkeeper said no. People were always trying to buy it, he said, "but it's a part of our charmin' atmosphere and I'm keepin' it."

Even so, those of us who are not genealogists, and those who are, could look around these docks and daydream of an early America, knowing or not knowing how many of our ancestors walked up those gangplanks onto sailing ships leaving for Boston and New York, and wondering what we would be and where we would be, if anywhere, had they not sailed out from Liverpool to America.

From there we went to London to the wharf where the *Mayflower* set sail in 1620, intending to land in Virginia to meet the Englishmen who had arrived thirteen years earlier, aboard the *Susan Con-*

stant and the *Godspeed,* but it was blown off course and landed in Plymouth, Massachusetts, by mistake. We saw the *Mayflower*'s dock on the Thames in London and found the space occupied by a pub of the same name. The proprietor said the docks were the same, but some parts were not original.

Trying to stick to our schedule and our assignment, we went to Palos, a small place in Spain where Christopher Columbus set sail in 1492 intent on proving the world was round, a theory then somewhat in doubt. There was not much to put on television film but a rather bland monument to the admiral.

Hoping for something more interesting, we took our film crews down southward to the west coast of Africa, to Senegal and its capital, Dakar, and beyond, the source of millions of involuntary immigrants—slaves shipped to America to be sold to farmers to work in their fields of cotton, tobacco and indigo, to Americans in cities north and south eager to buy servants for house and yard work. Africans captured in tribal wars were held as slaves by the victors in wars and sold to the first outsiders to penetrate the interior, Arab traders. They were then marched down to the Atlantic coast and sold to shippers, mostly Dutch, looking for cargo to carry across the Atlantic, at a price. A story the White House was never willing to deny was that these Dutch slave shippers included ancestors of Franklin D. Roosevelt.

Senegal's minister of tourism heard we were in town and invited me to come with him for a walk around the town to admire the beauties of Dakar. I did not see any beauties. What I did see was the town park—a concrete slab surrounded by about a dozen wooden benches, all of them occupied by blind, lame, armless, legless beggars. I think the minister misunderstood my mission and assumed I was planning to use American television to urge thousands of rich American tourists to come to Senegal and spend money. When we strolled through the park, the minister apologized and said, "Mr. Brinkley, this is a serious problem for us. Every few weeks we gather up all these people and take them out to sea on a barge and push them over the side. But when we come back here, the benches are filled up again. It's a problem."

Dakar's one remnant of its terrible past was an island called Gorée, and on it the building, still carefully preserved today, where the African slaves marched down to the city from the interior, were held in leg irons while awaiting a ship to take them across the Atlantic Ocean. The cells and leg irons were still displayed as artifacts of Senegalese history. A sad, spooky and unsettling sight, and an affecting film sequence for our program, was the door at the back of the building opening directly out to the deep water of the Atlantic, where ships tied up and human beings sold as articles of merchandise marched out the door and into the hold of a ship about to sail to North or South America, where they would be sold again. Up and down the East Coast of the United States auctions were held in cities with slave markets when shiploads of Africans arrived. One was in my hometown, Wilmington, where a substantial building beside the Cape Fear River was used only for a slave market. The building is gone, but the name remains to this day: Market Street.

Within our film crew we had a problem of our own but did not yet know it. A unit manager is a network employee who travels with news film crews. His job is to reserve hotel rooms and airplane seats, rent the cars and pay all the bills. In traveling from country to country in odd parts of the world, as we did, the only form of payment acceptable everywhere was American cash, and so all of NBC's unit managers had to carry briefcases filled with currency, each usually holding many thousands of dollars. While we were finishing work in Senegal, we sent him farther down the African coast to make arrangements in Ghana, where we planned to do some filming. He returned the next day deeply upset. He said people at the airport in ragtag uniforms demanded to know what was in his briefcase. When he resisted, he said, they seized his case at gunpoint and told him he was in violation of Ghana's currency control laws and they were required by law to seize the case and its contents—thirty thousand dollars.

It was, we all agreed, another case of what was a common experience among people accustomed to working in Africa and dealing with its constant difficulties. With a little help from the American embassy we told NBC in New York what happened to our money and asked to have the thirty thousand dollars replaced. ''How?'' they asked. ''We can send you thirty thousand but how can we get it to you in American currency?'' The embassy did not have that much in cash. NBC had no banking connection in Senegal. Sending the money by courier would take several days, and we couldn't wait. We had to skip Ghana and cancel any further shooting and leave Africa, the last stop on our shooting schedule, and make do with the film we had.

We went home and put the documentary together, and it went on the air during the network's special program for the bicentennial. The critics and others said it was good. Somehow I never had a chance to see it and still haven't.

Meanwhile, my luck was running out at NBC. I was doing a magazine program I never really liked, but there was nothing else around. And it was put on the air opposite one of the highest-rated programs in television history, *Dallas*. On the night *Dallas* earned its most explosive ratings with a sequence some will remember, a series called ''Who Shot JR?'' and after they had let it run on for weeks while the suspense and publicity were built higher and higher, on the autumn night when the question

would be answered, CBS had most of the television
audience with its highest rating in years. Finally,
when the red-hot secret came out on CBS, who was
on NBC in the same airtime, opposite a program
that was attracting this tremendous audience? I was.
And I opened my program by saying to the audience: "You don't have to tune in CBS to see who
shot JR. Just stay where you are and when they give
the answer, we'll give it to you right here where
you are."

Cute, maybe, but it didn't help.

NBC agreed finally to let me off the magazine
program and even further agreed to let me organize
and own a weekly discussion program with several
Washington journalists. The key word here is
"own." If I owned a program I could have it syn-
dicated, pay the expenses myself and after expenses
take the income, if any. As it was, with NBC owning my program, we were all salaried employees,
and if we did a broadcast well enough to make it
successful, as *Huntley-Brinkley* had done for years,
however much money it brought in, many millions,
all Huntley and I ever saw were our regular paychecks, by television standards quite modest.

I still recall a conversation with my friend Julian
Goodman after he became president of NBC and
Huntley-Brinkley was flying high. The lawyers and
other correspondents' agents (I never had an agent;
never liked the idea of it; maybe I was wrong) told
me that what they were paying me was ridiculous,

that others bringing in far less than we were earning for NBC were paid far more. I asked Julian about this and he said, ''Yes. You are grossly underpaid. How much do you want?''

I hemmed and hawed, having never before been in position to name my own salary. He said, ''Just name a figure. I'll pay you anything you want. Any amount. We owe it to you. But I should remind you that whatever we pay you the federal income tax will take seventy percent of it and the District of Columbia where you live will take another ten percent. So with all of that and other odds and ends in the tax law you will wind up with maybe fifteen cents on the dollar.'' Under my breath I cursed the House Ways and Means Committee and the Senate Finance Committee and all their members for what I saw was greedy and abusive politicians committing an outrage on the American people and decided it made no sense to accept a pay increase and to become simply an unwilling conduit to the federal tax collector. I was urged by NBC's tax lawyers to defer money. I did. I deferred some just in time to watch the inflation of the Jimmy Carter years destroy half its value. But I went ahead with organizing a half-hour discussion program on Sundays.

I was interrupted here by this news: NBC learned what happened to the thirty thousand dollars the unit manager said was taken from him in Africa, in Ghana. It was not taken from him. He stole it. He hid it in his baggage and brought it home when we

returned to the United States. He was found out because a number of unit managers had been caught
stealing from the company, and each one, when ap-
prehended, named others. It was a humiliating scandal for a much-admired network.

This all led NBC to hire a woman of grace, charm
and talent, an officer of the IBM corporation named
Jane Cahill Pfeiffer, and to bring her in as chairman
of the board. It was a resounding title but with
limited powers, since the real power lay not with
NBC's board but with the board of the network's
owner, RCA. She was a splendid woman, yes, but
however much she knew about IBM's computers
her knowledge of journalism and broadcasting was
zero or less. But she was given the task of cleaning
up the scandal among the unit managers, finding the
guilty and firing them. She did. Many thought she
was overzealous in hanging people who had stolen
nothing but who had failed to inform on others who
had. The network stonewalled in public, trying to
avoid embarrassment. Its decision was to fire those
who stole the money but not to prosecute them.
Court trials with lawyers and accusations and denials and massive press coverage would have run
on for weeks or months. It was decided to recover
whatever money could be found (very little) and to
get it off the front pages as quickly as possible.
Pfeiffer's next task was to deal with me. She organized a lunch for me and the top executives of
the news department, "for a discussion," she said.

A discussion? Of what? If they were planning to fire me, fine. It would be good news. My contract had years to run, and if they let me go they would have had to continue paying me anyway even if I worked somewhere else. I could even go back to Wilmington, live happily on the beach, work on the *Star-News* while continuing to cash NBC's paychecks. The more I thought about this the better it seemed, and I was halfway hopeful they would fire me. But no. The purpose of the meeting was to tell me that in spite of our agreement, I would not be allowed to own and syndicate a weekly talk program, which was what I wanted. Why not? Nobody would answer. The program I was planning went on without me, and it is on the air today as *The McLaughlin Group*. But for Pfeiffer it would have been *The Brinkley Group* or some such. I don't know what was in Pfeiffer's mind, if anything. So what was I to do? Carry on with the magazine program, *NBC Magazine with David Brinkley*, I was already doing. That was the reason for the shrimp and the teacups and the politely pointless conversation about nothing while I waited just to see why I was there. I was disappointed not to be fired.

It got worse. Pfeiffer colluded with a pleasant enough corporate lawyer named Richard Salant, then an officer of NBC, who knew little more about news than she, and the two of them resolved—without asking or telling any of us—that what NBC News needed was to hire a third-level news executive from CBS named William Small and make him president of NBC News. My wife called a friend at CBS and asked him what he knew about the new man. His response: "Small is small."

Later I was told that as a CBS executive Small had tried to get some degree of control over *60 Minutes*. Its executive producer, Don Hewitt, was king of the CBS hill, running the most successful news-oriented program on television, as he still is, and in effect refused to pay any attention to Small. And politely let him know his opinions were not welcome. In television when your program is at the very top in the ratings and earning piles of money, you can speak that way.

When he arrived at NBC as head of news, he very quickly moved in on *NBC Magazine with David Brinkley*, our nearest equivalent to *60 Minutes* but not as good, and began trying to dictate to me what I should put on it. For example, on my magazine program, like all of those on the air then and now, we did news-feature stories prepared days in advance. Small argued that I should include whatever spot news developed late on the day of our broadcast, Friday. I tried to explain to him it was impossible. In a given amount of airtime, one hour in this case, it was extremely difficult to fit in three, four, five features, six commercials, and openings and closings, and to have it all fit into the allotted airtime with a variance of not more than a second or two. Force items of more or less last-minute news into this package late on the day of the broadcast and something has to go. If the material in a magazine program has been put together skillfully, no element can be cut without damaging it. Moreover, trying to do a program as Small insisted was silly. I was on the air shortly after the regular evening news programs, and whatever fresh news there was, if any, would already have been told minutes before on the evening news before I could get to it. Trying to explain all this to Small was frustrating. It seemed to me by now as if he might be trying to establish his authority as head of NBC at my expense. And at the same time it looked as if he were busily trying to turn NBC News into CBS News by hiring one after another newsperson from CBS and installing them at NBC. Roger Mudd, Marvin and Bernard Kalb and others. Nobody minded that. Most of the people he brought over were highly qualified professionals. What I did mind very much were his suggestions that NBC was inferior to CBS, all the more infuriating because in those years most of the time CBS had been a poor second. With ordinary common sense and sensitivity all of this could easily have been worked out. It never was. Again, having no choice, I wanted to quit NBC. Thornton Bradshaw, a highly civilized man, and his wife, Pat, were friends of Susan's and mine before he became chairman of RCA. When Small was hounding me and I was in need of help, I went to Bradshaw and asked him to allow me to leave NBC.

In effect, but not in these words, I asked Bradshaw, ''Fire him or fire me.''

Days before, there had been some corporate up-heaval in the RCA boardroom, and far too many executives were being fired for reasons never clearly explained. In 1981 the *Wall Street Journal* reported all this in embarrassing detail on page one, column six, calling what was happening ''blood on the carpet at RCA.'' It was so messy the board re-sponded with a flat order that nobody anywhere in the company was to be fired for any reason. The publicity was too ugly and RCA wanted no more of it.

Bradshaw responded in his typically gentlemanly fashion that Small probably should be removed, but in the current climate he was under orders not to get rid of anyone. But he would ask NBC to release me from my contract and allow me to leave. After I tried to get fired and failed, I was allowed to quit. Emotionally, it was a rending, wrenching experi-ence, inducing tears for Susan and me for several unhappy hours in our New York hotel room. To leave my working home of most of my life, thirty-eight years, after having a part in bringing television news to America, of being present at the creation, was it going to end like this?

No, it was not. Roone Arledge and Richard Wald of ABC News were calling. Arledge then was build-ing a news department that in time became the best in broadcasting, the leader. For the moment, he said he wanted to improve, to rebuild, a Sunday-morning ABC interview program called *Issues and Answers.* Its tired and boresome format, like that of NBC's *Meet the Press* and CBS's *Face the Nation*, then consisted of one or several reporters interviewing a politician or two and struggling to draw out some insights, thoughts or even once in a while a little news. They usually failed. But the programs were cheap to produce, and they could be entered in the networks' logs under the rubric "public service," a category loosely construed and looking good when it came time to renew their broadcast licenses. And the old Sunday-morning programs were at times used to give a favored politician airtime to promote himself or some legislation he was pushing, perhaps some legislation beneficial to the network. And beyond all that, late Sunday morning is for television an inconvenient hour, but the time has to be filled with *something.* For all these reasons one of them, *Meet the Press*, is the longest-running program on the air, any air. It began in radio days, the work of Lawrence Spivak, who may have been the first man in America to festoon his entire house with NO SMOKING signs, and a woman named Martha Rountree, later a fervent admirer of Senator Joe McCarthy. She said to me one day, leaning against the mantel in somebody's living room, "When you're trying to save America as I am, you have to take some chances." The two of them moved their program to television, inviting newspaper reporters to question the guests, since the program's title referred only to the press and when it began newspapers were the only news medium widely circulated and trusted. Plus the fact newspaper reporters were willing to work free, thinking it might be helpful to them professionally if their publishers across the country saw them in Washington publicly interviewing some big-time politician. On television as it had been on radio, all three of the Sunday-morning interview/talk programs had gone stale, tired and tiresome. Roone Arledge was the first network executive to see this and to demand something better. He and Wald asked if I would be interested in working for them on a new Sunday-morning program they had already planned and designed. They said it would be an hour, the cast would include me as a moderator, plus two other Washington journalists, and we would question two, three or four guests, give a background report on the week's topic and finally an ad-lib discussion for the remaining time among the three of us and a fourth correspondent, a different one every week. I signed up and moved to ABC.

Then there occurred a small miracle. A fairly complex television program plotted and planned in advance in dozens of meetings over many months appeared on the network in September 1981 with everything in it broadcast exactly as discussed in all those meetings. Arledge even chose a title, *This Week with* ————, the blank to be filled in when he decided who would preside over the program. In choosing the title Arledge gave himself a little protective edge. If the show was a flop they could change the moderator's name without having to change anything else. Thanks to Bill Small I was unemployed at the moment, and the name they wrote in was mine. Down to the last ABC remembered that, as always, every television program is expensive and every one is a gamble. Failure is always possible, probably even likely, considering that all broadcasting is relentlessly competitive. But the existing Sunday-morning programs, including ABC's, were so lacking in energy or ideas that they offered little competition, and ours was a quick success. We took the lead in the ratings and have held it almost every week since, for about fourteen years now. NBC and CBS responded, of course. CBS created a new Sunday-morning version of its program, *Face the Nation*, with Bob Schieffer, a solid veteran of the television wars, and NBC brought *Meet the Press* into the twentieth century with a new format and a new, very talented and aggressive moderator, Tim Russert. All three programs were vastly improved, and while we won the ratings, the real winner was the audience. Why did we win? Because ABC had assembled a group of newspeople with formidable skills.

Sam Donaldson, who came to Washington from Texas, in time became White House correspondent for ABC News, arriving there to find the press corps, like everything else in Washington, had swollen beyond recognition. Where in the past, during my years of working there, two or three dozen reporters showed up at the White House on the days of presidential press conferences, now there were a hundred or more, and the sessions with the president came to resemble used-car auctions with a room full of reporters shouting to be recognized. Sam studied this scene and concluded that the only way he could ever be noticed, stand out in what had nearly become a mob scene, ever get to ask a question of the president, ever to help ABC News rise from a puny third in the television news world, was to be a little louder, more pushy, more aggressive than anyone else. He was. It worked, yes, not because he was loud but because he was good. He kept himself well informed, and he was not so eager to be welcomed in Washington's social salons that he was unwilling to ask the one tough, ugly question that every president hoped nobody would ask. Sam asked it. Of course, there was some grumbling among the other reporters, complaints that Sam could be rude and embarrassing, and whatever happened to courtesy, to manners, to the old-time presidential press conference as a sweet and respectful intellectual tea dance? It was gone. But more often than not, it was Sam's tough question that produced the lead story on that night's television news and in the next morning's newspapers. Rude or not, he produced the goods. And he is still the same today. Since we have no rehearsals whatever, on Sunday mornings I often wonder what on earth Sam will ask. The folklore is that an occasional guest has refused to appear on our program in fear of Sam's questions. Since no public figure would ever admit this, I don't know if it's true, but I doubt it. Anyone tough enough and smart enough to be invited to appear on our program would be tough enough to deal with Sam.

George Will, on the other hand, is not a reporter and never was, and he is not a member of the ABC News staff. He is an all-purpose intellectual who works for us on Sunday mornings and on other occasions—elections, conventions and so on. That, incidentally, is why when I am away on vacation or otherwise, George does not replace me as moderator. ABC insists that job be filled by a full-fledged staff member and no one else. One may not in any way represent our news department without being legally, morally and contractually allied to it, as George is not. He does all kinds of work outside of ABC. He writes prodigiously—columns for newspapers and for *Newsweek*, books—lectures, travels the world and in his own crystalline prose reports what he finds. Conservative? Yes. He feels government is too big and too expensive and the bureaucracy intent on expanding its own power beyond its abilities. But who wants a discussion program filled with one more liberal love fest?

In these terms, I do not really know what I am. I decline to wear any label other than fairness and decency, since I know from long and intimate observation that neither political party, right or left, has the answers to our rapidly growing and increasingly dangerous social problems. As for the Republicans and Democrats, in dealing honestly with the country's real problems, I find one to be about as bad as the other and both pretty bad.

Cokie Roberts, our newest club member, brings a fresh view that no male could ever match or would try to match. She came with us about the time, or soon after, that American women finally were becoming major figures in this country's public affairs. It is not a point that needs laboring, but what about this one for size: the enormous state of California represented in the United States Senate in the midnineties by not one woman but two—Dianne Feinstein and Barbara Boxer. Cokie's late father was an esteemed member of Congress, Hale Boggs, representing a district in New Orleans. Her mother took her husband's seat when he was killed in an airplane crash in Alaska, and she held the seat until she decided to retire. Cokie is herself a correspondent covering Congress for National Public Radio. ("I do a morning radio program from home still in my nightgown.") In my opinion she knows more about the Congress than any one of its members. On the air or off, I've never asked her a question about the nuts and bolts of complicated issues before the Congress that she did not answer quickly and clearly. The truth is that the members themselves often seek her advice. Of course, Cokie is not really her name. It appeared in her childhood because her real name is a bit of a mouthful. Her full name is Mary Martha Corinne Morrison Claiborne Boggs Roberts. Of New Orleans. She is a knowledgeable woman with the longest name in television, and we could not do without her.

And it took some time in the beginning, some trial and error, to find three people, men or women, journalists or otherwise, because the demands are quite severe. The program is totally ad-lib, with no script, no rehearsal, no notes. They have to get through an hour of Washington and world affairs while millions watch, relying on whatever they had in their heads when they walked into the studio. Not everyone can do it.

If our Sunday-morning program is successful, these three, along with our production staff and our executive producer, Dorrance Smith, proud product of Houston, Texas, and among the best in television, are the reasons why.

However much we knew, and we thought we knew it all and carefully did not include a single shrinking violet in our on-the-air group, we did learn more about the political animal. We had known many Washington politicians long before our Sunday program started. All the way back to my late and entirely unlamented *America United*, I had interviewed many politicians on the radio, and it was so intensely boring that when NBC canceled it, there was not one word, one letter, one phone call of complaint, since it looked as if nobody even noticed. But now with our Sunday mornings on television the audience began to grow rapidly and the pols noticed, since they read the Nielsen ratings in John Carmody's columns in the Washington *Post* as carefully as we did. We began to see that when we invited them to appear on the air, they accepted immediately. And long letters from Congress members began arriving, describing new legislative ideas they were pushing, and saying, "If you think this would be a topic for your Sunday program, please call me." It was another case of success breeding success—they saw that our guests included presidents, cabinet members, the leadership of Congress, national leaders from around the world brought in to us by satellite, business and academic figures. ABC made it even a little more attractive by having a chef in our green-room kitchen every Sunday morning to serve what we believed was the best brunch in town. Guests? We wound up having to turn them away. And those who agreed to come first called in their speech writers, public relations persons, advisers and consultants, brainstorming in their offices on Saturdays and trying to guess what Sam would ask, what approach George would take, and what they thought was on Cokie's mind, and carefully working out their answers to the questions they thought would be asked. Most arrived in the studio with some kind of verbal set piece in mind, carefully worked out, repeated aloud a few times to decide about the sound of it, and including more or less clever, catchy sentences they hoped would become a sound bite and be picked up and repeated on other programs later and quoted in the press Monday morning. It was true that the wire services and the big newspapers assign reporters to tune in the Sunday discussion programs and take notes of any news we have made and send it out to be printed, usually with credit grudgingly placed far down in the story. Other television news agencies may simply tape our program off the air and choose a few quotes for their own use. That is why the program names and graphics are so prominently displayed in the background, to assure that whoever swipes our news off the air will have to let the audience see where he got it. And that accounts for the small, round "bug" in the lower right corner showing the initials of the network originating the picture. If you want to take our picture, you have to take our bug and show it on your screen. Roone Arledge said some time ago there were so many cable and broadcast programs now—fifty and more—that without the bug many in the audience would not know what channel they were watching. The networks spend millions trying to distinguish themselves from their competitors, knowing that people often forget or ignore the network's name, and the bug is there to remind them.

Through all this our Sunday guest arrives in the

studio primed and ready, having checked his notes again and worked over his sound bite again, and reassures himself that it's good enough. One I remember from a congressman in the Midwest was this: "Before I'll vote for this tax increase I'll go home to Iowa and jump off the barn." Hardly a candidate for *Bartlett's Quotations* but having the virtues of brevity, clarity and simplicity. Fine, but in the cut and thrust on the air, while he waits for a chance to throw out his rehearsed and carefully nurtured sound bite, it may happen that the question he needs is not asked. In that case, a more aggressive approach is required, like this: "Sam, if you were to ask me about this tax increase, I would tell you this." Then comes the answer he's been saving and waiting to use, and of course it has to do with jumping off the barn. Thought up on the spur of the moment, apparently. So it is that political speech has become a manufactured commodity, like sausage. And as with sausage, it includes some dubious and invisible ingredients best not described.

One of the more energetic practitioners of this simple art form was President Clinton. In 1992 the Democrats nominated him, the most verbose politician in modern times, and a reporter traveling with him estimated that during his campaign he talked at the rate of close to forty thousand words a day. At the previous convention, while still governor of Arkansas, he made a speech so long, so boring, it surely must have set a new indoor record for wordiness and tedium. Less than halfway through it, the audience stopped listening. As Peter Jennings and I were in our booth in the convention hall itching to get out before the restaurants closed, looking at the clock and waiting for Clinton to finish, he ran on and on, and what looked to be more than half of the delegates did not wait. They left their seats and wandered around the hall visiting and shaking hands. Or sat there and read newspapers. Some slept sitting up. It was in the Texas delegation, I believe, that I spotted two delegates playing gin rummy, using an empty chair for a card table. When I asked for a camera to move in on them for a close-up shot, they looked guilty and put the cards away. The only time the audience applauded Clinton was when he said, "In conclusion . . ."

I expect the next set of conventions to be my last, and this is the time to to recall some further thoughts and recollections from twenty-two of them.

In 1992 Senator Ted Kennedy tried to get a litany going with the question, "Where was George?"— referring to George Bush. He listed a series of political failures and ended each with the same shouted question, trying to get the audience to join him and shout along with him, "Where was George?" They did join in, while the Republicans privately offered their answer, "Dry, sober and home with his wife."

A new law in 1992 said members of Congress could keep their leftover campaign money and take it home with them if they retired from Congress that year. Representative Stephen Solarz of Brooklyn had more than a million dollars left over. Had he retired he could have taken the money home. But no, he ran for another term, confident of winning. His district in Brooklyn was predominantly Jewish, as he was. He told me when he ran for Congress the first time the polls showed him running far behind because the voters, looking at his unusual name, thought he was not Jewish. "But they came around when I circulated a pamphlet giving my mother's recipe for gefilte fish," and he won. But in 1992 his district boundaries were changed; many new people were moved in and added to the voting rolls. Solarz lost his seat in Congress and his million.

Another member of Congress, whom out of charity I will not name, kept his seat and gave his left-over campaign money to endow a chair in a small college in his district with the understanding that when he left Congress the chair would be his.

I believe it was Mary Matalin who wrote a speech for George Bush saying that with the end of the cold war the Democrats were "busily beating swords into pork barrels." Nobody is sure now who wrote his vastly more famous campaign statement, "Read my lips. No new taxes." Not even the usually tolerant and forgiving American electorate would accept a promise so clearly stated and so quickly broken. Watching all this in 1988 from ABC's high perch in the New Orleans convention hall, it seemed to me no candidate could say that unless he truly meant it. Most politicians' offerings include so many escape hatches and ambiguities that what seems to be a flat promise turns out to be a fuzz ball that looks like something but on examination is found to be so empty and insubstantial that the first breeze will carry it away. When Bush's promise blew away, there was the usual stream of excuses—Congress promised to support a tax reduction by cutting spending but in the end refused to do so, Bush said he was talked into breaking his promise by Richard Darman, his financial adviser, and so on. In what passes for truth in politics, it was another of what the crime writers used to call a caper.

We assumed Bush's promise would be kept and that he would be a candidate to become a statue in the park, or a roosting place for pigeons.

The differences in our two political parties could be seen in their behavior at their conventions. Year after year, Republican conventions were mostly alike, only some of the names and faces being changed. The Democrats could never leave anything alone. Not anything. Every year there were new rules on voting, new requirements on how many minorities had to be seated in the convention hall, which states followed the party's rules and their demands that each delegation must include this many women, this many physically handicapped, and this many of this and that many of that. It was very annoying at times. The chairman of the Massachusetts delegation complained the only way he could meet the party's requirements would be to cut some of his delegates in half. Not even the Democrats would allow this, and the perfect, mathematically determined "fairness" the Democrats wanted was never achieved and probably never will be. There is something in the Democrats' political bloodstream that wants to force people to be happy whether they like it or not, whether they want it or not, whether their definition of happiness is the same as the Democratic party's. All these ambitions, along with a faint, wispy and sticky belief that whatever anybody says, money will buy happiness. Of course it will. It absolutely will. Won't it? Only a Republican could deny that. Right?

Another memory I took away from Houston was of a woman wearing a huge mound of blond hair, driving a pink Cadillac convertible with the top down and carrying a Bible bound in mink fur.

IN JUNE 1994 ABC sent me and our Sunday program, along with about a hundred others, to France, to Normandy, to report from Omaha Beach on the fiftieth anniversary observance of D Day, June 6, 1944, when Americans, British, Free French, Dutch, Polish, Norwegians and Belgians fought their way ashore and straight into the muzzles of the German guns awaiting them—set, loaded, aimed, cocked and ready. Fifty years later Americans and others looked back with great respect to this day of bravery—yes, truly incredible bravery and self-sacrifice. With modern weaponry and military strategy an event like this is unlikely ever to be seen again, or needed again. The fighting on the beach was so bloody and bitter because the Germans' commander, Erwin Rommel, knew and said repeatedly that if the Allied forces were able to get even a small foothold ashore, the Germans would lose the war. Behind the Americans were about as many fighters and bombers as the skies could hold, and lined up for a thousand miles in a train of ships extending all the way across the Atlantic and back to America and now only waiting impatiently for room to come ashore was the most massive assemblage of military power in the history of the world. As Rommel said, if they were able to get ashore nothing on earth could stop them.

ABC and other networks and others from around the world arrived with their usual army of cameras and crews, producers, directors, technicians, twenty-million-dollar control rooms installed in trailers, the staffs of eight or nine different television news programs, including mine, from ABC alone, plus what appeared to be about all the television technical gear on the entire globe, mountains of it, feeding our pictures and sound to the top of a flimsy-looking, cobwebby steel tower rising 250 feet into the air and from there to our satellites 20,000 miles in space and then back to earth. The tower would only be used for three or four days and then dismantled and hauled away. Altogether, something like a thousand of us, a few famous faces but most of us unknown.

None of us had ever seen Omaha Beach, the scene of the most vicious fighting and the heaviest American casualties, and now a place of somber beauty with a clipped and manicured and perfectly maintained American military cemetery for thirty-five thousand men and three women (Army nurses) lying forever beside white marble crosses row on row for half a mile.

We had not known that Omaha Beach sloped directly from the surf up into French farmland and that the area for miles around was entirely rural. There was not a city or even a town of any size for miles. The farmland had been cultivated for maybe five hundred years and so meticulously maintained that when it rained, as it did, the top foot or two of topsoil turned into a gelatinous, thick, black, slimy mud no doubt great for growing crops to feed France, but impossible for us to move around in. ABC had to send out to buy rubber knee boots for us. There being no American troops remaining in France, the U.S. Army flew a contingent over from Germany, a group of uniformed men and women too young to remember D Day, but they were altogether splendid. They took charge, politely controlled the crowds, untangled the traffic on French country roads so narrow two cars could barely pass. Each driver tried desperately to stay on the pavement and out of the mud. If either car moved over enough to let the other pass easily, it risked having two wheels sunk out of sight, forcing a wait for a tow. We had to learn that most French highways have no shoulders. The thinking is that adding several feet of unused land alongside every highway would, collectively, use up hundreds of thousands of acres, more than a smallish country is willing to give up—an oddity for Americans accustomed unthinkingly to using land lavishly and wastefully. For us and our heavy trucks, the Army brought in the kind of steel grating designed for hurriedly building landing strips in the jungles, laid it down for several hundred yards and allowed us to drive in and out. At dinner in our hotel mess hall each night the speculation was that we would eventually disappear, gurgling and gasping and expiring in the mud, leaving nothing behind but rusting cameras and work spaces occupied by roosting chickens.

In time everything was in place, and here came the Americans who landed here fifty years before, all of them now in their seventies or more. And we contemplated the frightening details of what they had done, as told to me by the survivors. Listening to them, we tried to imagine this.

You are nineteen or twenty years old. It is midnight, pitch black. You are scrunched down shoulder to shoulder in a landing craft pitching and tossing in the windy English Channel. You have not an inch to spare for other young soldiers, all of them as miserable as you are. You are hungry. When you left England yesterday the Army handed you a little packet of something that, technically speaking, might have qualified as food, but in the terrible reality of the moment looks to have been created in some failed experiment in a test tube with heavy artificial coloring, a substance no supermarket would allow on its shelf. You are hungry, yes, but not quite hungry enough to eat that, whatever in God's name it is. You would give anything for a Snickers or a Baby Ruth. You are seasick and nauseous, but there is no place to vomit. If you can't hold it down you will have to throw up on somebody else or on yourself. When you need to urinate, try to forget it. There is no place for it. Somebody said the only urinal is your pants. Go ahead. Pee on yourself. Soon it will all be washed away in the English Channel anyway. Now you are so totally miserable that for a minute here and a minute there you are able to forget the near certainty that in a matter of hours you will be shot to death by a German gunner you never knew and never saw. You wonder how long it will take to die and how much it will hurt. When you are ordered to jump out of the landing craft and try to wade ashore you know that if the water is over your head you will drown. Drowning is painless, they say. With the sixty to eighty pounds of military gear strapped to your body, you cannot swim. If you slip and fall you will be unable to get up with all the weight and you will drown. (Hundreds did. In a few landing craft, the pilots chickened out and tried to dump their men far from shore, in deeper water where they could not possibly survive, the pilots hoping to save their own asses from the German guns by staying far back and out of their range. In a few landing craft, it is unknown how many, the men had to kill their pilots and take over the boats themselves and drive them in closer to give themselves at least some small chance to survive.) With all of that, when the time comes to jump it is light enough that you can see the water is streaked in red with the blood of those already killed, their bodies floating away with the tide.

Knowing all that, when the order comes to jump, who will do it? *Who* will do it?

Military leaders know when a soldier risks his life knowing he is likely to lose it why he risks it. Does he do it for Mom, home, the flag, apple pie?

No. He does it for his friends, his buddies in uniform. When they work together, march together, fight together, eat together, live in tents or sleep on the ground together, removed from the life they once knew, and in wartime knowing that soon they may have to die together, there is a bonding of the highest order.

Knowing the risk, knowing the likelihood of death, who would jump out of a landing craft?

They would.

They did.

VII

—————⚘—————

OVER THE YEARS it began to seem an ugly black cloud had settled over the Brinkley family, and I wondered if our good days were over. When I was in third grade my father, a sweet, generous and trusting man, a fifty-two-year-old Peter Pan, died of a heart attack. Only then was it discovered—to Mama's fury—that he had lent his friends thousands of dollars of the family's money, keeping no record of who borrowed it or how much. Around the corporate headquarters of the Atlantic Coast Line Railroad where he worked we were told later he was known as the softest of soft touches, willing to lend anyone anything he had on any vague promise of repayment sometime somehow, vague promises never kept. Why was his carelessness and casualness with the family's money never known until he died? Because in the small-city South in those years married women literally were housewives in charge of the house, the children, the family's meals and very little else. A wife was not expected to know anything about her husband's money and had no idea of even how much he earned. Mama told me in later years she never knew. When she needed money, she asked Papa and he handed it to her, usually in cash. No household financial records were kept or required because at that time there were no income taxes and no need to account for every dime. Mama asked around among Papa's friends, inquiring about his loans and who got them and how much. Loans? What loans? Nobody was aware of anything. What Papa had lent out over these years would have been the inheritance for me and his other children, and none of us ever inherited a dime. And for years when one of Papa's friends bought a new house or a new car, the conjecture at our dinner table was "He must have bought it with our money."

Margaret, assistant to the president of the Tide Water Power Company, her office on the second floor with no elevator, fell down a flight of stairs and injured her back. She lived in pain for the rest of her life. The typical small-town family doctor, Houston Moore (pronounced "Houseton" Moore), a physician and not a surgeon, told Mama, "It's too dangerous to operate. Cut the wrong nerve and Margaret could be paralyzed for life. Just use pain killers and live with it." Having no choice, she did.

My oldest brother, Jesse, was a near genius in mathematics, able to add, subtract and multiply large numbers in his head, but during Prohibition his head also was filled with a desire for bootleg whiskey, always available, whatever the law said. Often he called me in and said, "David, go over to the back door on Chestnut Street, you know which one, and tell Casper to send me a fruit jar." Whiskey from the bootleggers was routinely sold in quart sizes of Ball Mason jars, normally used for home canning of fruits during the summer to be kept and served in the winter. Ball State University in Indiana was a beneficiary.

When I came to think I was old enough to imitate my older brothers, I and several of my high school friends resolved to follow our high school football team, the Wildcats, to their afternoon game in Fayetteville, an hour's drive up the highway. And at the age of about fifteen we agreed to take along a fruit jar of moonshine. That was what we saw our older brothers doing, wasn't it? And since I had now been appointed to the exalted post of exchange editor of the *Wildcat*, the New Hanover High School newspaper, wasn't I now mature enough to drink a little bootleg whiskey? Didn't the adults at football games bring whiskey in what were called hip flasks, usually silver plated and curved to fit unobtrusively around the buttock and slide into a hip pocket, the screw cap held on with a small chain, since if anyone emptied the hip flask he would be too drunk to find the cap and screw it back on? All true, of course. On one single occasion in her entire life, Mama was induced to take a swallow or two of moonshine whiskey. She hated it and swore her first taste would be her last. It was.

In Fayetteville there was to be a parade before the game, a marching band, flags of the two high schools, the campus queen and so on, and since somebody in our group had his father's new Cadillac, or maybe a LaSalle, General Motors' second most expensive car, we were invited to ride in the parade. One member of our group of high schoolers, not one of whom had ever owned a car, explained to me the complex manufacturing processes in the automobile industry.

"The LaSalle is made with the scraps left over when they make Cadillacs. Same way the Chevrolet is made from the scraps left over from the Pontiac. And the Pontiac from the scraps off the Buick." Trying to educate me, he told me all this nonsense with such confidence and assurance. I still remember it.

On the way to Fayetteville I sat in the backseat and drank whiskey for the first time in my life. Its appeal escaped me. The taste was vile and disgusting, and it was nearly impossible to swallow. But the exchange editor of the *Wildcat* could not chicken out in front of his peers, could he? Of course not.

A little joke circulating then was that one man stopped another on the sidewalk, pulled a gun, handed the man a fruit jar of whiskey and ordered him on pain of being shot to take a drink of it. He did, gagging and wheezing and snorting at the truly horrible taste. Then the first man took the fruit jar back, handed the gun to the other and said, "Now force me to take a drink."

As our parade moved down the main street of

Fayetteville behind the brass band, I was feeling manly and thought I had to prove my manhood by taking several swallows from our fruit jar. Shortly, we rolled past the reviewing stand, the band playing, the flags flying, all the cheerleaders shouting and waving, and there I was hanging out the new car's window vomiting all over the upholstery and down the outside of the car and out into the street. It is not my favorite memory.

My brother William, red-haired and handsomer than any movie star and of course always called Red, drank very little. His interest was in pursuing women with such determination that his employer said to my mother, ''Red's a good man but he can't keep his pants on.'' Then he fired him. Whereupon the employer's wife became hysterical and demanded that William be rehired immediately. He was hired back quickly. I have no details on this event, but I can easily imagine some.

William's sexual successes mounted ever higher, and he became a bedroom phenomenon when it was learned that he had a low sperm count or something like that, and the women around town discovered he could not father a child. In a time when abortion was a criminal act and a doctor willing to perform one impossible to find, the women found William even more appealing because he could do everything else but he could not induce a pregnancy. He died of natural causes after a fruitless but extremely happy life.

It did seem to me now there were fewer Brinkleys every day. Mary, retired from Senator McCarthy's office, was beginning to be forgetful. Often she put a pot or a pan on the kitchen stove and forgot it was there until it began to smoke and burn. We worried she would torch her house. When I came to visit, she kept asking me, "David, will you drive me out to see Mama?" when Mama had been dead for ten years, and it was unbearably pathetic. Her Alzheimer's was gradually growing worse, and in time she did not recognize me, her only living brother and the only family member surviving from 801 Princess where we began.

My mother suffered grievously among her Presbyterian church members for bringing me into the world when she was forty-two. The church ladies thought it improper for a woman to be pregnant this late in life. I never was sure if they disapproved of my being born or of the salacious behavior that led to it. They never let up on her, and she suffered all her life. However many Presbyterian ladies were annoyed by my arrival, I was glad to be here and to be the youngest family member by almost twenty years, and giving me the terrible privilege of being around to watch my family disintegrate one by one, while I was still young enough to attend all their funerals. Mama's was the last Brinkley funeral I was to see. She died at eighty-seven.

This depressing period in our lives was not over. Eight years after I was divorced from my wife, Ann, she was operating her own antiques shop and, among much else, selling off the paintings, furniture, carpets and other stuff I had bought and left behind when I moved out, including a beautiful walnut pool table I had to leave because I had no room big enough to hold it. All of us laughed when she ran an ad in the paper and sold my pool table to the Montgomery County, Maryland, police department for its recreation room, where it remains. We laughed about this and the fact that when she sold my table she kept the $1,500 she got for it and then sent me the bill for the newspaper ad. I paid it, but we remained good friends.

But the laughter was brief. Eight years after our divorce and four years after I was married again Ann began to have trouble speaking, and soon we could not understand anything she said. We bought her a sort of computer-like keyboard that allowed her to type out on a screen anything she wanted to say. But soon that was of no use because she lost the ability to control her fingers. Finally, the diagnosis: amytrophic lateral sclerosis, otherwise known as Lou Gehrig's disease. All of us, adults, children, grandchildren, had to learn the horrible truth about ALS, as it is called. Gradually, it destroyed her nervous system so completely that she can no longer turn her head or move a finger or make a sound, and, even worse, leaving her mind unaffected so she is completely conscious and aware of the horrors slowly happening to her. The end result is a live, aware, thinking woman trapped in a totally lifeless body. Before she lost all ability to communicate—by moving her eyes, and in time even that went away—my sons and I asked each other how a merciful God could inflict such extreme cruelty on a more than decent, innocent woman. We have never found an answer.

BY 1971, divorced and a bachelor, I was living in Washington about a block from John Chancellor, who had rented a house nearby on Woodley Road, and one night he invited the NBC staffers to a party. About forty of us, maybe, including Douglas Kiker, another southerner, the pride of Griffin, Georgia, formerly of the New York *Herald Tribune* and hired at NBC for his suave and polished writing skills. He, too, was divorced and for the same reason many of us were—away from home too much. It is destructive to a marriage when the children graduate from grade school and their father is not there to congratulate them because he is looking for news in some place on the other side of the world. And for their birthdays, family celebrations, sports successes and awards, their father not only is not home, he is in some godforsaken place unable even to send good wishes to his children by telephone, television being about the only business that runs continuously around the clock every day of the year. Kiker brought to Chancellor's party his woman friend, Jeanne Daly, and her beautiful, talented roommate, Susan Benfer, an engaging midwestern mixture of French and Dutch. That was in September, I asked Susan out, it was all wonderful, she was and is one of the truly great women, and we were married the following June. Since I was a member of the Board of Trustees of Colonial Williamsburg, was and am devotedly interested in architecture, historic preservation and American history, we were able to have our wedding in Williamsburg's Carter's Grove mansion, which some think is the handsomest house in America. We brought Susan's and my friends and family from Washington and New York. We were married at the foot of the grand stairway beside what Williamsburg calls the Refusal Room, where it is said that first George Washington and then Thomas Jefferson proposed marriage to the daughter of the owner of the house, and she refused them both in the thought neither would ever amount to much.

Williamsburg was and is filled with wonderful stories. Later, I became chairman of its Raleigh Tavern Society, named for the building, now reconstructed, where Washington, Jefferson, George Wythe and others smoked clay pipes, drank rum and—for the first time anywhere—discussed the possibility of refusing to remain a British colony, breaking away and becoming an independent country to be called the United States of America. The society members were those of us willing to work and to contribute to keeping the little town's history alive.

After the wedding, Carl Humelsine, then chairman of Williamsburg and one of this country's great citizens, installed us and our guests in the beautifully restored little eighteenth-century houses kept for overnight guests. A breakfast was served at the Williamsburg Inn, overlooking the James River and near Jamestown, where the first permanent English settlers put ashore in 1607, and a bus decorated with flowers and with a caterer aboard rode our guests back to Washington or to the airport. Susan, meticulously, had arranged all this to perfection as she always did and still does. When the guests left she and I drove to my little country place near Woodville, Virginia, where several years before two of my sons, Joel and John, and I had a wonderful time hammering and nailing and sawing and building with our own hands a tiny house on some mountain land I had bought. We stayed there the first few nights of our marriage, at the conclusion of one of the great, or greatest, weeks of my life.

Now, years later, I am blessed with a wife I not only love, but respect. When she decides to work at it she is vastly competent in the kitchen and she also works part-time as a talented interior designer.

We have three sons and a daughter: Alan, the oldest, a history professor at Columbia University and winner of the American Book Award; Joel, an editor of *The New York Times* who spent years as a correspondent and won a Pulitzer Prize; John, the youngest, the one with movie-star looks and a writer for the Scripps-Howard newspaper chain; and Alexis, our only daughter, a graduate of the University of North Carolina in Chapel Hill and now holding a master's in special education.

Among our children's other triumphs, it was Joel, at about the age of twelve, who on a summer night ran around our front yard catching fireflies, or lightning bugs, and collecting them in a quart milk bottle. When it was filled with flashing little bugs, he put it into a paper sack, bought a ticket and carried the bottle into the Avalon movie theater down the street, set it on the floor, took it out of the bag, moved several aisles away and waited. In a few minutes the bugs began flying all around inside the theater and flashing their little lights in the dark. The audience burst into laughter. The management had to stop the movie and open all the exit doors to let the bugs fly out. The Avalon's manager may not have thought so, but I thought it was funnier than anything Hollywood ever put into his theater.

With all of this, I am blessed beyond anything that in my days in Wilmington, North Carolina, I could ever have expected or even imagined. Credit it all to luck, modest talent and chancing to be in the right place at the right time to start modestly in a new and promising industry, television, and to grow with it as it grew to its overwhelming presence today.

VIII

―⁂―

LIVING AND WORKING in Washington, it took me
some time to understand that our national capital
could be seen as the world's largest ATM—automatic teller machine—always ready to dump out
millions and billions to anyone who could push the
right buttons. So many have pushed so many buttons so many times our debt has risen to five trillion
dollars, so high we cannot pay it. We can only pay
the interest, now 15 percent of Washington's tax
income, and rising. If your ordinary ATM runs out
of money it shuts down and emits a nasty little buzz.
When our grand national ATM runs out there is no
buzz. There is no sound at all. Quietly and almost
shamefacedly we refill it with money borrowed at
the going rate of interest from Japan and Germany.
In time, will the Germans and Japanese be in a position to dictate to our government and set the terms
we must meet if we want to borrow more money?
Unless something radical and drastic is done, yes.

Whatever is said in the Fourth of July speeches,
whatever is said in Congress in remarks carefully
crafted, or assembled from spare parts, by professional speechwriters, however many times the warm
and loving symbols of gray-haired mothers and the
grand old flag are called up in support of a faltering

speech, in Washington in peace and war, it's always money.

IN JANUARY 1925 Calvin Coolidge explained to any remaining doubters that "the business of government is business." Until Franklin Roosevelt and the New Deal, it was. The real centers of power, all business-oriented conservatives, were a few members of Congress, none more influential than Republican Senator Nelson Aldrich of Rhode Island, whose name was to live on beyond him in the person of Nelson Aldrich Rockefeller, governor of New York and unsuccessful candidate for president. Aldrich was as near as the Senate ever came to having a boss. As a rooster watches over his hens, he watched over the interests of domestic business and industry. His most effective way of defending and enriching them was the tariff, the tax on imported goods. Aldrich preached that if Congress kept the tariffs high enough, American manufacturers would not have to bother about price competition from what he saw as a gang of foreign cutthroats smelling of garlic. And Americans would be free to do business and make money behind a protective wall of tariffs, setting prices as high as they liked. In time, ordinary and predictable greed pushed prices so high they brought hostile and strident political oratory from the Democrats. There were so many complaints about Aldrich's high-handedness he felt

a need to cool down his critics by promising to reduce or eliminate a few tariffs and allow some foreign goods to be sold here at reasonable prices.
Aldrich made some changes, nearly all of them
laughable and absurd and best described by Finley
Peter Dunne's Mr. Dooley: ''Th' Republican party
has been true to its promises. If you don't believe
it look at the list of free items they will let come in
without tariffs. Practically everything necessary to
existence comes in free. Here's the list: curling
stones, teeth, sea moss, newspapers, nux vomica,
Pulu [?], canary bird seed, hog bristles, marshmallows, silkworm eggs, stilts, skeletons and leeches.
The new tariff puts these familiar items within the
reach of all.''

Aldrich retired from the Senate in 1911 and died
four years later, living just long enough to see that
he and his political methods were coming to be history. In these early years of the twentieth century,
the country was outgrowing him and his gouging of
the public. The United States by now was being
pushed or invited or forced into other countries'
wars and was accumulating thousands of wounded
veterans needing hospitals and pensions, coming to
be too big and its costs too high to go on living on
tariffs squeezed out of foreign manufacturers trying
to sell their goods to the rich new country in the
West. It had to raise money on its own.

ON AN EARLY spring night, March 24, 1910, nine
hundred members of the New York Economic Club
gathered in the ballroom of the Astor Hotel in
Times Square. They were served a nine-course dinner of soup, a consommé with sherry, fish, fowl and
beef, four French wines plus a thirty-five-year old
port with a fruit and cheese course of Stilton and
brandied pears. The diners, all rich, displayed
varying degrees of overweight. Some of the heavier
club members were known to wear corsets. Without
exception, all wore the obligatory vest with four
pockets, ornamented by a gold chain draped from a
left pocket across the stomach, or paunch, through
a buttonhole to a right pocket and the obligatory
gold watch, either a Waltham, an Elgin, a Hamilton
or an Illinois. When my father wore this regalia, he
favored an Illinois, commonly known as a railroad
watch, weighing about half a pound. On its back
was an engraving of a locomotive flying down the
rails, its plume of smoke trailing back to the edge
of the watch. He liked it because when it had to be
reset it required a little project. He had to unscrew
the gold ring holding the crystal in place, pull a tiny
lever out from one side of the movement, turn the
stem to change the hands to the correct time, push
the lever back in and then screw the crystal back
on. After my father died I always wondered what
happened to his watch. But he lived long enough to
explain to me why it was made this way, why it
was so complicated. A railroad legend, he said, was

that a train's conductor, pulling his watch in and out of his vest pocket, somehow snagged the stem and moved the hands, causing his train to pull out of the station twenty minutes early, leaving the passengers with their luggage stranded on the platform, whereupon the Atlantic Coast Line Railroad fired him.

The Economic Club's dinner in the Astor Hotel proceeded in stately fashion. Nearly all the nine hundred smoked Cuban cigars, creating air pollution of such density that those sitting at one round table could barely see those at the next. The men in their heavy black woolens were not so much dressed as they were upholstered, beginning next to the skin with a union suit, so called because it was all in one piece—cotton underwear beginning at the neck with a collarless shirt buttoned up the front and continuing on downward into knee-length pants with fly front and a drop seat, meeting all of a man's personal needs in one piece. From there their garb worked outward to detachable high-neck stiff collars, black grenadine bow ties loosely tied in a contrived casualness, a scene out of Edith Wharton.

The Economic Club members were gathered to hear a debate on the great question of the day: Should the pending amendment to the Constitution permitting a federal income tax be adopted?

Far beyond the Astor's ballroom the idea, or threat, of an income tax was already afloat and already warmly detested by the prosperous. Ward

McAllister, the New York social leader who invented the term "the Four Hundred," the number of socialites refined enough to be received in Mrs. Astor's private ballroom, had already declared that if the income tax became law he would leave the United States. His threat might have terrorized the social world, but it was never tested. He died first.

When a spoon was rapped on a glass, the club members squirmed around in their chairs to face the head table and hear the speakers. First was Austen G. Fox, a club member and New York lawyer and an opponent of the very idea of an income tax. He rose, ground out the stub of his cigar in the dregs of his coffee and said, "I do not revere the Constitution because I revere the dead but because I fear the power of the living. In the first place, for the first time in our history we are invited to clothe the central government with the power of taxation unlimited . . . we are told the Congress will not exercise this power arbitrarily, or perhaps at all except in time of war. Well, gentlemen, does anyone believe that clothing the national government with a great new power is the best way to prevent its use?" (APPLAUSE)

Another lawyer and club member, William D. Guthrie, said he wondered why the Washington government, already awash in multimillion-dollar surpluses, needed more money. He said, "As Hamilton pointed out, the states were to perform the principal functions of government. They were to provide schools and colleges and asylums and hospitals. The states were to perform the functions of police. The states were to furnish funds for public improvements. The states were to perform nine tenths of the duties performed by national governments in other countries. . . .''

Yes, all true. But for the great majority of Americans, the more appealing fact was that in the tax law as then written, personal incomes below four thousand dollars (equal to about thirty-five thousand dollars in 1990s dollars) would be totally exempt and would pay no tax at all. Higher incomes would pay a maximum of 2 percent. Hardscrabble dirt farmers in the South, ranchers and Basque sheepherders in the West and even the despised sodbusters and the great majority of the American people almost never saw four thousand dollars in any year, and so it was clear that five or six prosperous industrial states in the Northeast would have to pay nearly all of whatever tax was imposed. California in 1910 was not yet developed enough to be a factor. And everyone understood when Representative James Monroe Miller of Kansas said, ''I stand here as a representative of the Republican party of the central West to pledge you my word that the great western states will be found voting with you for an income tax. Why? Because they will not pay it!''

Beneath the surface of the income tax debate could be seen one of the less attractive and less sensible features of the emerging American char-

acter, envy and resentment of wealth. It came to
these shores with the cold and unforgiving Puritans
who began arriving in the new world in the seventeenth century. They were English Protestants, so
furious they were willing to cross the Atlantic and
abandon their homes and their country because they
thought the churches of England were too lenient,
even going to the intolerable extreme of allowing
their members to accumulate more money than the
church thought they should have. In their Presbyterian and Episcopalian Sunday sermons, the message every week and every day was that money was
evil and it was evil to pursue it. Their spoor is still
with us. And so when the income tax was sold to
voters in the western states as a way to attack "the
luxurious incomes in the East," it was voted into
law by people who were confident it would punish
the rich they despised while they themselves would
never have to pay it. Envy and resentment carried
the day. In the U.S. Congress it still does.

EVEN THOUGH I was in Washington covering the
White House for the last years of Franklin Roosevelt's presidency and reported from the White
House every day when there was any news and
traveled with him on several trips, we only knew,
as everyone knew, the U.S. Treasury paid him one
hundred thousand dollars a year. And I was aware
that the Internal Revenue Service had investigated

the financial dealings of a Roosevelt friend and ordered him to pay twenty thousand dollars in fines,
interest and penalties. The president thought it was
too much, telephoned the director of Internal Revenue and told him, ''Cut his fine to three thousand.
I think that's enough.'' It is diverting to imagine the
scandal today if a president ordered the IRS to reduce a fine for a friend and it was duly leaked to
the Washington *Post*, as it would be. But in Roosevelt's case he made the call in the hearing of some
of us in the press corps, and nobody seemed to think
it was news or even very interesting. Perhaps because the city and its news media were not yet so
obsessed with money and not yet so curious and in
the habit of intruding into every person's private
finances. Perhaps because so few Americans then
lived on payments from Washington. Or because
the computer had not yet arrived and it was not
possible to load every American and every monetary detail of his life into the bottomless maw of
mainframe computers. We had not yet reduced, and
that is the word, reduced the entire population of
the United States into the computer's rows of 1s and
0s. And nobody laughed when we read Oliver Wen-
dell Holmes's opinion that taxes were the price we
paid for civilization. It was easy for him to be so
warm and generous when the top tax rate was 10
percent.

As for Roosevelt's personal finances, once in a
while we reporters saw his mother, Sara Delano

Roosevelt, walk smartly into his office, hand him an envelope and walk out, saying nothing. Press Secretary Steve Early told us it was his "allowance."

IN THE LATE thirties, the income tax now familiar and firmly in place, the law was that money owed the government from last year had to be paid this year in quarterly installments. Every taxpayer began each new year in debt to the government for the previous year's taxes and was allowed twelve months to pay up. It was a creaky and archaic system designed in another age and grossly inadequate for one of the world's great powers now deep in depression and slipping and sliding into world war. With taxes rising rapidly, what happened when a man, the head of a family, died? He left behind a year of debt but no income to pay it. What happened when a man with high income was sent into the Army when the draft began in 1940 and was paid the Army's stipend of twenty-one dollars a month? Clearly all this was an impossible mess until the answer offered by Beardsley Ruml, an economist and member of the New York Federal Reserve board and chairman of R. H. Macy and Company. His plan was accepted but only after great difficulty, argument and nastiness by the Congress and by Roosevelt.

"Pay as you go," Ruml said. Employers would

deduct the taxes from each employee's paycheck, and at the end of a year they will all have been paid. But if it was to be started on January 1, taxes for the previous year would have to be forgiven. Otherwise, the taxpayers would have to pay for two years in one year, impossible for most.

Forgive a year of taxes? Roosevelt erupted in vituperative fury. Let those big-business bastards get away with this highway robbery? Get out of paying a whole year of taxes? Never! He so hated the leaders of American big business because they all hated him. He called them "economic royalists." He thought they sat around in their boardrooms and their private clubs and told nasty, bitter jokes about him. He was right. And he hated them for trying every day in every possible way to block, obstruct and if possible destroy his New Deal programs, all of them. And it was noted that the Vanderbilts built a mansion far grander than the president's home in Hyde Park, New York, and built it just next door. Perhaps over the years it stood there mocking him.

It was explained to Roosevelt over and over that the business fat cats he despised would still have to pay their taxes in full each year. If there was any benefit for them in skipping a year of taxes they would not see it until the last year of their working lives. Finally and angrily, he relented; the withholding tax was introduced, to the working people of America and, not incidentally, to the U.S. Congress.

This change, combined with the wartime tax rates that eventually reached 92 percent in the top bracket, turned Washington into a money machine, an ATM.

THE WAR OVER, Roosevelt dead, President Harry Truman held a quiet, informal White House meeting with the leaders of Congress, mainly to decide what they should do about the Niagaras of money the withholding tax was pumping into Washington. As Vice President Alben Barkley described it to me later (here relying on my fairly good memory since I have no notes on this), he said the congressmen were restless and irritable.

"They went through the dry years of the war. Roosevelt reveling in being the boss. And lording it over us. He was running the war and all Congress could do was step aside and let him run it while we had to give him whatever he wanted. If we looked to be interfering with the war for political reasons the public would have torn us to pieces. We told Harry [Truman] we wanted to keep the money coming for a while. During the war we could do nothing for our people at home. A congressman couldn't even build a post office with his name on the front. All the money had to go to the war. We couldn't even argue. Now it's over and we want the post offices. We want money for our people who got nothing during the war. Everything was rationed. Now we want the roads and bridges and the hospitals. And we want our names on them.''

From this meeting the word went out: Congress was open for business again and had money again. Truman had spent years in the Senate, as Roosevelt never had, and he understood the psychic needs and the pains and pressures and night sweats afflicting a member of Congress, each representing somewhere near five hundred thousand citizens, most of whom wanted something. They agreed in the White House meeting that everyone had suffered enough in the war years, and now they were ready to let the good times roll.

THERE BEGAN a brutal, bare-knuckled assault on the lives and property and privacy of the American people. The withholding tax poured in more money than Beardsley Ruml could ever have imagined, partly because government soon learned what automobile and real estate salesmen already knew— if you talk to the customer about monthly payments, never mentioning the total price, it is much easier to sell a car or a house. In tax collections, the term ''take-home pay'' entered the language, and soon it was clear the government could take in far more without serious complaint if it deducted the money before the taxpayer ever saw it. If the immense sums being collected had to be handed over in one lump sum, surely there would have been a revolt. The withholding tax allowed government to keep the rates high, around 70 percent in the top brackets, long after the war was over, but Congress was so enthralled with its new money it was unwilling to give it up, and for twenty-five years it held on to it, an artesian well spouting cash, computers to count it and disburse it, an automatic, power-driven money machine never seen before and a true wonder of the world. With all this money theirs to spend, congressmen could buy votes and build post offices and roads and bridges and reelect themselves almost interminably. They did.

They also hired more staff, the population of Capitol Hill rising perilously close to thirty thousand souls. In addition to traffic jams and fights over parking spaces, they spent their idle hours writing wordy speeches and sending them to me and the others broadcasting news in the hope one of us would invite them to be on the air and explain why it was essential to have a new federal agency in his home state with a staff of perhaps forty thousand with a budget in the billions to perform some public service not previously known to be needed.

Here, for the record, are a few of the outrages inflicted on the American people in the name of taxation: a paragraph of instructions saying, ''Subparagraph B in section 1 G 7, relating to income included on parents' returns, is amended (1) by striking $1,000 in clause i and inserting twice the amount described in 4 A ii I and (2) by amending subclause (capital II) of clause small ii to read as follows. . . ."

What did that mean? Could anyone tell? In the thousands of pages of the tax codes were thousands of examples of this kind of tortured, or shattered, English. And thousands of examples showing how badly—no, horribly—our language was distorted, twisted out of shape and beyond comprehension in instructions we were required, on pain of imprisonment, to obey. Why does a decent, democratic country like ours run its tax collection system with tricky, indecipherable rules and regulations written in the nonlanguage of idiots, as foreign to English as Urdu, and daring you to make a mistake and threatening you with fines and imprisonment? My own judgment is that this qualifies as unconstitutional cruel and unusual punishment. We all know we have to pay taxes and most of us do it willingly, so why does the U.S. Congress and the House Ways and Means Committee—the guilty party here, not the IRS—operate its tax system in such an unwholesome atmosphere of fear, threat and menace?

Two reasons. One is that a former assistant secretary of the Treasury and "tax expert" named Randolph Paul, now deceased, devoutly believed and preached in the early 1940s that the purpose of taxation was not simply to raise money for government, but also to manipulate the American public's behavior. He preached that activities the government wished to approve should be rewarded with tax benefits and whatever it disapproved should be punished with one or another kind of adverse tax treatment. These were not moral judgments. One wishing to be critical could call them judgments based entirely on greed. Not greed for personal enrichment but greed for power. In the early days of the income tax, burglars, prostitutes, gamblers and others with money from illegal sources asked, through their lawyers, if they would be prosecuted if they reported their profits and reported where they came from. The answer was no. If they paid the tax they could give the source as "other income," no questions would be asked and no information would be given to the police. This remains true today. You can import a shipload of cocaine and sell it for millions, and if you pay the taxes it will remain your secret. This is defended on the ground that if the crooks' occupations were made public they would refuse to pay any taxes and government would have to track them down, gather the evidence, prosecute them and then collect whatever money it could. It is seen as preferable and much quicker and easier and far more profitable to take their money and keep quiet. Of course, if law enforcement agencies find out somehow on their own, they will prosecute, but with no help from the tax collectors.

The other reason our system is such a mess is that Congress's members love to tinker with the tax code, adding one benefit here and another one there for friends, supporters and large givers of campaign money. One of many egregious examples is this: A friend of a senator on the Finance Committee owned a house in Augusta, Georgia, standing immediately beside the famous Masters Golf Course. Each year during the Masters Tournament he was able to rent his house for two weeks to some rich golf enthusiast for an enormous sum. Now a line or two in the federal law allows him and everyone else to rent a house for two weeks a year with the rent tax free. Senator Bill Bradley of New Jersey says that Finance Committee staffers estimate this little favor to a friend has cost the government $330 million over five years. My guess is the golf club, golf ball and equipment manufacturers who pay golfers in televised tournaments to wear caps and shirts with their names on them rent this house for two weeks and pay tremendous rents and use it to entertain their customers during the Masters. Since this provision is still in the law, anyone anywhere can rent his house to anyone for two weeks for whatever price he can get and whatever he gets is tax free.

There is one outrage after another. A study by the Tax Foundation described in the *Wall Street Journal* says for 90 percent of the smaller American corporations it costs more to comply with the hideous complexities of the tax code than it costs to pay the taxes. Hiring the lawyers, accountants and tax advisers costs on average 390 percent more than the taxes. Or, for every $100 paid by a small corporation another $390 has to be spent for legal and accounting paperwork. If this is not abuse of the American people, what is it?

As one of the more sensible members of the Senate, Robert Kerrey of Nebraska, said, "Our fiscal problems do not exist because wealthy Americans are not paying enough taxes. Our fiscal problems exist because of the rapid, uncontrolled growth in programs that primarily benefit the middle class." He is right. The top 5 percent of income earners pay about half of the total tax load and the top 10 percent pay about 60 percent.

This plain fact has been explained to Congress and the public a thousand times. But fantasies that soaking the rich will solve all problems continue even now to float through the dreams of the descendants of the Puritans who hated money so long as it belonged to someone else. Demonstrably wrong as this is, Congress simply could not avoid trying once more to force the rich to pay the bills for everyone. Instead of assaulting the wealthy head-on (after all, they do give campaign money) they moved in sidewise and attacked the symbols of wealth, the symbols they believe the ribbon clerks and assistant bookkeepers dream about: furs, diamonds, yachts and expensive cars. The maneuver took the form of a 10 percent "luxury tax." The new tax proved again that for years Congress and the Treasury have stubbornly refused to consider or even to discuss publicly the fact that taxes cause changes in the public's behavior. They have studied this, but they refuse to say what they have learned. It is too inconvenient and troublesome to predict the public response to a new tax, but even so they continue to count the money even before it is collected. But in this case we know the answer. The results of the 10 percent luxury tax are clear. The sale of yachts fell by 73 percent and boatyards died. The rich bought many fewer furs, diamonds and luxury cars. The cost to government: nine thousand jobs and $20 million in tax collections. Slowly and reluctantly, in a rare display of common sense, Congress began repealing the luxury tax. In every session they have to learn all over again that Americans will look for ways to protect their property about as fast as Congress looks for ways to take it away from them.

In the early days of television I made a documentary tracing the movement of Western civilization from Egypt around the shores of the Mediterranean to Spain and the town of Palos, where Columbus set sail for the West. This whole area is, of course, strewn with Egyptian, Greek and Roman artifacts, and we photographed a great many of them. In the hills above Beirut, Lebanon, formerly Phoenicia, there was an ancient Greek and Roman town called Baalbek. The Greeks called it Heliopolis, city of the sun. Standing on its hilltop was a magnificent Roman temple nearly intact, looking like a Parthenon recently built and the best preserved of all the Roman temples. We hauled our cameras up to the hilltop to record it on film. Along the way we saw a stunning sight—beside the little road was a block of beautiful white marble about the size of a Volkswagen Beetle lying on its size at a crooked angle in a field of weeds. Engraved on the block were the words DIVO VESPASIANO. The great Vespasian. Emperor of Rome from a.d. 69 to a.d. 79. The legend is that about two thousand years ago the marble block was being dragged up the hill to be placed inside the temple, but for some reason lost to history the effort was abandoned partway up the hill —perhaps because Vespasian died—and the block was simply left lying there in an open field where it has remained for twenty centuries.

When I wrote the script for my documentary I did not know enough about Vespasian to be sure I had it all right. In the library I learned a small fact I recall now because it describes one of mankind's early attempts to extract tax money from the public efficiently and painlessly. Vespasian installed urinals on the streets of Rome and charged a fee for using them—a truly essential, not to say critical, service provided by government for a small tax. The House Ways and Means Committee should learn from this.

It does not. In its constant and ill-conceived and somewhat ignorant pursuit of new ways, or tricks, to soak the rich and carry on class warfare through the tax code, Congress voted a new rule saying if a business pays its chief executive officer more than $1 million a year, the amount above the million cannot be deducted as a business expense, even though the entire amount would then be taxable to the CEO as personal income. The rule will produce little new money but will afford the blue-suit-rimless-glasses bureaucrats on the tax-writing committees the pure, sensual pleasure of taking still more money away from businesspeople who make more than they do, and who produce wealth rather than consume it.

So silly is this new and puritanical rule that, in just one example, Chicago's Tribune Company cannot deduct on its tax return the full salary of its CEO if it exceeds $1 million, but it can deduct every dime of the $7 million the same company pays its Chicago Cubs second baseman Ryne Sandberg. Is this tax collection or punishment? Class warfare? Greed? All three?

I HAVE consulted, read or talked with one Washington tax authority after another, *not including members of Congress*. Not including them because whatever their other virtues, they are always under political pressure from their voters at home and from the givers of campaign money. And every word they say in public must be acceptable to both. It is difficult.

What I have found is that only one idea for tax

reform comes anywhere close to genuinely wide acceptance by the taxpayers, and that is the flat tax.

Why? Many reasons. One is that every tax we already have in America, except the income tax, is a flat tax. Taxes on sales, gasoline, real estate, airplane tickets, sales of houses—flat taxes every one, the same price to all regardless of personal wealth or lack of it. Its greatest virtue is simplicity. All a taxpayer needs to know at year's end is his total income for the year, multiplies by some percentage to be determined—18, 19, 20 percent or something like that—and the job is done.

In antiquity and often still, church members tithe—give 10 percent of their incomes to the church and it is always the same percentage, regardless of the church member's wealth; if in the past it sometimes was entirely in the form of cattle, sheep, goats or acres of wheat. The tithe is not a tax, but effectively it is the same. And so the flat tax is hardly a new idea.

The objections are that the flat tax is seen as regressive, a greater burden on those with low incomes. There is some truth in this. And in fairness it would have to be dealt with. The best answer would be to give those with low incomes a free ride with no taxes at all on their first fifteen, eighteen or twenty thousand or some amount to be determined, one that works fairly.

Deduction for the mortgage interest on your residence? Yes, if politically unavoidable, as it may be, but it would require the flat tax rate to be a point or two higher, a benefit to home mortgage holders at the expense of those who rent or whose home loans are paid off. We do elect politicians to make difficult decisions like this.

YEARS LATER, when I had lived in Washington for years, I drove down to Wilmington on a little nostalgic trip. I drove out Princess Street to Eighth for a look at our old house where, because Mama thought electric lights attracted mosquitoes, I had been told to go out and sit on the curb and read under the streetlight. I wondered how our old house looked now, who owned it and if by chance it might be for sale. If so, I thought I might buy it, not to live in it but simply as a resting place, to keep our family's memories warm and alive; maybe even a place for my children and grandchildren to stay when in future years they came down for vacations at the beach. As I drove southward from Washington, the more I thought about this the more I liked it. I resolved there at the steering wheel I would buy the house and hire somebody to look after it. And to do everything possible to restore and maintain the flower garden that in life Mama loved so deeply. She raised roses, dahlias, cyclamens, azaleas, camellias, peonies and other flowers whose names I never knew, all arrayed against a white fence of one-inch-square spokes ending in little pyramids on top. And the ineradicable memory of Shep, the collie of my childhood, sailing over the fence with such ease, grace and suavity that he seemed to ignore gravity. All these recollections flew around in my head as I drove down U.S. 17, the so-called Ocean Highway. I would renovate the house, I told myself, and make it into a convenient little private hotel for all the Brinkleys vacationing at the beach. A private place for our children and their friends and ours, a few special people from my television studios.

I drove south on Market to Ninth, turned right to Princess and south on Princess to 801, stopped the car and looked around at one of the saddest sights of my life: 801 was not even there. Torn down a year or two ago, they said. Replaced by a small, hideous one-story brick building with a sign on the front saying something stupid and infuriating about insurance. Our house, gone. The white fence, gone. Mama's flower garden covered over in concrete. The majestic two-hundred-year-old oak tree whose branches protectively reached out over us and our house for most of our lives, gone. They cut it down to make room for parking. Parking! Parking where Margaret ate her meals under the dining room table? Parking where one night Mary said she had a date with a traveling salesman for Kellogg's cereals, and when he arrived to pick her up in a panel truck with KELLOGG'S PEP BRAN FLAKES painted on the sides, where Mama took one look and said Mary was forbidden to go out in it? Mary argued. She lost. Where at times I'd had to sit on the curb to read under the streetlight?

The streetlight was still there, the only physical fragment left from a rich and pungent family life.

A Note About the Author

David Brinkley was born in Wilmington, North Carolina, and was educated at the University of North Carolina and Vanderbilt University. His career as a disseminator and interpreter of the news began early—while still in high school he wrote for his hometown paper, the Wilmington *Morning Star*. After his army service in World War II he worked for United Press and then joined NBC News, becoming White House correspondent before the end of the war. In 1956 he and Chet Huntley launched their celebrated news program *The Huntley-Brinkley Report*, which during its fourteen years won them every major broadcasting award. He then became coanchor (with John Chancellor), and subsequently commentator, on *NBC Nightly News*, and since 1981 has conducted his own program of news commentary and interviews, *This Week with David Brinkley*, on Sunday mornings. He has been the recipient of ten Emmy Awards and three George Foster Peabody Awards. He lives with his wife, Susan, in Washington, D.C.

LARGE PRINT EDITIONS

Look for these at your local bookstore

American Heart Association, *American Heart Association Cookbook, 5th Edition* (abridged)

Barbara Taylor Bradford, *Angel* (paper)

John Berendt, *Midnight in the Garden of Good and Evil* (paper)

Joe Claro, editor, *The Random House Large Print Book of Jokes and Anecdotes* (paper)

Michael Crichton, *Disclosure* (paper)

Michael Crichton, *The Lost World* (paper)

Michael Crichton, *Rising Sun*

E. L. Doctorow, *The Waterworks* (paper)

Dominick Dunne, *A Season in Purgatory*

Fannie Flagg, *Daisy Fay and the Miracle Man* (paper)

Fannie Flagg, *Fried Green Tomatoes at the Whistle Stop Cafe* (paper)

Ken Follett, *A Place Called Freedom* (paper)

Robert Fulghum, *From Beginning to End: The Rituals of Our Lives*

Robert Fulghum, *It Was on Fire When I Lay Down on It* (hardcover and paper)

Robert Fulghum, *Maybe (Maybe Not): Second Thoughts from a Secret Life*

Robert Fulghum, *Uh-Oh*

Gabriel García Márquez, *Of Love and Other Demons* (paper)

Martha Grimes, *The Horse You Came In On* (paper)

David Halberstam, *The Fifties* (2 volumes, paper)

Katharine Hepburn, *Me* (hardcover and paper)

P. D. James, *The Children of Men*

Pope John Paul II, *Crossing the Threshold of Hope*

(continued)

Pope John Paul II, *The Gospel of Life* (paper)
Dean Koontz, *Dark Rivers of the Heart* (paper)
Judith Krantz, *Lovers* (paper)
John le Carré, *Our Game* (paper)
Anne Morrow Lindbergh, *Gift from the Sea*
Cormac McCarthy, *The Crossing* (paper)
Audrey Meadows with Joe Daley, *Love, Alice* (paper)
James A. Michener, *Mexico* (paper)
James A. Michener, *Miracle in Seville* (paper)
James A. Michener, *Recessional* (paper)
James A. Michener, *The World Is My Home* (paper)
Richard North Patterson, *Degree of Guilt*
Luciano Pavarotti and William Wright, *Pavarotti: My World* (paper)
Louis Phillips, editor, *The Random House Large Print Treasury of Best-Loved Poems*
Colin Powell with Joseph E. Persico, *My American Journey* (paper)
Ruth Rendell, *Simisola* (paper)
Andy Rooney, *My War* (paper)
Margaret Truman, *Murder on the Potomac* (paper)
Anne Tyler, *Ladder of Years* (paper)
Anne Tyler, *Saint Maybe*
Phyllis A. Whitney, *Daughter of the Stars* (paper)

The New York Times Large Print Crossword Puzzles (paper)

Will Weng, editor, Volumes 1–3
Eugene T. Maleska, editor, Volumes 4–7
Eugene T. Maleska, editor, Omnibus Volume 1